Hadoop® 2
Quick-Start Guide

 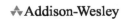

Hadoop® 2 Quick-Start Guide

Learn the Essentials of Big Data Computing in the Apache Hadoop® 2 Ecosystem

Douglas Eadline

✦✦ Addison-Wesley

New York • Boston • Indianapolis • San Francisco
Toronto • Montreal • London • Munich • Paris • Madrid
Capetown • Sydney • Tokyo • Singapore • Mexico City

For information about buying this title in bulk quantities, or for special sales opportunities (which may include electronic versions; custom cover designs; and content particular to your business, training goals, marketing focus, or branding interests), please contact our corporate sales department at corpsales@pearsoned.com or (800) 382-3419.

For government sales inquiries, please contact governmentsales@pearsoned.com.

For questions about sales outside the United States, please contact international@pearsoned.com.

Visit us on the Web: informit.com/aw

Library of Congress Cataloging-in-Publication Data

Eadline, Doug, 1956-author.
  Learn the essential aspects of big data computing in the Apache Hadoop 2 ecosystem / Doug Eadline.
      pages   cm
  Includes bibliographical references and index.
  ISBN 978-0-13-404994-6 (pbk. : alk. paper)—ISBN 0-13-404994-2 (pbk. : alk. paper)
  1. Big data. 2. Data mining. 3. Apache Hadoop. I. Title.
  QA76.9.B45E24 2016
  006.3'12—dc23
                                                              2015030746

ISBN-13: 978-0-13-404994-6
ISBN-10: 0-13-404994-2
Text printed in the United States on recycled paper at RR Donnelley in Crawfordsville, Indiana.
First printing, November 2015

Contents

Foreword

Apache Hadoop 2 introduced new methods of processing and working with data that moved beyond the basic MapReduce paradigm of the original Hadoop implementation. Whether you are a newcomer to Hadoop or a seasoned professional who has worked with the previous version, this book provides a fantastic introduction to the concepts and tools within Hadoop 2.

Over the past few years, many projects have fallen under the umbrella of the original Hadoop project to make storing, processing, and collecting large quantities easier while integrating with the original Hadoop project. This book introduces many of these projects in the larger Hadoop ecosystem, giving readers the high-level basics to get them started using tools that fit their needs.

Doug Eadline adapted much of this material from his very popular video series *Hadoop Fundamentals Live Lessons*. However, his qualifications don't stop there. As a coauthor on the in-depth book *Apache Hadoop™ YARN: Moving beyond MapReduce and Batch Processing with Apache Hadoop™ 2*, few are as well qualified to deliver coverage of Hadoop 2 and the new features it brings to users.

I'm excited about the great wealth of knowledge that Doug has brought to the series with his books covering Hadoop and its related projects. This book will be a great resource for both newcomers looking to learn more about the problems that Hadoop can help them solve and for existing users looking to learn about the benefits of upgrading to the new version.

—*Paul Dix, Series Editor*

Preface

Apache Hadoop 2 has changed the data analytics landscape. The Hadoop 2 ecosystem has moved beyond a single MapReduce data processing methodology and framework. That is, Hadoop version 2 offers the Hadoop version 1 methodology to almost any type of data processing and provides full backward compatibility with the vulnerable MapReduce paradigm from version 1.

This change has already had a dramatic effect on many areas of data processing and data analytics. The increased volume of online data has invited new and scalable approaches to data analytics. As discussed in Chapter 1, the concept of the Hadoop data lake represents a paradigm shift away from many established approaches to online data usage and storage. A Hadoop version 2 installation is an *extensible platform* that can grow and adapt as both data volumes increase and new processing models become available.

For this reason, the "Hadoop approach" is important and should not be dismissed as a simple "one-trick pony" for Big Data applications. In addition, the open source nature of Hadoop and much of the surrounding ecosystem provides an important incentive for adoption. Thanks to the Apache Software Foundation (ASF), Hadoop has always been an open source project whose inner workings are available to anyone. The open model has allowed vendors and users to share a common goal without lock-in or legal barriers that might otherwise splinter a huge and important project such as Hadoop. All software used in this book is open source and is freely available. Links leading to the software are provided at the end of each chapter and in Appendix C.

Focus of the Book

As the title implies, this book is a quick-start guide to Hadoop version 2. By design, most topics are summarized, illustrated with an example, and left a bit unfinished. Indeed, many of the tools and subjects covered here are treated elsewhere as completely independent books. Thus, the biggest hurdle in creating a quick-start guide is deciding what *not* to include while simultaneously giving the reader a sense of what is important.

To this end, all topics are designed with what I call the hello-world.c experience. That is, provide some background on what the tool or service does, then provide a beginning-to-end example that allows the reader to get started quickly, and finally, provide resources where additional information and more nitty-gritty details can be found. This approach allows the reader to make changes and implement variations that move away from the simple working example to something that solves the reader's particular problem. For most of us, our programming experience started from applying incremental changes to working examples—so the approach in this book should be a familiar one.

Who Should Read This Book

The book is intended for those readers who want to learn about Hadoop version 2, but not get mired in technical details. New users, system administrators, and devops personnel should all be able to get up to speed with many of the important Hadoop topics and tools by working through this text. In particular, readers with no Hadoop experience should find the book highly usable, even if they have no Java programming experience. Experience with Linux command-line tools is helpful, as all of the examples involve command-line interaction with Hadoop.

Users and administrators who are currently using Hadoop version 1 should find value as well. The changes in Hadoop version 2 are rather substantial, and this book's discussion of YARN and some of the changes in the MapReduce framework is important.

Book Structure

The basic structure of this book was adapted from my video tutorial, *Hadoop Fundamentals LiveLessons, Second Edition* and *Apache Hadoop YARN Fundamentals LiveLessons* from Addison-Wesley. Almost all of the examples are identical to those found in the videos. Some readers may find it beneficial to watch the videos in conjunction with reading the book as I carefully step through all the examples.

A few small pieces have been borrowed from *Apache Hadoop™ YARN: Moving beyond MapReduce and Batch Processing with Apache Hadoop™ 2*, a book that I coauthored. If you want to explore YARN application development in more detail, you may want to consider reading this book and viewing its companion video.

Much of this book uses the Hortonworks Data Platform (HDP) for Hadoop. The HDP is a fully open source Hadoop distribution made available by Hortonworks. While it is possible to download and install the core Hadoop system and tools (as is discussed in Chapter 2), using an integrated distribution reduces many of the issues that may arise from the "roll your own" approach. In addition, the Apache Ambari graphical installation and management tool is too good to pass up and supports the Hortonworks HDP packages. HDP version 2.2 and Ambari 1.7 were used for this book. As I write this preface, Hortonworks has just announced the launch of HDP version 2.3 with Apache Ambari 2.0. (So much for staying ahead of the curve in the Hadoop world!) Fortunately, the fundamentals remain the same and the examples are all still relevant.

The chapters in this text have been arranged to provide a flexible introduction for new readers. As delineated in Appendix B, "Getting Started Flowchart and Trouble-shooting Guide," there are two paths you can follow: read Chapters 1, 3, and 5 and then start playing with the examples, or jump right in and run the examples in Chapter 4. If you don't have a Hadoop environment, Chapter 2 provides a way to install Hadoop on a variety of systems, including a laptop or small desk-side computer, a cluster, or even in the cloud. Presumably after running examples, you will go back and read the background chapters.

Chapter 1 provides essential background on Hadoop technology and history. The Hadoop data lake is introduced, along with an overview of the MapReduce process found in version 1 of Hadoop. The big changes in Hadoop version 2 are described, and the YARN resource manager is introduced as a way forward for almost any computing model. Finally, a brief overview of the many software projects that make up the Hadoop ecosystem is presented. This chapter provides an underpinning for the rest of the book.

If you need access to a Hadoop system, a series of installation recipes is provided in Chapter 2. There is also an explanation of the core Hadoop services and the way in which they are configured. Some general advice for choosing hardware and software environments is provided, but the main focus is on providing a platform to learn about Hadoop. Fortunately, there are two ways to do this without purchasing or renting any hardware. The Hortonworks Hadoop sandbox provides a Linux virtual machine that can be run on almost any platform. The sandbox is a full Hadoop install and provides an environment through which to explore Hadoop. As an alternative to the sandbox, the installation of Hadoop on a single Linux machine provides a learning platform and offers some insights into the Hadoop core components. Chapter 2 also addresses cluster installation using Apache Ambari for a local cluster or Apache Whirr for a cloud deployment.

All Hadoop applications use the Hadoop Distributed File System (HDFS). Chapter 3 covers some essential HDFS features and offers quick tips on how to navigate and use the file system. The chapter concludes with some HDFS programming examples. It provides important background and should be consulted before trying the examples in later chapters.

Chapter 4 provides a show-and-tell walk-through of some Hadoop examples and benchmarks. The Hadoop Resource Manager web GUI is also introduced as a way to observe application progress. The chapter concludes with some tips on controlling Hadoop MapReduce jobs. Use this chapter to get a feel for how Hadoop applications run and operate.

The MapReduce programming model, while simple in nature, can be a bit confusing when run across a cluster. Chapter 5 provides a basic introduction to the MapReduce programming model using simple examples. The chapter concludes with a simplified walk-through of the parallel Hadoop MapReduce process. This chapter will help you understand the basic Hadoop MapReduce terminology.

If you are interested in low-level Hadoop programming, Chapter 6 provides an introduction to Hadoop MapReduce programming. Several basic approaches are covered, including Java, the streaming interface with Python, and the C++ Pipes interface. A short example also explains how to view application logs. This chapter is not essential for using Hadoop. In fact, many Hadoop users begin with the high-level tools discussed in Chapter 7.

While many applications have been written to run on the native Hadoop Java interface, a wide variety of tools are available that provide a high-level approach to programing and data movement. Chapter 7 introduces (with examples) essential Hadoop tools including Apache Pig (scripting language), Apache Hive (SQL-like language), Apache Sqoop (RDMS import/export), and Apache Flume (serial data import). An example demonstrating how to use the Oozie workflow manager is also provided. The chapter concludes with an Apache HBase (big table database) example.

If you are interested in learning more about Hadoop YARN applications, Chapter 8 introduces non-MapReduce applications under Hadoop. As a simple example, the YARN Distributed-Shell is presented, along with a discussion of how YARN applications work under Hadoop version 2. A description of the latest non-MapReduce YARN applications is provided as well.

If you installed Hadoop with Apache Ambari in Chapter 2, Chapter 9 provides a tour of its capabilities and offers some examples that demonstrate how to use Ambari on a real Hadoop cluster. A tour of Ambari features and procedures to restart Hadoop services and change system-wide Hadoop properties is presented as well. The basic steps outlined in this chapter are used in Chapter 10 to make administrative changes to the cluster.

Chapter 10 provides some basic Hadoop administration procedures. Although administrators will find information on basic procedures and advice in this chapter, other users will also benefit by discovering how HDFS, YARN, and the Capacity scheduler can be configured for their workloads.

Consult the appendixes for information on the book webpage, a getting started flowchart, and a general Hadoop troubleshooting guide. The appendixes also include a resources summary page and procedures for installing Apache Hue (a high-level Hadoop GUI) and Apache Spark (a popular non-MapReduce programming model).

Finally, the Hadoop ecosystem continues to grow rapidly. Many of the existing Hadoop applications and tools were intentionally not covered in this text because their inclusion would have turned this book into a longer and slower introduction to Hadoop 2. And, there are many more tools and applications on the way! Given the dynamic nature of the Hadoop ecosystem, this introduction to Apache Hadoop 2 is meant to provide both a compass and some important waypoints to aid in your navigation of the Hadoop 2 data lake.

Book Conventions

Code and file references are displayed in a monospaced font. Code input lines that wrap because they are too long to fit on one line in this book are denoted with this symbol: ➡. Long output lines are wrapped at page boundaries without the symbol.

Accompanying Code

Please see Appendix A, "Book Webpage and Code Download," for the location of all code used in this book.

Acknowledgments

Some of the figures and examples were inspired and derived from the Yahoo! Hadoop Tutorial (https://developer.yahoo.com/hadoop/tutorial/), the Apache Software Foundation (ASF; http://www.apache.org), Hortonworks (http://hortonworks.com), and Michael Noll (http://www.michael-noll.com). Any copied items either had permission for use granted by the author or were available under an open sharing license.

Many people have worked behind the scenes to make this book possible. Thank you to the reviewers who took the time to carefully read the rough drafts: Jim Lux, Prentice Bisbal, Jeremy Fischer, Fabricio Cannini, Joshua Mora, Matthew Helmke, Charlie Peck, and Robert P. J. Day. Your feedback was very valuable and helped make for a sturdier book.

To Debra Williams Cauley of Addison-Wesley, your kind efforts and office at the GCT Oyster Bar made the book-writing process almost easy. I also cannot forget to thank my support crew: Emily, Marlee, Carla, and Taylor—yes, another book you know nothing about. And, finally, the biggest thank you to my patient and wonderful wife, Maddy, for her constant support.

About the Author

Douglas Eadline, Ph.D., began his career as a practitioner and a chronicler of the Linux cluster HPC revolution and now documents Big Data analytics. Starting with the first Beowulf how-to document, Doug has written hundreds of articles, white papers, and instructional documents covering virtually all aspects of HPC computing. Prior to starting and editing the popular ClusterMonkey.net website in 2005, he served as editor-in-chief for *ClusterWorld Magazine*, and was senior HPC editor for *Linux Magazine*. He has practical, hands-on experience in many aspects of HPC, including hardware and software design, benchmarking, storage, GPU, cloud computing, and parallel computing. Currently, he is a writer and consultant to the HPC industry and leader of the Limulus Personal Cluster Project (http://limulus.basement-supercomputing.com). He is author of *Hadoop Fundamentals LiveLessons* and *Apache Hadoop YARN Fundamentals LiveLessons* videos from Addison-Wesley and book coauthor of *Apache Hadoop™ YARN: Moving beyond MapReduce and Batch Processing with Apache Hadoop™ 2*.

1

Background and Concepts

Apache Hadoop represents a new way to process large amounts of data. Rather than a single program or product, Hadoop is more of an approach to scalable data processing. The Hadoop ecosystem encompasses many components, and the current capabilities of Hadoop version 2 far exceed those of version 1. Many of the important Hadoop concepts and components are introduced in this chapter.

Defining Apache Hadoop

The name *Hadoop* has grown to mean many different things. In 2002, it began as a single software project to support a web search engine. It has since grown into an ecosystem of tools and applications that are used to analyze large amounts and types of data. Hadoop should no longer be considered a monolithic single project, but rather an "approach" to data processing that is radically different from the traditional relational database model. A more pragmatic definition of Hadoop is an ecosystem and framework of open (and closed) source tools, libraries and methodologies for "Big Data" analysis. Some of the features that shape Hadoop data processing are as follows:

- Core parts are open source under the Apache License (see the sidebar "The Apache Software Foundation").

- Analysis usually involves large unstructured (i.e., nonrelational) data sets sometimes in the petabyte (10^{15} bytes) range.

- Traditionally, data is stored across multiple servers using the scalable Hadoop Distributed File System (HDFS). Some new designs use storage fabrics or network-based storage subsystems.

- Many applications and tools are based on the Hadoop version 1 (V1) MapReduce programming model.

- Hadoop MapReduce jobs can scale from a single server to thousands of machines and tens of thousands of processor cores.

- Other programing models (including V1 MapReduce) are supported in Hadoop version 2 (V2) with YARN (Yet Another Resource Negotiator).

- Hadoop core components were designed to run on commodity hardware and the cloud.

- Hadoop offers many fault-tolerant features that enable operation over large numbers of servers.

- Many projects and applications are built on top of the Hadoop infrastructure.

- Although the core components are written in Java, Hadoop applications can use almost any programing language.

The core components of a Hadoop installation include HDFS and the YARN resource manager. While the HDFS file system is robust, redundant, and able to provide distributed access to data across a Hadoop cluster, it should not be considered a high-performance parallel file system. It was designed to meet the needs of Big Data processing, such as large-block streaming access. YARN is responsible for managing cluster resources. In one sense, it can be considered a cluster operating system with data locality services. (In other words, YARN can schedule jobs on nodes that contain specific data in HDFS.) Hadoop applications, including those that use the MapReduce engine, run as application frameworks on top of YARN.

The Apache Software Foundation

The Apache Software Foundation (ASF), a U.S. 501(c)(3) nonprofit corporation, provides organizational, legal, and financial support for more than 150 open source software projects covering a broad range of areas. The ASF provides an established framework for intellectual property and financial contributions that simultaneously limits potential legal exposure for its project committers. Through a collaborative and meritocratic development process known as The Apache Way, Apache projects deliver enterprise-grade, freely available software products that attract large communities of users. The pragmatic Apache License makes it easy for all users—commercial and individual—to deploy Apache products.

The mission of the ASF is to provide software for the public good. It does so by providing services and support for many like-minded software project communities of individuals.

Apache projects are defined by collaborative, consensus-based processes, an open, pragmatic software license, and a desire to create high-quality software that leads the way in its field. More information can be found at http://www.apache.org/.

A Brief History of Apache Hadoop

Hadoop was started at Yahoo! to provide a data processing infrastructure to the Apache Nutch web search engine. The project was started by Doug Cutting and Michael J. Cafarella in 2005. The name Hadoop came from Cutting, whose son had given his toy elephant the name "Hadoop."

A portion of the technical inspiration came from the Google File System (GFS) and a 2004 Google paper on the MapReduce algorithm. Yahoo! began embracing Hadoop in 2006, and by 2008 the Yahoo! search index was being generated by Hadoop. One key design decision was to use low-cost, commodity servers for both computing and storage. Indeed, one of the important principles of early Hadoop MapReduce processing was the capability to "move the computation to the data" because it was faster than moving data from server to server. The design also required that Hadoop software be scalable, handle large amounts of data, and tolerate hardware failures.

The Hadoop design also sacrifices some efficiency in favor of massive scalability. At a small scale, Hadoop may present an inefficient approach for some problems. Other tools may, in fact, provide better performance in these cases. As the problem or data set scales to massive proportions, however, Hadoop begins to show its ability to handle problems of sizes that are impossible to manage on other systems. Some areas where Hadoop is used include the following:

- Social media
- Retail web commerce
- Financial services
- Web search
- Government
- Research and development
- Many others

Some prominent users include the following:

- Yahoo!
- Facebook
- Amazon
- EBay
- American Airlines
- *The New York Times*

- Federal Reserve Board of Governors
- Chevron
- IBM
- Many others

Defining Big Data

Big Data, as the name implies, suggests large-volume data processing—often measured in petabytes (10^{15} bytes). Big Data, however, does not have to be "big." There are, according to *Wikipedia* (http://en.wikipedia.org/wiki/Big_data), several characteristics that define Big Data:

- Volume: Large volumes clearly define Big Data. In some cases, the sheer size of the data makes it impossible to evaluate by more conventional means.
- Variety: Data may come from a variety of sources and not necessarily be "related" to other data sources.
- Velocity: The term *velocity* in this context refers to how fast the data can be generated and processed.
- Variability: Data may be highly variable, incomplete, and inconsistent.
- Complexity: Relationships between data sources may not be entirely clear and not amenable to traditional relational methods.

Many organizations may not need to process large volumes of data, yet may still have several of the data processing needs mentioned here. The notion that all companies are sitting on petabytes of unanalyzed data is not necessarily valid. Consider the blog post entitled "Big Data Surprises" (http://www.sisense.com/blog/big-data-surprises), where the author mentions research indicating Big Data's sweet spot starts at 110 gigabytes (10^9 bytes) and that the most common amount of data the average company has under management is between 10 and 30 terabytes (10^{12} bytes). Also of note is the paper, "Nobody Ever Got Fired for Using Hadoop" (http://research.microsoft.com/pubs/163083/hotcbp12%20final.pdf), where it is documented that at least two analytics production clusters at Microsoft and Yahoo! have median job input sizes of less than 14 gigabytes and that 90% of jobs on a Facebook cluster have input sizes of less than 100 gigabytes. Some examples of what may be considered "Big Bata" follow:

- Media including video, audio, and photos
- Web data including system/web logs, click trails, and text messages/email
- Written documents, periodicals, and books
- Scientific research data including simulations results and human genome data
- Stock transactions, customer data, and retail purchases
- Telecommunications including phone records

- Public records including federal, state, and local government resources
- The Internet of Things (data from all connected devices)
- Real-time sensor data including traffic or transportation logistics

The list of data will continue to grow as more data is stored online. The data may be private or public.

Hadoop as a Data Lake

Before examining how Hadoop can process Big Data, it is important to understand how modern data storage systems operate. One of the Big Data features not mentioned earlier, but certainly implied, is a central storage depot for all data. As some data may not be amenable to storage in a relational database, most data will need to be stored in raw form. This characteristic is what often distinguishes Hadoop data processing from more traditional methods. Often called a "data lake," the idea is to create a vast repository for all raw data and use it as needed.

Contrast this approach with that of a traditional relational database or data warehouse. Adding data to the database requires data to be transformed into a *predetermined* schema before it can be loaded into the database. This step is often called extract, transform, and load (ETL) and can consume both time and cost before the data can be used. Most importantly, decisions about how the data will be used must be made during the ETL step. In addition, some data are often discarded in the ETL step because it does not fit into the data schema or is deemed un-needed.

Hadoop focuses on using data in its raw form. Essentially, what looks like the ETL step is performed when the data is accessed by Hadoop applications. This approach, called **schema on read,** enables programmers and users to enforce a structure to suit their needs when they access data. The traditional data warehouse approach, called **schema on write,** requires more upfront design and assumptions about how the data will eventually be used.

With respect to Big Data, as described previously, the data lake offers three advantages over a more traditional approach:

- All data remains available. There is no need to make any assumptions about future data use.
- All data is sharable. Multiple business units or researchers can use all available data, some of which was not previously available due to data compartmentalization on disparate systems.
- All access methods are available. Any processing engine can be used to examine the data (e.g., MapReduce, graph processing, in-memory tools).

To be clear, Hadoop is not destined to replace the data warehouse. Data warehouses are valuable business tools; however, the traditional data warehouse technology was developed before the data lake began to fill up quite so rapidly. The growth of new

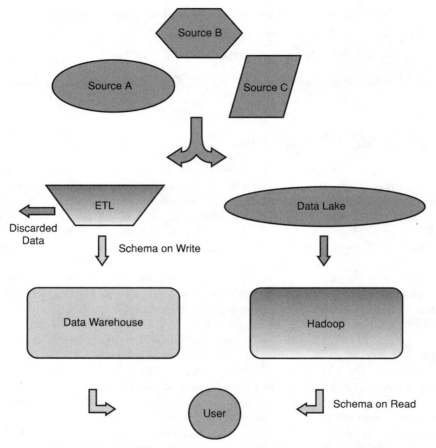

Figure 1.1   The data warehouse versus the Hadoop data lake

data streams from disparate sources, including social media, click trails, sensor data, and others, has increased the flow into the data lake.

The difference between a traditional data warehouse and Hadoop is depicted in Figure 1.1. In the figure, different data can be seen entering either an ETL process or a data lake. The ETL process places the data in a schema as it stores (writes) the data to the relational database. The data lake simply stores the raw data. When a Hadoop application uses the data, the schema is applied when it reads the data from the lake. Note that the ETL step often discards some data as part of the process.

Using Hadoop: Administrator, User, or Both

An Apache Hadoop installation can mean many things to different people. There are many modes in which individuals can interact with Hadoop. Traditionally, systems administrators are in charge of installation, monitoring/managing, and tuning Hadoop software. In addition, the traditional user would develop Hadoop applications, work with data, and use the various Hadoop tools that are discussed in this book. Depending on the size of your installation, the lines between administrator and user may blur and may blend into a new role commonly referred to as "devops." Hadoop can be explored on a laptop, in a large cluster, or anywhere in between. Thus, your role may change depending on your goals and scale of your project. This book provides enough resources so that you can quickly get up to speed on both aspects. The following essential tasks will be discussed in the subsequent chapters.

- **Administrators**
  - Install Hadoop and manage packages
  - Basic cluster management
  - Monitor/manage the Hadoop services
  - Tune the Hadoop services (and installed tools/packages)
- **End Users**
  - Use existing Hadoop tools to examine work flow and storage
  - Create Hadoop applications using MapReduce tools
  - Write non–MapReduce applications that work directly with YARN
  - Import/export data to/from HDFS by hand
  - Use Hadoop tools to automatically import and export data into HDFS

First There Was MapReduce

The first version (V1) of Apache Hadoop provided a monolithic MapReduce processing engine in which both cluster resource management and MapReduce processing were combined. This situation changed in the second version (V2) of Hadoop. Instead of operating as a single entity, the MapReduce processing was split from the resource management. The capability to run V1 MapReduce applications in V2 was retained, however. MapReduce has become an application framework that is managed by the YARN resource manager.

Because many applications and tools use the MapReduce engine, understanding how this component fits into both Hadoop V1 and V2 is important. Further details about MapReduce processing are presented in Chapter 5, "Hadoop MapReduce Framework."

Apache Hadoop Design Principles

Apache Hadoop V1 was designed to efficiently process large volumes of information by connecting many commodity computers together to work in parallel. There are some important principles that influenced this design. Many of these design principles carried over to Hadoop V2.

First, as mentioned earlier, one of the key aspects of Hadoop is the idea that moving computation is cheaper than moving data. Thus, an underlying principle is that keeping data on disk instead of moving blocks of data to servers provides faster performance. The Hadoop MapReduce paradigm enables this to be done in a scalable and transparent fashion. The bottleneck of a single disk drive can be resolved by applying the same tasks to many disks, each holding a different portion or slice of the overall data.

Hadoop is designed to use large numbers of commodity servers for both computation and storage. As the number of machines increases, so does the chance that something will fail. (Statistically speaking, a failure is almost certain to happen.) Hadoop V1 MapReduce was designed to accommodate hardware failures so that tasks can keep working. In a similar fashion, the V2 YARN resource manager offers dynamic run-time management capabilities so new applications can choose to build in some level of fault tolerance.

The MapReduce paradigm has no dependency on how it is executed. That is, it can be executed sequentially on one processor and hard drive, or it can be executed in parallel using many processors and hard drives. From the user's perspective, there is no difference in the semantics of the problem because the execution details of MapReduce are hidden from the user. Thus, all tools built on top of MapReduce are scalable.

Since Hadoop deals with large data sets, HDFS file access is optimized for sequential access (streaming) rather than random access. In addition, Hadoop uses a simple file system coherency approach that employs a write-once/read-many model. Finally, as part of the data lake concept, all original data should remain intact and should not be changed by the MapReduce process.

Apache Hadoop MapReduce Example

MapReduce is a two-step process that includes a mapping step followed by a reducing step. An example will help explain how Hadoop performs this task.

A preliminary step in performing a Hadoop MapReduce query is to place the data in a distributed file system such as HDFS. Note that HDFS is not strictly needed for MapReduce, but it is probably the best choice due to its design.

As shown in Figure 1.2, when data is copied into HDFS, it is automatically sliced and placed on different nodes (or servers). Each slice is a different part of the whole data set. This process is transparent to the user, and when the user looks at the file in HDFS, it "looks" like the original file (i.e., if one were to ls a file, it would be listed as one file and not multiple slices).

After files are loaded into HDFS, the MapReduce engine can use them. Consider the following simplified example. If we were to load the text file *War and Peace* into HDFS, it would be transparently sliced and remain unchanged from a content perspective.

The mapping step is where a user query is "mapped" to all nodes. That is, the query is applied to all the slices independently. Actually, the map is applied to logical splits of the data so that words (or records, or some other partitions) that were physically split by data slicing are kept together. For example, the query "How many times

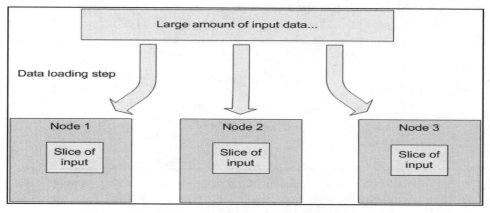

Figure 1.2 Loading data into HDFS (Adapted from Yahoo
Hadoop Documentation)

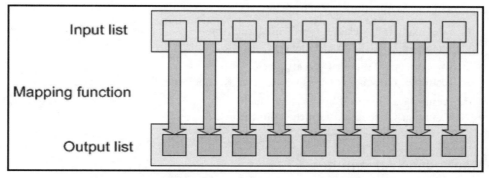

Figure 1.3 Applying the mapping function to the sliced data (Adapted from
Yahoo Hadoop Documentation)

is the name Kutuzov mentioned in *War and Peace*?" might be applied to each text slice
or split. This process is depicted in Figure 1.3. In this case, the mapping function takes
an input list (data slices or splits) and produces an output list—a count of how many
times Kutuzov appears in the text slice. The output list is a list of numbers.

Once the mapping is done, the output list of the map processes becomes the input
list to the reduce process. For example, the individual sums, or the counts for Kutuzov
from each input list (the output list of the map step), are combined to form a single
number. As shown in Figure 1.4, the resulting data *reduced* in this step. Like the mapping
function, the reduction can take many forms and, in general, collects and "reduces" the
information from the mapping step. In this example, the reduction is a sum.

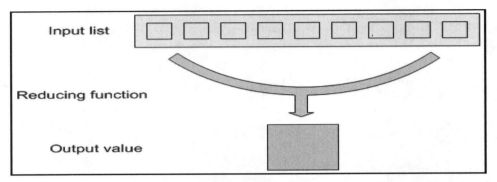

Figure 1.4   Reducing the results of the mapping step to a single output
value (Adapted from Yahoo Hadoop Documentation)

MapReduce is a simple two-step algorithm that provides the user with complete control over the mapping and reducing steps. The following is a summary of the basic aspects of the MapReduce process:

1. Files loaded into HDFS (performed one time)
   Example: Load *War and Peace* text file.

2. User query is "mapped" to all slices
   Example: How many times is the name Kutuzov mentioned in this slice?

3. Results are "reduced" to one answer
   Example: Collect and sum the counts for Kutuzov from each map step. The answer is a single number.

MapReduce Advantages

The MapReduce process can be considered a **functional approach** because the original input data does not change. The steps in the MapReduce process only create new data. Like the original input data, this intermediate data is not changed by the MapReduce process.

As shown in the previous section, the actual processing is based on a single one-way communication path from mappers to reducers (you can't go back and change data!). Since it is the same for all MapReduce processes, it can be made transparent to the end user. There is no need for the user to specify communication or data movement as part of the MapReduce process. This design provides the following features:

- *Highly scalable.* As input data size grows more nodes can be applied to the problem (often linear scalability)

- *Easily managed work flow.* Since all jobs use the same underlying processes, the workflow and load can also be handled in a transparent fashion. The user does not need to manage cluster resources as part of the MapReduce process.

- *Fault tolerance.* Inputs are immutable, so any result can be recalculated because inputs have not changed. A failed process can be restarted on other nodes. A single failure does not stop the entire MapReduce job. Multiple failures can often be tolerated as well—depending on where they are located. In general, a hardware failure may slow down the MapReduce process but not stop it entirely.

MapReduce is a powerful paradigm for solving many problems. It is often referred to as a data parallel problem or a single instruction/multiple data (SIMD) paradigm.

Apache Hadoop V1 MapReduce Operation

Although almost all-new development is taking place in Hadoop V2, understanding how V1 operates can be helpful when the new YARN layer is discussed later. In general, the MapReduce process presented previously provides a basic programmer's view of the system progress. To understand how MapReduce is executed on a cluster, consider Figure 1.5.

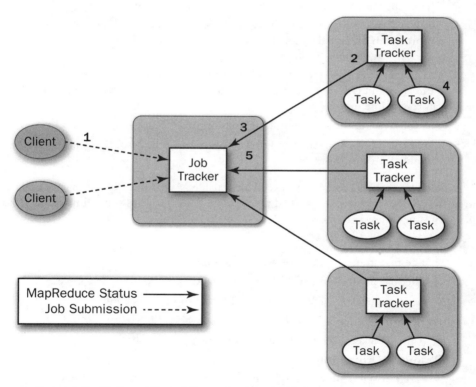

Figure 1.5 Hadoop V1 workflow using monolithic Job Tracker and multiple Task Trackers in a cluster (From Arun C. Murthy, et al., *Apache Hadoop™ YARN*, copyright © 2014, p. 36. Reprinted and electronically reproduced by permission of Pearson Education, Inc., New York, NY.)

In Figure 1.5, the master control process for a Hadoop V1 cluster is the Job Tracker. This process usually runs on its own server (or cluster node), but it can be run along with other Hadoop services on the same hardware. The single Job Tracker schedules, launches, and tracks all MapReduce jobs on the cluster. The Task Tracker nodes are where the actual work gets done on the cluster. Each Task Tracker receives work from the Job Tracker and manages sub-jobs on the local cluster node. The sub-job work consists of mapping tasks and then reducing tasks as part of the MapReduce process described earlier. Note that modern multicore servers can easily run multiple sub-jobs—all under the control of the local Task Tracker.

Keep in mind that many (if not all) Task Tracker nodes are often HDFS nodes. Thus, each cluster node provides both computation and storage services. There is no requirement that they be the same. However, Hadoop MapReduce is designed to take advantage of data locality where possible.

As shown in Figure 1.5, a typical job progresses as follows:

1. Clients submit MapReduce jobs to the monolithic Job Tracker.
2. The Job Tracker assigns and schedules cluster resources for the users' jobs. The resources can include data locality, so that sub-jobs are placed on nodes where the users' data resides (in HDFS).
3. The Job Tracker works with the Task Trackers on cluster nodes in collecting status data and tracking progress. If a node (or nodes) go down, the Job Tracker can reschedule jobs.
4. The Job Tracker supports only MapReduce jobs.
5. When the job is complete, the Job Tracker releases the resources and makes them available for other work.

While Hadoop V1 provided an excellent scalable MapReduce platform, the growth in both use cases and job size pushed the original design toward some limitations. The primary issues were as follows:

- **Scalability**
  - The maximum cluster size was about 4000 nodes.
  - The maximum number of concurrent tasks was about 40,000 processes.
  - Coarse synchronization in the Job Tracker limited scalability.
- **Availability**
  - A Job Tracker failure kills all queued and running jobs.
- **Resource Utilization**
  - Fixed or static allocation of resources for map and reduce processes often results in low resource utilization.
- **Support for Alternative Programming Paradigms and Services**
  - Iterative applications implemented using MapReduce are 10 times slower.
  - Non-MapReduce applications are needed.

Moving Beyond MapReduce with Hadoop V2

Work on a more robust Hadoop platform began in 2005 at Yahoo! Arun C. Murthy started a new project as a way to address the issues mentioned previously. The solution was to split the Job Tracker's responsibilities:

- Scheduling and resource management are done apart from the actual jobs that are running on the cluster. This component is called YARN (Yet Another Resource Negotiator) and is a pure scheduler.

- MapReduce is a separate application that relies on YARN for cluster services. This part is called MRv2 or the MapReduce applications framework.

- Perhaps most importantly, YARN presents a generalized interface so any application can take advantage of the Hadoop infrastructure. These new applications are called **application frameworks** and can include almost any kind of application written in any kind of programming language.

Hadoop V2 YARN Operation Design

In contrast to the Hadoop V1 operation, Hadoop V2 with YARN uses a separate Resource Manager to schedule and manage all jobs on the cluster. Worker nodes are managed by a Node Manager process that works with the Resource Manager. Job resources are portioned out in containers. A container is a computing resource usually defined by one processing core and an amount of memory. The Resource Manager and the Node Managers have no information about the actual jobs. They manage the containers running on the cluster and are *task neutral*. Each application must start an Application Master that manages the actual tasks for the job. The Application Master runs in a container scheduled by the Resource Manager and managed by the Node Manager.

To run the actual application, the Application Master container must request additional containers from the Resource Manager. These containers are where the actual work gets done in the cluster. The Resource Manager/Application Master relationship can be dynamic in nature where containers can be requested and released at run time. Of course, the Resource Manager is the final arbiter of container requests, and on a loaded cluster it may not be possible to satisfy all container requests. As shown in Figure 1.6, a typical Hadoop V2 MapReduce job progresses as follows:

1. Clients submit jobs to the Resource Manager.
2. The Resource Manager selects a node and instructs the Node Manager to start an Application Master (App Mstr).
3. The Application Master (running in a container) requests additional containers (resources) from the Resource Manager.
4. The assigned containers are started and managed on the appropriate nodes by the Node Managers.
5. Once the Application Master and containers are connected and running, the Resource Manager and Node Managers step away from the job.

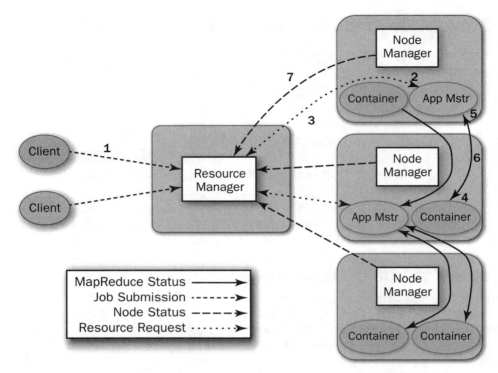

Figure 1.6   Hadoop V2 MapReduce workflow using Resource Manager,
Application Master, and Node Managers (From Arun C. Murthy, et al., *Apache
Hadoop™ YARN*, copyright © 2014, p. 39. Reprinted and electronically
reproduced by permission of Pearson Education, Inc., New York, NY.)

6. All job progress (e.g., MapReduce progress) is reported back to the
   Application Master.

7. When a task that runs in a container is completed, the Node Manager makes the
   container available to the Resource Manager.

The separation of user jobs from the scheduler has enabled Hadoop V2 to run more
jobs, with each job being managed by its own Application Master, and still remain
backward compatible with Hadoop V1 MapReduce applications. The net result were
advances along five major fronts:

1. *Better scale.* A separate scheduler allows a much larger number of nodes and
   jobs to run.

2. *New programming models and services.* Since the scheduler is task neutral, any type
   of programming model can be run on the cluster and have access to the data lake.
   These models include applications such as graph processing (Apache Giraph), in-
   memory models (Apache Spark), and even the Message Passing Interface (MPI).

3. *Improved cluster utilization*. Dynamic container allocation enables applications such as MapReduce to adjust the number of mappers and reducers and not rely on the fixed allocations strategies in Hadoop V1.

4. *Application agility*. New and updated applications can be improved and tested on the same cluster that is running production jobs.

5. *Move beyond Java*. Removing the application tasks from the scheduler enables applications to be written/created in any programming language and run on a Hadoop V2 cluster.

The Apache Hadoop Project Ecosystem

One of the biggest challenges facing new Hadoop users is the plethora of projects and sub-projects that fit under the Hadoop umbrella. Indeed, as the last two sections have shown, Hadoop is no longer a one-trick pony offering only a MapReduce engine. Instead, it is an ecosystem or platform on which to build applications that need to swim in the data lake.

At first glance, the number of sub-projects and components for Hadoop might seem overwhelming. (Particularly because, like Hadoop, the names have little relation to what the application actually does!) The good news is you will not use all of them at the same time, and your applications will probably ever use only a subset of the various tools and projects.

Like Hadoop, most of the sub-projects are part of the Apache Software Foundation (ASF) and are open source (see the sidebar "The Apache Software Foundation"). There are also many closed source projects that can coexist with the projects using the Apache License.

Currently, the major Hadoop distribution/service players include Cloudera, Hortonworks, MapR, and others. Each of these commercial organizations offers various support and packaging options. Hortonworks is the biggest contributor to the Apache Hadoop code base and maintains a totally open software stack and a commitment to the ASF 2.0 license.

Figure 1.7 illustrates the relationship between many of the Apache projects and the core Hadoop components (in gray). The major Apache applications in the figure can be categorized as follows. By no means is this a complete list, however.

- **Core Components**
  - **HDFS** is the Hadoop Distributed File system, which is used for storing data in a Hadoop cluster. HDFS is a redundant and highly reliable distributed file system.
  - **YARN** is Yet Another Resource Manager, which provides all scheduling and resource management for the cluster.
  - **MapReduce** is a YARN application framework that provides MapReduce functionality for the cluster. It is compatible with Hadoop V1 MapReduce and serves as the basis for many of the higher-level Hadoop tools.

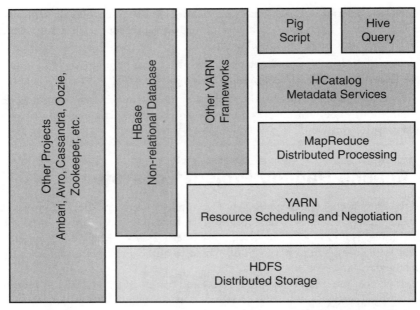

Figure 1.7   Example of the Hadoop V2 ecosystem (From Arun C. Murthy, et al., *Apache Hadoop™ YARN*, copyright © 2014, p. 34. Reprinted and electronically reproduced by permission of Pearson Education, Inc., New York, NY.)

- **Hadoop Database**
  - **Apache HCatalog** is a table and storage management service for data created using Hadoop. The table abstraction removes the need for the user to know where data is stored.
  - **Apache HBase** is the Hadoop database and is a distributed and scalable, column-oriented database similar to Google Big Table. HBase provides random, real-time access to data in the cluster. HBase is designed for hosting very large tables with billions of rows and millions of columns.
- **MapReduce Query Tools**
  - **Apache Pig** is a high-level language that enables programmers to write complex MapReduce transformations using a simple scripting language. Pig Latin (the actual language) defines a set of transformations on a data set such as aggregate, join, and sort. It is often used for extract, transform, and load (ETL) data pipelines, quick research on raw data, and iterative data processing. This language improves programming productivity with respect to Java programming of MapReduce jobs.
  - **Apache Hive** is a data warehouse infrastructure built on top of Hadoop for providing data summary, ad hoc queries, and the analysis of large data sets

using an SQL-like language called HiveQL. Hive transparently translates queries into MapReduce jobs that are executed in HBase. Hive is considered the de facto standard for interactive SQL queries over petabytes of data using Hadoop.

- **Data Import Export**
  - **Apache Sqoop** is a tool designed for efficiently transferring bulk data between HDFS and relational databases. Once placed in HDFS, the data can be used by Hadoop applications.
  - **Apache Flume** is a distributed, reliable service for efficiently collecting, aggregating, and moving large amounts of dynamic serial data (e.g., log data).
  - **Apache Avro** is a serialization format that makes it possible for data to be exchanged between programs written in any language. It is often used to connect Flume data flows.
- **Workflow Automation**
  - **Apache Oozie** is a workflow/coordination system to manage multistage Hadoop jobs. It enables workflow decisions based on job dependencies. Oozie is best for designing job execution graphs.
  - **Apache Falcon** enables automation of data movement and processing for ingest, pipelines, and replication operations. Falcon can trigger a job start when data changes or becomes available.
- **Administration**
  - **Apache Ambari** is a web-based tool for provisioning, managing, and monitoring Apache Hadoop clusters.
- **YARN Application Frameworks**
  - Application frameworks are applications that are written specifically for the YARN environment. The core MapReduce framework is one example. Other projects include applications like Apache Giraph (graph processing), Apache Spark (in-memory processing), Apache Storm (stream processing), and others. See Chapter 8, "Hadoop YARN Applications," for a more detailed discussion of YARN application frameworks.
- **Other**
  - **Apache ZooKeeper** is a centralized service used by applications for maintaining configuration, health, and other status elements on and between nodes. It maintains common objects needed in large cluster environments, including configuration information, hierarchical naming space, and so on. Applications can use these services to coordinate distributed processing across Hadoop clusters. Zookeeper also provides application reliability. If an Application Master dies, Zookeeper spawns a new Application Master to resume the tasks.
  - **Apache Mahout** is a scalable machine-learning library that implements many different approaches to machine learning.

Summary and Additional Resources

The Apache Hadoop project has evolved from a powerful MapReduce engine to a full Big Data platform running under the YARN resource manager. Unlike data warehouse methods, Hadoop favors a data lake concept where data is stored unchanged in raw form. Any extract, transform, and load steps (ETL) are postponed until the application run time.

The Hadoop V1 distributed MapReduce engine helped launch many new Big Data applications, but it encountered limitations as the number of concurrent jobs grew bigger and the application space grew wider. Hadoop V2 resolved many of these problems by splitting the resource manager from the MapReduce job engine. The Hadoop YARN platform provides scalable cluster resource management for all types of applications, including full Hadoop V1 MapReduce compatibility. The Hadoop ecosystem include many open source projects that provide for data import and export, workflow automations, SQL-like access, administration, and many new non-MapReduce applications.

Additional background on basic Hadoop history, design and use can be obtained from the following resources:

- Main Apache Hadoop website: http://hadoop.apache.org.
- Apache Hadoop documentation website: http://hadoop.apache.org/docs/current/index.html.
- Wikipedia: http://en.wikipedia.org/wiki/Apache_Hadoop
- Book: Murthy, Arun C., et al. 2014. *Apache Hadoop YARN: Moving beyond MapReduce and Batch Processing with Apache Hadoop 2*, Boston, MA: Addison-Wesley, http://www.informit.com/store/apache-hadoop-yarn-moving-beyond-mapreduce-and-batch-9780321934505.
- Video Training: *Hadoop Fundamentals LiveLessons,* second edition, http://www.informit.com/store/hadoop-fundamentals-livelessons-video-training-9780134052403.

## 2

Installation Recipes

In This Chapter:

- The Core Apache Hadoop services and configuration files are introduced.
- Background on basic Apache Hadoop Resource planning is provided.
- Step-by-step single-machine installation procedures for a virtual Apache Hadoop sandbox and a pseudo-distributed mode are provided.
- A full cluster graphical installation is performed using the Apache Ambari installation and modeling tool.
- A cloud-based Apache Hadoop cluster is created and configured using the Apache Whirr toolkit.

Installing Hadoop is an open-ended subject. As mentioned in Chapter 1, "Background and Concepts," Hadoop is an expanding ecosystem of tools for processing various types and volumes of data. Any Hadoop installation is ultimately dependent on your goals and project plans. In this chapter, we start by installing on a single system, then move to a full local cluster install, and finish with a recipe for installing Hadoop in the cloud. Each installation scenario has a different goal—learning on a small scale or implementing a full production cluster.

Core Hadoop Services

Regardless of the scope and direction that your installation takes, there will be a few common core services you will need to run. These services are Java applications that provide the basic Hadoop functionality. The first service is the Hadoop Distributed File System (HDFS). The second is the resource manager (YARN) that manages the jobs across the cluster.

HDFS includes two major components. The first is the process that manages the entire file system, called the NameNode. The second component comprises the processes that manage the actual data, which are called the DataNodes. There needs to be at least one DataNode for HDFS to work. In a typical Hadoop cluster, all of the worker machines in the cluster (often referred to as nodes) are running the DataNode service that reports to the central NameNode. The NameNode is often run on a separate machine from other Hadoop processes. It can be run in federated and/or failover modes as well.

There is also a process called the SecondaryNameNode. This process is not a backup NameNode and is best described as a CheckPointNode (NameNode failover is discussed in Chapter 3, "Hadoop Distributed File System Basics"). The SecondaryNameNode periodically fetches the in-memory HDFS edits from the NameNode and then merges and returns them to the NameNode. The in-memory design allows the NameNode to work quickly without having to commit file system changes directly to disk.

The second core service is the YARN workflow scheduler. Two main YARN services are required to run a program on a Hadoop cluster. The first is the ResourceManager, which is the single master scheduler for all cluster jobs. The ResourceManager works by communicating with the NodeManager service running on worker nodes. The NodeManager manages all the actual work done on the cluster nodes. There needs to be at least one NodeManager running for Hadoop jobs to run. Both the ResourceManager and the NodeManagers are job neutral—that is, they have no knowledge or interest in what the actual user job is doing. In addition, some history servers can be run as a part of YARN. These services are not essential for jobs to run, but they make job tracking much easier. The JobHistoryServer is used for MapReduce job history collection. The ApplicationHistoryServer is a more general history server that can be used by non-MapReduce jobs.

Depending on your installation scheme, these services can be run in a variety of ways. For instance, in a single-machine installation, all the services are run on a single machine with a single DataNode and single NodeManager processes. In a full cluster installation, the NameNode, SecondaryNameNode, ResourceManager, and history servers may all be run on separate machines. In other designs, some of the services may overlap and run on the same machine. Each of the worker machines usually has both a DataNode and a NodeManager service running. As will be shown in the following installation scenarios, the core Hadoop services can be deployed in a flexible fashion and tuned to your needs.

Hadoop Configuration Files

All core Hadoop services use XML files for storing parameters. These files are usually located under /etc/hadoop. For instance, both HDFS and YARN have their own XML files (i.e., hdfs-site.xml and yarn-site.xml). The sheer number of options is too numerous to cover here. The Hadoop documentation page (https://hadoop.apache.org/docs/stable/; scroll down to the lower lefthand corner under Configuration) has a full listing of each file with the option name, value, and a description.

If you are installing from the Apache sources, you will need to edit these files by hand (see the single-node Apache source installation process in the section "Installing

Hadoop from Apache Sources"). The XML files have the following internal format. All configuration properties are placed between `<configuration>`,`</configuration>` tags. Each property takes the following form:

```
<property>
   <name>dfs.replication</name>
   <value>1</value>
 </property>
```

In this case, the property name is `dfs.replication` and the value is `1`. If the XML configuration file is changed while the service is running, the service must be restarted for the new configuration to take effect. Most Hadoop tools and applications use a similar method for assigning properties. If you are using an automated tool such as Apache Ambari (see the section "Installing Hadoop with Ambari"), the XML files are preconfigured and can be modified from the Ambari web GUI.

The `/etc/hadoop` configuration directory also contains environment files (`*.sh`) that are used to set up the proper environment and Java options for a particular service. Similar to the XML files, changes take effect only when the service is restarted.

Planning Your Resources

As will be described in this chapter, Hadoop installation options can range from a single system with the core services to large clusters with a full array of Hadoop services and applications. A full treatment of these evolving options is beyond the scope of this chapter. The following discussion provides some basic guidelines for Hadoop resource planning.

Hardware Choices

The first hardware choice is often whether to use a local machine or cloud services. Both options depend on your needs and budget. In general, local machines take longer to procure and provision, require administrative and power costs, but offer fast internal data transfers and on-premises security. For their part, cloud-based clusters are quickly procured and provisioned, do not require on-site power and administration, but still require Hadoop administration and off-site data transfer and storage. Each option has both advantages and disadvantages. There is often a cloud-based feasibility stage for many Hadoop projects that start in the cloud and end up in production on an internal cluster. In addition, because Hadoop uses generic hardware, it is possible to cobble together several older servers and easily create an internal test system.

Hadoop components are designed to work on commodity servers. These systems are usually multicore x86-based servers with hard drives for storing HDFS data. Newer systems employ 10-gigabit Ethernet (GbE) as a communication network. The Hadoop design provides multiple levels of failover that can tolerate a failed server or even an entire rack of servers. Building large clusters is not a trivial process, however; it requires designs that provide adequate network performance, support for failover strategies, server storage capacity, processor size (cores), workflow policies, and more.

The various Hadoop distributers provide freely available guides that can help in choosing the right hardware. Many hardware vendors also have *Hadoop recipes*. Nevertheless, using a qualified consultant or Hadoop vendor is recommended for large projects.

Software Choices

The system software requirements for a Hadoop installation are somewhat basic. The installation of the official Apache Software Hadoop releases still relies on a Linux host and file system such as ext3, ext4, XFS, and btrfs. A Java Development Kit starting with the later versions of 1.6 or 1.7 is required. The officially supported versions can be found at http://wiki.apache.org/hadoop/HadoopJavaVersions. Various vendors have tested both the Oracle JDK and the OpenJDK. The OpenJDK that comes with many popular Linux distributions should work for most installs (make sure the version number is 1.7 or higher). All of the major distributions of Linux should work as a base operating system; these include Red Hat Enterprise Linux (or rebuilds like CentOS), Fedora, SLES, Ubuntu, and Debian.

Hadoop versions 2.2 and later include native support for Windows. The official Apache Hadoop releases do not include Windows binaries (as of July 2015). However, building a Windows package from the sources is fairly straightforward.

Many decisions go into a production Hadoop cluster that can be ignored for small feasibility projects (although the feasibility projects are certainly a good place to test the various options before putting them into production). These decisions include choices related to Secure Mode Hadoop operation, HDFS Federation and High Availability, and checkpointing.

By default, Hadoop runs in non-secure mode in which no actual authentication is required throughout the cluster other than the basic POSIX-level security. When Hadoop is configured to run in secure mode, each user and service needs to be authenticated by Kerberos to use Hadoop services. More information on Secure Mode Hadoop can be found at http://hadoop.apache.org/docs/current/hadoop-project-dist/hadoop-common/SecureMode.html. Security features of Hadoop consist of authentication, service level authorization, authentication for web consoles, and data confidentiality.

HDFS NameNode Federation and NameNode HA (High Availability) are the two important decisions for most organizations. NameNode Federation significantly improves the scalability and performance of HDFS by introducing the ability to deploy multiple NameNodes for a single cluster. In addition to federation, HDFS introduces built-in high availability for the NameNode via a new feature called the Quorum Journal Manager (QJM). QJM-based HA includes an active NameNode and a standby NameNode. The standby NameNode can become active either by a manual process or automatically. Background on these HDFS features is presented in Chapter 3.

Installing on a Desktop or Laptop

A minimal production Hadoop installation usually entails several servers running in a data center. Acquiring even a small cluster can be a rather large barrier to entry if a user wants to explore the Hadoop ecosystem. To help circumvent this problem, there are ways to install Hadoop on a desktop or laptop for personal use. Although not usable for larger jobs and with larger amounts of data, actual Hadoop software can be studied and investigated without large system startup overhead.

In the next two sections, we provide instruction on how to install two freely available single-machine Hadoop versions. The first is the Hortonworks HDP (Hortonworks Data Platform) Sandbox, which provides a fully running Hadoop environment with a full suite of tools and utilities. This environment is distributed as a virtual machine that can be easily installed on modern Apple or Microsoft operating systems.

The second method, while a bit more detailed, installs the official Apache Hadoop software in a *pseudo-distributed mode*. Once installed, this version more closely mimics how you would might install and use Hadoop on a real cluster.

Either environment will enable you to run and modify the majority of the examples presented in this book. Of course, where true parallel operation is required, a full installation of Hadoop will be used.

Installing Hortonworks HDP 2.2 Sandbox

The Hortonworks Hadoop Sandbox is a freely available virtual machine that will run in the VirtualBox, VMware, or Hyper-V environments. The virtual machine uses the same software in the professional (also freely available) Hortonworks Data Platform. If you choose to use the web interface to the virtual machine, Hortonworks will ask for a no-obligation registration. There is no registration needed to connect via the command line.

In this example, VirtualBox will be used to run the Hadoop sandbox on a MacBook Pro. There are versions for Linux and Windows machines as well. VirtualBox can be downloaded from https://www.virtualbox.org. The VirtualBox base packages (everything but the extension pack) are released under the GNU General Public License V2.

Once VirtualBox is installed on your system, you can download the virtual machine from http://hortonworks.com/hdp/downloads. As per the Hortonworks web page, the minimum requirements are as follows:

- 32-bit and 64-bit OS (Windows XP, Windows 7, Windows 8, and Mac OSX)
- Minimum 4GB RAM (8GB required to run Ambari and HBase)
- Virtualization enabled on BIOS
- Browser: Chrome 25+, Internet Explorer 9+, or Safari 6+ recommended. (The Sandbox will not run on Internet Explorer 10.)

In this example, we are using version 2.2 of the Hortonworks Sandbox. The virtual machine file is called `Sandbox_HDP_2.2_VirtualBox.ova` and is 4.9GB in size. There is also an installation guide available from Hortonworks.

What Is a Virtual Machine?

A virtual machine is an image of a running computer that runs inside a physical computer. This arrangement allows the virtual machine to run a different operating system (and in some cases hardware) from the host computer. The Hortonworks Sandbox is delivered as a virtual machine that consists of the Linux operating system, configuration settings, Hadoop software, and applications that work together as they would on a real machine. When not running, the virtual machine exists as a file (disk image). To run on a virtual machine on a host requires a virtualization environment that simulates a running computer. These environments are created by packages like VirtualBox, VMWare, and Hyper-V. When encapsulated as a virtual machine, an entire Hadoop installation can be preconfigured and tested before distribution to users. Thus, a single-machine turnkey Hadoop sandbox can be configured without the need to customize it for each operating system.

Step 1: Start Virtual Box

After it is installed, click on VirtualBox from the Applications window. The Virtual-Box Manager window, shown in Figure 2.1, will open.

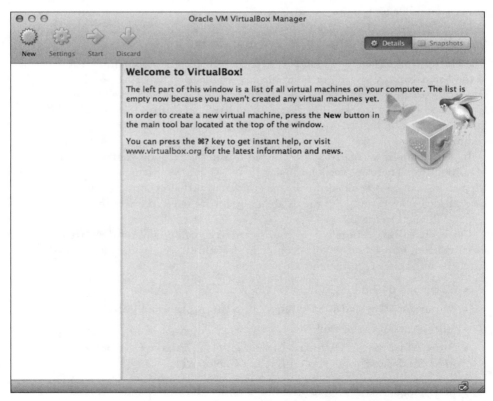

Figure 2.1   The VirtualBox Manager window

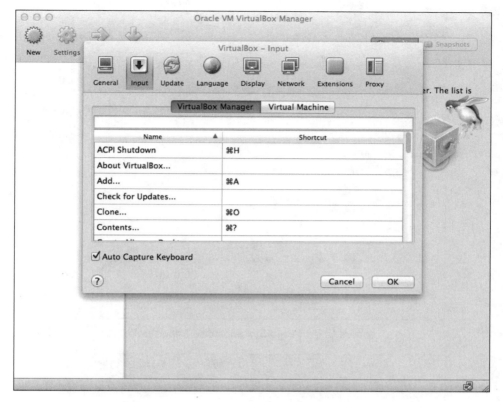

Figure 2.2   VirtualBox Preferences—Input options

Before the sandbox is loaded and started, we need to make a few changes. From the VirtualBox main menu, select File/Preferences. When the box in Figure 2.2 appears, check Auto Capture Keyboard at the bottom and click OK.

Step 2: Load the Virtual Machine

From the main VirtualBox window, select File/Import Appliance. A box, as shown in Figure 2.3, will open that allows you to browse for the .ova file (in this example, the file name is Sandbox_HDP_2.2_VirtualBox.ova).

Once you have selected the file, click Continue and the window in Figure 2.4 will be presented. The various appliance settings can be changed at this point, such as the number of CPUs or the amount of RAM to use for the virtual machine. It is best not to decrease the default values, however.

When the settings are confirmed, the virtual machine can be imported by clicking the Import button. A progress window like the one shown in Figure 2.5 should appear.

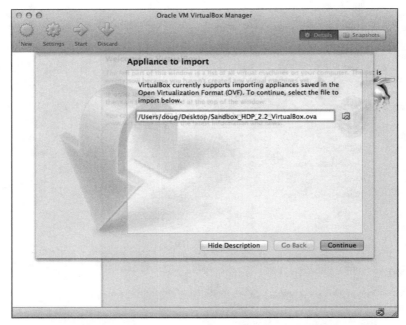

Figure 2.3   VirtualBox appliance import box

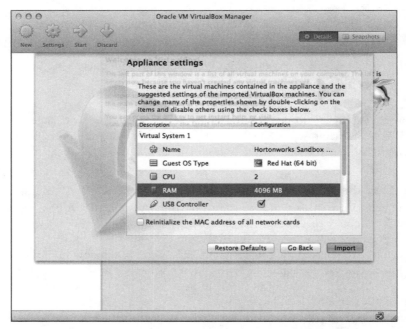

Figure 2.4   VirtualBox Appliance settings window

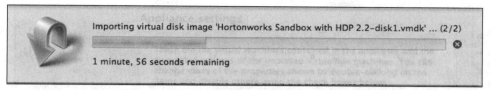

Figure 2.5   VirtualBox import progress window

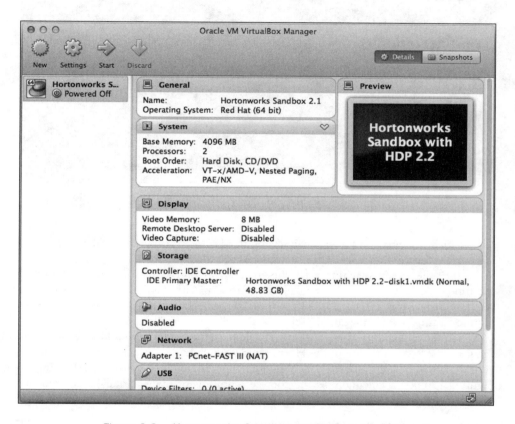

Figure 2.6   Hortonworks Sandbox appliance loaded into
VirtualBox Manager

Once the Sandbox appliance has been imported, the VirtualBox Manager, shown in Figure 2.6, should show the virtual machine as Powered Off (see the lefthand column). At this point, you may wish to adjust the Base Memory for your virtual machine. If your host system has 4GB of memory, it is best to set the Base Memory to 2048MB (2GB) so the host operating system does not run out of memory. The virtual machine will start and run in 2GB, but some of the applications (e.g., Ambari and HBase) may not function or may function too slowly. If you have more than 8GB

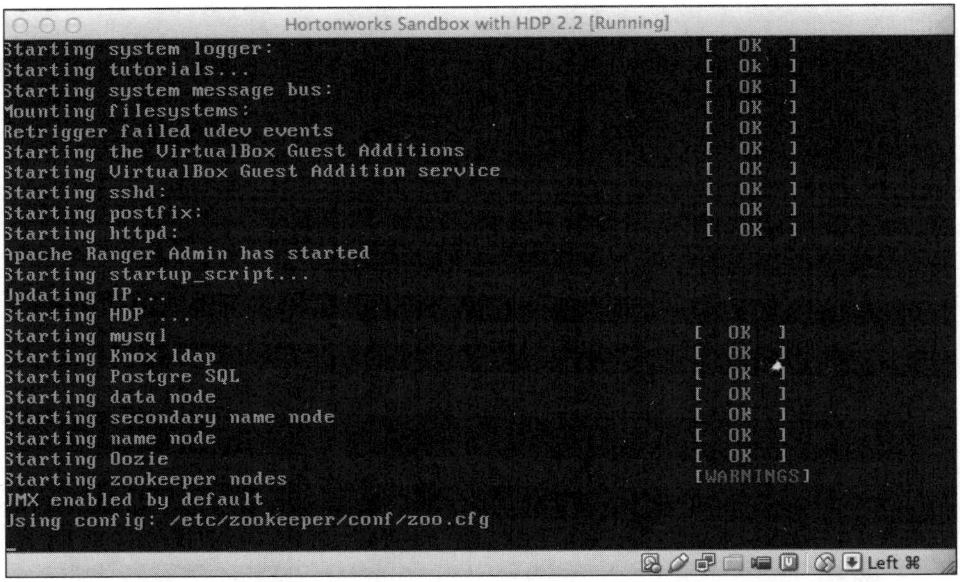

Figure 2.7   Hortonworks Sandbox appliance booting in console window

of host memory, you can increase the setting to 8192MB (or higher). Make sure you leave room for the host operating system, however.

To start the virtual machine, click the green arrow on the main menu bar. A virtual machine console window will open and the virtual machine will start to boot up. This window is shown in Figure 2.7 and produces the exact boot up screen for appliance. (Those familiar with Linux boot process will notice it immediately.)

When the appliance is done booting, the next virtual window should look like the Figure 2.8. Normal use of the Hortonworks Sandbox does not require you to use your keyboard or your mouse inside the Hortonworks Sandbox console window in Figure 2.7. If you accidentally let the console capture your mouse or keyboard, you can release them back to the host machine by pressing the Ctrl key and then clicking OK.

Step 3: Connect to the Hadoop Appliance

There are two ways to connect to the Hadoop appliance. The first is to simply use ssh and log into the new machine. (Remember the virtual appliance is a separate running instance of a complete machine.) To log in, open a terminal window on your system and enter the following command:

```
$ ssh root@127.0.0.1 -p2222
```

The password is hadoop. Once you are logged in, you can use all of the Hadoop features installed in the appliance. You can also connect via a web interface by entering http://127.0.0.1:8888 into your host browser. On first use, there is a

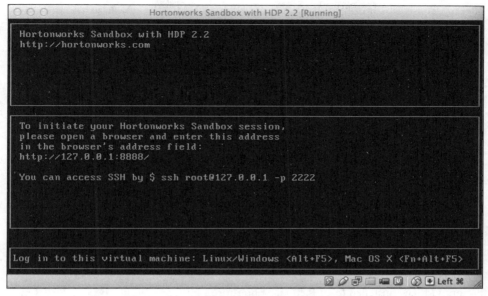

○ ○ ○   Hortonworks Sandbox with HDP 2.2 [Running]

Hortonworks Sandbox with HDP 2.2
http://hortonworks.com

To initiate your Hortonworks Sandbox session,
please open a browser and enter this address
in the browser's address field:
http://127.0.0.1:8888/

You can access SSH by $ ssh root@127.0.0.1 -p 2222

Log in to this virtual machine: Linux/Windows <Alt+F5>, Mac OS X <Fn+Alt+F5>

Figure 2.8   Hortonworks Sandbox ready for use by either a web browser
or ssh

Hortonworks registration screen that requests some basic information. Once you enter
the information, the web GUI is available for use.

Step 4: Shutting Down or Saving the Hadoop Sandbox

When you are finished using the Hadoop Sandbox, the virtual machine can be either
shut down or saved. If you select Machine/Close from the VirtualBox menu bar, you
will be presented with three options. If you select Power Off, the machine will be
stopped immediately; this option is similar to pulling the plug on the machine. The
original image will then be rebooted the next time the appliance is started (i.e., all
changes and files will be gone). The second option is ACPI shutdown. This option is
supposed to shut down the appliance gracefully. If it does not work, you can log into
the appliance as root and enter poweroff; the appliance will then shut down. As with
a real system, all changes will be saved and available on the next startup. The final
option is Save State. If you use Save State, you can quickly save and restore the state of
the machine (including any changes you made to the system). The save/restore process
is usually much quicker than starting/stopping the virtual machine.

Installing Hadoop from Apache Sources

Although the Hadoop Sandbox provides an easy way to install a working single-
machine Hadoop system, installing from the Apache sources also has some benefits.
A hands-on installation provides some insights into how a production Hadoop system

operates and is configured. A basic Apache Hadoop YARN release has two core components:

- The Hadoop Distributed File System for storing data
- Hadoop YARN for running and implementing applications to process data

Both of these components and the MapReduce framework are included in the Apache Hadoop release obtained from https://hadoop.apache.org. This section presents the steps to install a single-machine version of Hadoop. A full cluster install is covered in the Ambari section of this chapter. We will also install the Pig and Hive packages so you can run these applications in other chapters.

Steps to Configure a Single-Node YARN Server

The following type of installation is often referred to as pseudo-distributed because it mimics some of the functionality of a distributed Hadoop cluster. A single machine is, of course, not practical for any production use, nor is it parallel. A small-scale Hadoop installation can provide a simple method for learning Hadoop basics, however.

The recommended *minimal* installation hardware is a dual-core processor with 2GB of RAM and 2GB of available hard drive space. The system will need a recent Linux distribution with Java installed (e.g., Red Hat Enterprise Linux or rebuilds, Fedora, Suse Linux Enterprise, OpenSuse, Ubuntu). CentOS version 6.5 is used for this installation example. A bash shell environment is also assumed. The first step is to download Apache Hadoop.

Note that the following commands and files are available for download from the book repository. See Appendix A, "Book Webpage and Code Download," for details.

Step 1: Download Apache Hadoop

Download the latest distribution from the Hadoop website (https://hadoop.apache.org/). For example, as root give the following commands:

```
# cd /root
# wget http://mirrors.ibiblio.org/apache/hadoop/common/hadoop-2.6.0/hadoop-
2.6.0.tar.gz
```

Next, extract the package in /opt:

```
# cd /opt
# tar xvzf /root/hadoop-2.6.0.tar.gz
```

Step 2: Set JAVA_HOME and HADOOP_HOME

For Hadoop 2, the recommended version of Java can be found at http://wiki.apache.org/hadoop/HadoopJavaVersions. In general, a Java Development Kit 1.6 (or greater) should work. For this install, we will use Open Java 1.7.0_51, which is part of CentOS Linux 6.5. Make sure you have a working Java JDK installed; in this case, it is the java-1.7.0-openjdk RPM. To include JAVA_HOME for all bash users (other shells must be set in a similar fashion), make an entry in /etc/profile.d as follows:

```
# echo 'export JAVA_HOME=/usr/lib/jvm/java-1.7.0-openjdk-1.7.0.51.x86_64/' > /etc/
profile.d/java.sh
```

In addition, to ensure that HADOOP_HOME is both defined and added to your PATH on login, execute the following command:

```
# echo 'export HADOOP_HOME=/opt/hadoop-2.6.0;export PATH=$HADOOP_HOME/bin:$PATH' >
/etc/profile.d/hadoop.sh
```

To make sure JAVA_HOME, HADOOP_HOME, and the updated PATH variable are defined for this session, source the new script:

```
# source /etc/profile.d/java.sh
# source /etc/profile.d/hadoop.sh
```

Step 3: Create Users and Groups

It is best to run the various daemons with separate accounts. Three accounts (yarn, hdfs, mapred) in the group hadoop can be created as follows:

```
# groupadd hadoop
# useradd -g hadoop yarn
# useradd -g hadoop hdfs
# useradd -g hadoop mapred
```

Step 4: Make Data and Log Directories

Hadoop needs various data and log directories with various permissions. Enter the following lines to create these directories:

```
# mkdir -p /var/data/hadoop/hdfs/nn
# mkdir -p /var/data/hadoop/hdfs/snn
# mkdir -p /var/data/hadoop/hdfs/dn
# chown -R hdfs:hadoop /var/data/hadoop/hdfs
# mkdir -p /var/log/hadoop/yarn
# chown -R yarn:hadoop /var/log/hadoop/yarn
```

Next, move to the YARN installation root and create the log directory and set the owner and group as follows:

```
# cd /opt/hadoop-2.6.0
# mkdir logs
# chmod g+w logs
# chown -R yarn:hadoop .
```

Step 5: Configure core-site.xml

From the base of the Hadoop installation path (e.g., /opt/hadoop-2.6.0), edit the etc/hadoop/core-site.xml file. The original installed file will have no entries other than the <configuration> </configuration> tags. Two properties need to be set. The first is the fs.default.name property, which sets the host and request port names for the NameNode (the metadata server for HDFS). The second is hadoop.http.staticuser.user, which will set the default user name to hdfs.

Copy the following lines to the Hadoop `etc/hadoop/core-site.xml` file and remove the original empty <configuration> </configuration> tags.

```
<configuration>
 <property>
    <name>fs.default.name</name>
    <value>hdfs://localhost:9000</value>
 </property>   <property>
    <name>hadoop.http.staticuser.user</name>
    <value>hdfs</value>
 </property>
</configuration>
```

Step 6: Configure hdfs-site.xml

From the base of the Hadoop installation path, edit the `etc/hadoop/hdfs-site.xml` file. In the single-node pseudo-distributed mode, we don't need or want the HDFS to replicate file blocks. By default, HDFS keeps three copies of each file in the file system for redundancy. There is no need for replication on a single machine; thus the value of `dfs.replication` will be set to 1.

In `hdfs-site.xml`, we specify the NameNode, SecondaryNameNode, and DataNode data directories that we created in Step 4. These are the directories used by the various components of HDFS to store data. Copy the following lines into Hadoop `etc/hadoop/hdfs-site.xml` and remove the original empty <configuration> </configuration> tags.

```
<configuration>
 <property>
    <name>dfs.replication</name>
    <value>1</value>
 </property>
 <property>
    <name>dfs.namenode.name.dir</name>
    <value>file:/var/data/hadoop/hdfs/nn</value>
 </property>
 <property>
    <name>fs.checkpoint.dir</name>
    <value>file:/var/data/hadoop/hdfs/snn</value>
 </property>
 <property>
    <name>fs.checkpoint.edits.dir</name>
    <value>file:/var/data/hadoop/hdfs/snn</value>
 </property>
 <property>
    <name>dfs.datanode.data.dir</name>
    <value>file:/var/data/hadoop/hdfs/dn</value>
 </property>
</configuration>
```

Step 7: Configure mapred-site.xml

From the base of the Hadoop installation, edit the `etc/hadoop/mapred-site.xml` file. A new configuration option for Hadoop 2 is the capability to specify a framework name for MapReduce using the `mapreduce.framework.name` property. In this install, we will use the value of yarn to tell MapReduce that it will run as a YARN application. First, however, we need to copy the template file to the `mapred-site.xml`:

```
# cp mapred-site.xml.template mapred-site.xml
```

Next, copy the following lines into Hadoop `etc/hadoop/mapred-site.xml` file and remove the original empty `<configuration>` `</configuration>` tags.

```
<configuration>
 <property>
   <name>mapreduce.framework.name</name>
   <value>yarn</value>
 </property>
 <property>
   <name>mapreduce.jobhistory.intermediate-done-dir</name>
   <value>/mr-history/tmp </value>
 </property>
 <property>
   <name>mapreduce.jobhistory.done-dir</name>
   <value>/mr-history/done</value>
 </property>
</configuration>
```

Step 8: Configure yarn-site.xml

From the base of the Hadoop installation, edit the `etc/hadoop/yarn-site.xml` file. The `yarn.nodemanager.aux-services` property tells NodeManagers that there will be an auxiliary service called `mapreduce.shuffle` that they need to implement. After we tell the NodeManagers to implement that service, we give it a class name as the means to implement that service. This particular configuration tells MapReduce how to do its shuffle. Because NodeManagers won't shuffle data for a non-MapReduce job by default, we need to configure such a service for MapReduce. Copy the following lines to the Hadoop `etc/hadoop/yarn-site.xml` file and remove the original empty `<configuration>` `</configuration>` tags.

```
<configuration>
 <property>
   <name>yarn.nodemanager.aux-services</name>
   <value>mapreduce_shuffle</value>
 </property>
 <property>
   <name>yarn.nodemanager.aux-services.mapreduce.shuffle.class</name>
   <value>org.apache.hadoop.mapred.ShuffleHandler</value>
 </property>
</configuration>
```

Step 9: Modify Java Heap Sizes

The Hadoop installation uses several environment variables that determine the heap sizes for each Hadoop process. These are defined in the `etc/hadoop/*-env.sh` files used by Hadoop. The default for most of the processes is a 1GB heap size; because we're running on a workstation that will probably have limited resources compared to a standard server, however, we need to adjust the heap size settings. The values that follow are recommended for a small workstation or server.

Edit the `etc/hadoop/hadoop-env.sh` file to reflect the following (don't forget to remove the # at the beginning of the line):

```
export HADOOP_HEAPSIZE="500"
export HADOOP_NAMENODE_INIT_HEAPSIZE="500"
```

Next, edit `mapred-env.sh` to reflect the following:

```
export HADOOP_JOB_HISTORYSERVER_HEAPSIZE=250
```

You will also need to edit `yarn-env.sh` to reflect the following:

```
JAVA_HEAP_MAX=-Xmx500m
```

Add the following line to `yarn-env.sh`:

```
YARN_HEAPSIZE=500
```

Finally, to stop some warnings about native Hadoop libraries, edit `hadoop-env.sh` and add the following to the end:

```
export HADOOP_COMMON_LIB_NATIVE_DIR=$HADOOP_HOME/lib/native
export HADOOP_OPTS="$HADOOP_OPTS -Djava.library.path=$HADOOP_HOME/lib/native "
```

Step 10: Format HDFS

For the HDFS NameNode to start, it needs to initialize the directory where it will hold its data. The NameNode service tracks all the metadata for the file system. The format process will use the value assigned to `dfs.namenode.name.dir` in `etc/hadoop/hdfs-site.xml` earlier (i.e., `/var/data/hadoop/hdfs/nn`). Formatting destroys everything in the directory and sets up a new file system. Format the NameNode directory as the HDFS superuser, which is typically the `hdfs` user account.

From the base of the Hadoop distribution, change directories to the `bin` directory and execute the following commands:

```
# su - hdfs
$ cd /opt/hadoop-2.6.0/bin
$ ./hdfs namenode -format
```

If the command worked, you should see the following near the end of a long list of messages:

```
INFO common.Storage: Storage directory /var/data/hadoop/hdfs/nn has been
successfully formatted.
```

Step 11: Start the HDFS Services

Once formatting is successfully completed, the HDFS services must be started.
There is one service for the NameNode (metadata server), a single DataNode (where
the actual data is stored), and the SecondaryNameNode (checkpoint data for the
NameNode). The Hadoop distribution includes scripts that set up these commands as
well as name other values such as PID directories, log directories, and other standard
process configurations. From the bin directory in Step 10, execute the following as
user hdfs:

```
$ cd ../sbin
$ ./hadoop-daemon.sh start namenode
```

This command should result in the following output (the logging file name has the
host name appended—in this case, the host name is limulus):

```
starting namenode, logging to /opt/hadoop-2.6.0/logs/hadoop-hdfs-namenode-limulus.out
```

The SecondaryNameNode and DataNode services can be started in the same way:

```
$ ./hadoop-daemon.sh start secondarynamenode
starting secondarynamenode, logging to /opt/hadoop-2.6.0/logs/hadoop-hdfs-
secondarynamenode-limulus.out
$ ./hadoop-daemon.sh start datanode
starting datanode, logging to /opt/hadoop-2.6.0/logs/hadoop-hdfs-datanode-limulus.out
```

If the daemon started, you should see responses that will point to the log file. (Note
that the actual log file is appended with .log, not .out.) As a sanity check, issue a jps
command to confirm that all the services are running. The actual PID (Java process
ID) values will be different than shown in this listing:

```
$ jps
15140 SecondaryNameNode
15015 NameNode
15335 Jps
15214 DataNode
```

If the process did not start, it may be helpful to inspect the log files. For instance,
examine the log file for the NameNode. (Note that the path is taken from the preceding command and the host name is part of the file name.)

```
vi /opt/hadoop-2.6.0/logs/hadoop-hdfs-namenode-limulus.log
```

As a test of the HDFS installation, the following commands will create a directory
for the MapReduce history server. These operations use the hdfs commands, which
are covered in Chapter 3:

```
$ hdfs dfs -mkdir -p /mr-history/tmp
$ hdfs dfs -mkdir -p /mr-history/done
$ hdfs dfs -chown -R yarn:hadoop  /mr-history
$ hdfs dfs -mkdir -p /user/hdfs
```

If you get warning messages that the system is "Unable to load native-hadoop library for your platform," you can ignore them. The Apache Hadoop distribution is compiled for 32-bit operation, and this warning often appears when it is run on 64-bit systems.

All Hadoop services can be stopped using the `hadoop-daemon.sh` script. For example, to stop the DataNode service, enter the following command (as user `hdfs` in the `/opt/hadoop-2.6.0/sbin` directory):

```
$ ./hadoop-daemon.sh stop datanode
```

The same can be done for the NameNode and SecondaryNameNode services.

Step 12: Start the YARN Services

As with HDFS services, the YARN services need to be started. One ResourceManager and one NodeManager must be started as user `yarn` (after exiting from user `hdfs`):

```
$ exit
logout
# su - yarn
$ cd /opt/hadoop-2.6.0/sbin
$ ./yarn-daemon.sh start resourcemanager
starting resourcemanager, logging to /opt/hadoop-2.6.0/logs/yarn-yarn-
resourcemanager-limulus.out
$ ./yarn-daemon.sh start nodemanager
starting nodemanager, logging to /opt/hadoop-2.6.0/logs/yarn-yarn-nodemanager-
limulus.out
```

The other service we will need is the MapReduce history server, which keeps track of MapReduce jobs.

```
$ ./mr-jobhistory-daemon.sh start historyserver
starting historyserver, logging to /opt/hadoop-2.6.0/logs/mapred-yarn-
historyserver-limulus.out
```

As when the HDFS daemons were started in Step 12, the status of the running daemons is sent to their respective log files. To check whether the services are running, issue a `jps` command. The following shows all the services necessary to run YARN on a single server:

```
$ jps
15933 Jps
15567 ResourceManager
15785 NodeManager
15919 JobHistoryServer
```

If there are missing services, check the log file for the specific service. Similar to the case with HDFS services, the YARN services can be stopped by issuing a stop argument to the daemon script:

```
./yarn-daemon.sh stop nodemanager
```

Step 13: Verify the Running Services Using the Web Interface

Both HDFS and the YARN ResourceManager have a web interface. These interfaces offer a convenient way to browse many of the aspects of your Hadoop installation. To monitor HDFS, enter the following:

```
$ firefox  http://localhost:50070
```

Connecting to port 50070 will bring up a web interface similar to Figure 2.9.

A web interface for the ResourceManager can be viewed by entering the following command:

```
$ firefox http://localhost:8088
```

A webpage similar to that shown in Figure 2.10 will be displayed.

Run a Simple MapReduce Example

To test your installation, run the sample pi program, which calculates the value of pi using a quasi-Monte Carlo method and MapReduce. First, make sure all the services started previously are still running. Next, change to user hdfs and enter the following commands:

```
# su - hdfs
$ export HADOOP_EXAMPLES=/opt/hadoop-2.6.0/share/hadoop/mapreduce
$ yarn jar $HADOOP_EXAMPLES/hadoop-mapreduce-examples-2.6.0.jar pi 16 1000
```

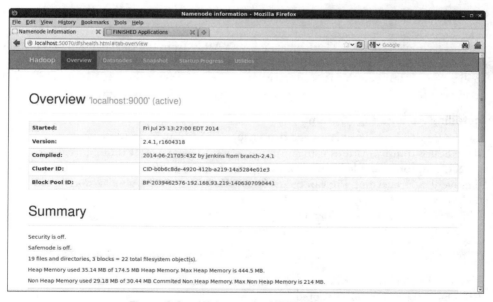

Figure 2.9   Webpage for HDFS file system

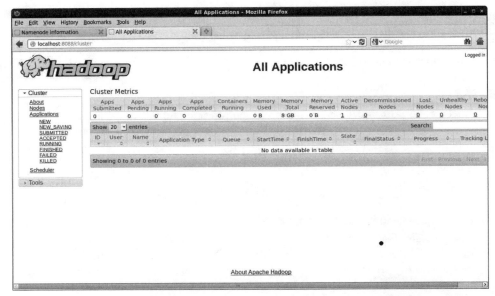

Figure 2.10   Webpage for YARN ResourceManager

If the program worked correctly, the following should be displayed at the end of the program output stream:

```
Estimated value of Pi is 3.14250000000000000000
```

This example submits a MapReduce job to YARN from the included samples in the share/hadoop/mapreduce directory. The master JAR file contains several sample applications to test your YARN installation. After you submit the job, its progress can be viewed by updating the ResourceManager webpage shown in Figure 2.10.

Installing Apache Pig (Optional)

Apache Pig is a high-level language that enables programmers to write complex MapReduce transformations using a simple scripting language. It is often used for extract, transform, and load (ETL) data pipelines, quick research on raw data, and iterative data processing. Pig can be easily installed for use on a pseudo–distributed Hadoop system.

The first step is to download the package. Note that there may be a more recent version. For this example, version 0.14.0 is used.

```
# wget http://mirrors.ibiblio.org/apache/pig/pig-0.14.0/pig-0.14.0.tar.gz
```

Once the Pig tar file is downloaded (we will assume it is downloaded into /root), it can be extracted into the /opt directory.

```
# cd /opt
# tar xvzf /root/pig-0.14.0.tar.gz
```

Similar to the case with the earlier Hadoop install, Pig defines may be placed in /etc/profile.d so that when users log in, the defines are automatically placed in their environment.

```
# echo 'export PATH=/opt/pig-0.14.0/bin:$PATH; export PIG_HOME=/opt/pig-0.14.0/;
PIG_CLASSPATH=/opt/hadoop-2.6.0/etc/hadoop/' > /etc/profile.d/pig.sh
```

If the Pig environment variables are needed for this session, they can be added by sourcing the new script:

```
# source /etc/profile.d/pig.sh
```

Pig is now installed and ready for use. See Chapter 7, "Essential Hadoop Tools," for examples of how to use Apache Pig.

Installing Apache Hive (Optional)

Apache Hive is a data warehouse infrastructure built on top of Hadoop for providing data summarization, ad hoc queries, and the analysis of large data sets using an SQL-like language called HiveQL. Hive can be easily installed for use on pseudo-distributed Hadoop systems.

The first step is to download the package. Note that there may be a more recent version. For this example, Hive version 1.1.0 is used.

```
# wget http://mirrors.ibiblio.org/apache/hive/hive-1.1.0/apache-hive-1.1.0-bin.
tar.gz
```

As before, the package is extracted into /opt:

```
# cd /opt
# tar xvzf /root/apache-hive-1.1.0-bin.tar.gz
```

Similar to the other packages, Hive defines may be placed in /etc/profile.d so that when users log in, the defines are automatically placed in their environment.

```
# echo 'export HIVE_HOME=/opt/apache-hive-1.1.0-bin/; export PATH=$HIVE_HOME/
bin:$PATH' >/etc/profile.d/hive.sh
```

Hive needs /tmp and /usr/hive/warehouse in HDFS. This task must be done as user hdfs. To create these directories, enter the following commands:

```
# su - hdfs
$ hdfs dfs -mkdir /tmp
$ hdfs dfs -mkdir -p /user/hive/warehouse
$ hdfs dfs -chmod g+w /tmp
$ hdfs dfs -chmod g+w /user/hive/warehouse
```

> **Note**
>
> If you are using Hadoop 2.6.0 and Hive 1.1.0, there is a library mismatch that will gener-
> ate the following error message when you start Hive:
>
> ```
> [ERROR] Terminal initialization failed; falling back to unsupported java.lang.
> IncompatibleClassChangeError: Found class jline.Terminal, but interface was
> expected
> ```
>
> This error arises because Hive has upgraded to Jline2, but Jline 0.94 exists in the Hadoop
> lib directory.
>
> To fix the error, perform the following steps:
>
> 1. Delete jline from the Hadoop lib directory (it's pulled in transitively from ZooKeeper):
>
>    ```
>    # rm $HADOOP_HOME/share/hadoop/yarn/lib/jline-0.9.94.jar
>    ```
>
> 2. Add the following to your environment:
>
>    ```
>    $ export HADOOP_USER_CLASSPATH_FIRST=true
>    ```

If the Hive environment variables are needed for this session, they can be added by
sourcing the new script:

```
$ source /etc/profile.d/hive.sh
```

Hive is now installed and ready for use. See Chapter 7, "Essential Hadoop Tools,"
for examples of how to use Apache Hive.

Installing Hadoop with Ambari

As can be seen from the single-machine pseudo-distributed installation process,
Hadoop installation is far from a turnkey operation. The steps become more
complex when a full cluster install is required. For this reason, larger cluster
installs should use the graphical Apache Ambari installation and management tool.
Ambari provides the means to handle the administrative and monitoring tasks by
employing an agent on each node to install required components, change configuration files, and monitor performance or failures of nodes either individually or as
an aggregate. Both administrators and developers will find many of the Ambari
features useful.

Installation with Ambari is faster, easier, and less error prone than manually setting
up each services configuration file. As demonstrated in this chapter, a four-node cluster install of the Hortonworks HDP Hadoop distribution can be accomplished in less
than one hour. Ambari can dramatically cut down on the number of people required
to install larger clusters and increases the speed with which development environments
can be created.

Configuration files are maintained by an Ambari service acting as the sole arbiter
of changes to the cluster. Ambari guarantees that the configuration files on all nodes
will be the same by redistributing them to the nodes every time you start or stop

the service. From an operational perspective, this approach provides peace of mind; you know that the entire cluster—from 4 to 4000-plus nodes—is always in sync. For developers, it allows for rapid performance tuning because the configuration files can be easily manipulated.

Monitoring encompasses the starting and stopping of services, along with reporting on whether a service is up or down, network usage, HDFS, YARN, and a multitude of other load metrics. Ganglia and Nagios report back to the Ambari server, monitoring cluster health in terms of issues ranging from utilization of services such as HDFS storage to failures of stack components or entire nodes. Administrative use of Ambari is covered in Chapter 9, "Managing Hadoop with Apache Ambari." Once Ambari is installed, users can also take advantage of the ability to monitor a number of YARN metrics such as cluster memory, total containers, NodeManagers, garbage collection, and JVM metrics. An example of the Ambari dashboard is shown in Figure 2.11.

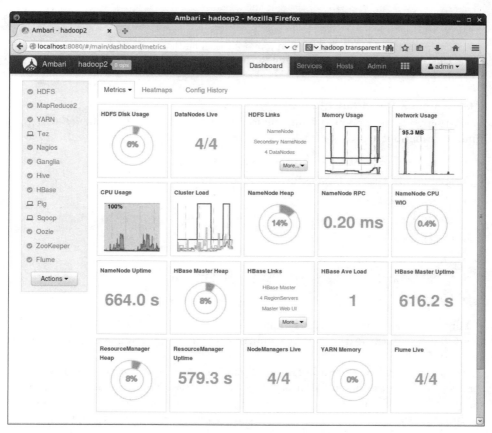

Figure 2.11   Ambari dashboard

Performing an Ambari Installation

Compared to a manual installation of Apache Hadoop 2, there are significantly fewer software requirements to meet and operating system tasks to perform when using Ambari. To manage the cluster with Ambari, two components are installed:

- The `ambari-server` (a Java process) that runs on its own node (if possible)
- An `ambari-agent` (a Python daemon) that runs on the remaining nodes of the cluster

For the purposes of this installation, we will use Apache Ambari 1.7.0 and the HDP 2.2 (Hortonworks Data Platform) distribution. Further documentation can be found by consulting the Ambari Installation Guide at http://docs.hortonworks.com/HDPDocuments/Ambari-1.7.0.0/Ambari_Install_v170/Ambari_Install_v170.pdf. Although Ambari may eventually work with other Hadoop installations, we will use the freely available HDP version to ensure a successful installation.

> **Note**
>
> Apache Ambari cannot be installed on top of an existing Hadoop installation. To maintain the cluster state, Ambari must perform the installation of all Hadoop components.

Step 1: Check Requirements

Ambari supports most popular Linux environments. As of version 1.7, the following Linux distributions are supported:

- Red Hat Enterprise Linux (RHEL) v6.x
- Red Hat Enterprise Linux (RHEL) v5.x (deprecated)
- CentOS v6.x
- CentOS v5.x (deprecated)
- Oracle Linux v6.x
- Oracle Linux v5.x (deprecated)
- SUSE Linux Enterprise Server (SLES) v11, SP1 and SP3
- Ubuntu Precise v12.04

For the following installation example, a Red Hat–derived distribution such as CentOS or an Oracle distribution is assumed. The following example uses the CentOS v6.x distribution.

As part of your base system install for all machines, make sure each node has `yum`, `rpm`, `scp`, `curl`, `wget` and an identical Java JDK. Additionally, `ntpd` should be running and provide the correct time on all nodes. If your cluster nodes do not have access to the Internet, you will have to mirror the Ambari and HDP repository and set up your own local repositories. In this installation recipe, we will assume all nodes have access to the Internet.

To assist with installation, the parallel distributed shell (pdsh) will be used. Although the pdsh package is not normally part of Linux distribution, it is a helpful tool for both the Ambari install and subsequent administration chores. A version of the pdsh package is distributed in the Extra Packages for Enterprise Linux (EPEL) repository. The following steps, performed as root, are needed to install the EPEL repository for the pdsh RPM:

```
# rpm -Uvh http://download.fedoraproject.org/pub/epel/6/i386/epel-release-6-8.
noarch.rpm
```

Next, the pdsh package can be installed.

```
# yum -y install pdsh-rcmd-ssh
```

The pdsh package needs to be installed only on the main Ambari server node. For pdsh to work properly, root must be able to ssh without a password from the Ambari server node to all worker nodes. This capability requires that each worker node has the Ambari server root public ssh key installed in /root/.ssh.

Step 2: Prepare Cluster Nodes

For this example, the cluster is assumed to have four nodes with node nicknames *limulus*, *n0*, *n1*, and *n2*. These node nicknames, along with their fully qualified domain names (FQDN), are also assumed to be in the /etc/hosts file of the Ambari server and worker nodes. In terms of Hadoop cluster size, this example is considered a small system. The purpose of the installation example is to show how to use Ambari to install Hadoop. A full production installation will undoubtedly have more server nodes.

To make the four-node example cluster more useful, the main node (limulus) will be overloaded as both a server node and a worker node. That is, it will run all the main services (e.g., NameNode ResourceManager, Oozie, Zookeeper) and also function as a DataNode for HDFS and a worker node running a NodeManager daemon. The overloaded configuration works well for a small system, but should not be replicated for larger clusters.

It is assumed that the cluster nodes have been configured as outlined in the previous step. If there are missing packages, pdsh can be used to add or remove packages from the nodes. It is also possible (and advisable) to create a kickstart install for the nodes where all configuration and packages mentioned here are installed automatically (including the steps presented in the following discussion).

If pdsh and /etc/hosts are installed and configured correctly, then pdsh can be used to install the Ambari repository on the nodes as follows:

```
# pdsh -w n[0-2] "wget http://public-repo-1.hortonworks.com/ambari/centos6/1.x/
updates/1.7.0/ambari.repo -O /etc/yum.repos.d/ambari.repo"
```

Next, the ambari-agent package is installed on the nodes:

```
# pdsh -w n[0-2] "yum -y install ambari-agent"
```

Once the Ambari agent is installed, the Ambari server host name must be set on all nodes. Substitute _FQDN_ in the line below with the name of your Ambari server (the server node nickname should work as well). Again, this task is easily accomplished with pdsh.

```
# pdsh -w n[0-2] "sed -i 's/hostname=localhost/hostname=_FQHN_/g' /etc/ambari-
agent/conf/ambari-agent.ini"
```

Finally, the Ambari agents can be started across the cluster. (Hint: Placing a |sort after a pdsh command will sort the output by node.)

```
# pdsh -w n[0-2] "service ambari-agent start" | sort
```

Step 3: Install the Ambari Server

Like the nodes, the Ambari repository needs to be made available. This step can be accomplished as follows:

```
# wget http://public-repo-1.hortonworks.com/ambari/centos6/1.x/updates/1.7.0/
ambari.repo -O /etc/yum.repos.d/ambari.repo
```

Next, the ambari-server and ambari-agent are installed on the Ambari host machine using yum. Recall that this machine is overloaded with both master services and worker node daemons. In general, this is not done on a production machine.

```
# yum -y install ambari-server
# yum -y install ambari-agent
```

Next, we set up the server. At this point, you can decide whether you want to customize the Ambari server database; the default is PostgreSQL. You will also be prompted to accept the Oracle JDK license unless you specify the --java-home option with an alternative path for the JDK on all nodes in the cluster. In this example, the OpenJDK provided with the Linux distribution will be used.

```
ambari-server setup -j /usr/lib/jvm/java-1.7.0-openjdk.x86_64
```

The following is an example Ambari server dialog (inputs are in **bold**). In this system, iptables has been configured to allow all traffic on the internal cluster network.

```
Using python  /usr/bin/python2.6
Setup ambari-server
Checking SELinux...
SELinux status is 'disabled'
Customize user account for ambari-server daemon [y/n] (n)? n
Adjusting ambari-server permissions and ownership...
Checking firewall...
```

```
WARNING: iptables is running. Confirm the necessary Ambari ports are accessible.
Refer to the Ambari documentation for more details on ports.
OK to continue [y/n] (y)? y
Checking JDK...
WARNING: JAVA_HOME /usr/lib/jvm/java-1.7.0-openjdk.x86_64 must be valid on ALL hosts
WARNING: JCE Policy files are required for configuring Kerberos security. If you
plan to use Kerberos, please make sure JCE Unlimited Strength Jurisdiction Policy
Files are valid on all hosts.
Completing setup...
Configuring database...
Enter advanced database configuration [y/n] (n)? n
Default properties detected. Using built-in database.
Checking PostgreSQL...
Running initdb: This may take upto a minute.
Initializing database: [  OK  ]

About to start PostgreSQL
Configuring local database...
Connecting to local database...done.
Configuring PostgreSQL...
Restarting PostgreSQL
Extracting system views...
.ambari-admin-1.7.0.169.jar
.
Adjusting ambari-server permissions and ownership...
Ambari Server 'setup' completed successfully.
```

Finally, the Ambari server and agent can be started on the main node by entering the following commands:

```
# service ambari-agent start
# ambari-server start
```

Step 4: Install Using the Ambari Console

Log into the Ambari server web console by using a local web browser pointing to http://localhost:8080. For example, if you were using Firefox, you would give this command:

```
# firefox http://localhost:8080 &
```

If everything is working properly, you should see the sign-in screen shown in Figure 2.12. The default username is admin and the password is admin. The password should be changed after the cluster is installed.

After you sign in, the welcome screen in Figure 2.13 will be shown. Click on Launch Install Wizard to continue.

The next window, as shown in Figure 2.14, will be the Getting Started panel where you enter the name of your cluster. In this example, the cluster is named Hadoop2. Click Next when you're finished.

Figure 2.12   Ambari sign-in screen

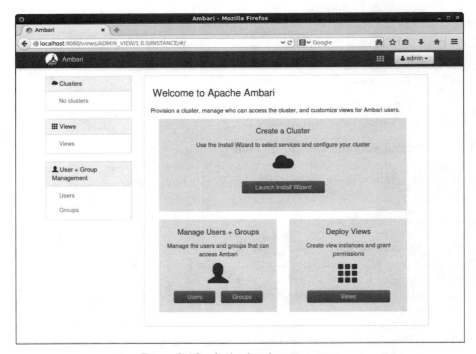

Figure 2.13   Ambari welcome screen

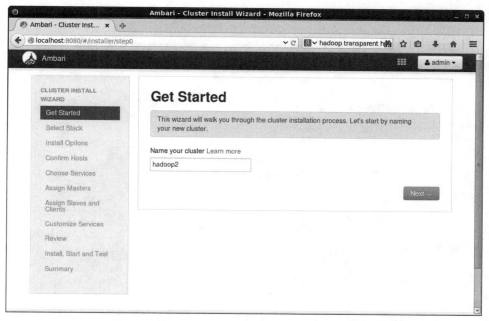

Figure 2.14   Select a name for the Hadoop cluster

The next choice is to select the Hadoop software stack. Currently, only the HDP stack is supported. As shown in Figure 2.15, it is suggested that you use HDP version 2.2. Ambari will set up the correct HDP repository based on this choice. Click Next when you're finished.

Once the stack is selected, the next window, shown in Figure 2.16, will ask for the node names. These are entered one name per line in the window. Note that Ambari requests fully qualified domain names. In this example, the node nicknames are used for simplicity. With a large number of nodes, it is possible to use pattern expressions to reduce the number of entries that must be made. (Move the mouse over the Pattern Expressions text on the window for more information.)

The next step is to pick one of two possible ways to install and start the Ambari agents. The first (default) way is to provide the ssh private key to automatically register hosts listed in the window. The other or manual method (used here) assumes the Ambari agent is running on all the cluster nodes (see Step 2).

Select Manual registration, and then click Register and Confirm. If you did not use FQDNs, Ambari will warn you and ask you to continue. Click OK to continue. Another window will be displayed that reminds you to make sure the Ambari agent is running on all the nodes. When you click OK, the Confirm Hosts screen shown in Figure 2.17 should appear.

At this point, the Ambari host is attempting to contact the Ambari agents on the nodes. If this step is successful, the progress bars should turn green. Sometimes,

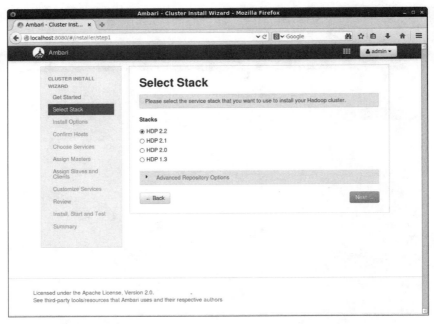

Figure 2.15   Choose the Hadoop software stack

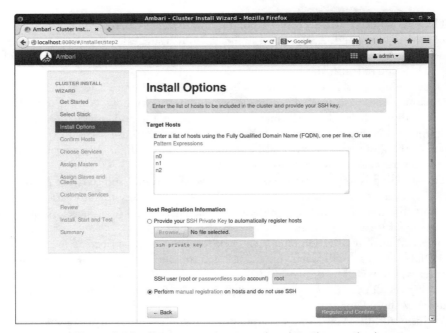

Figure 2.16   Enter target hosts and registration method

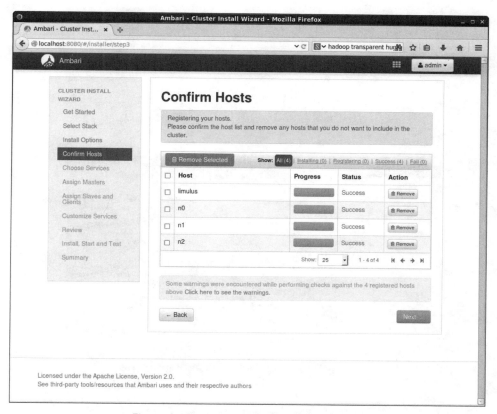

Figure 2.17   Ambari Confirm Hosts screen

however, Ambari may detect some node configuration issues with the nodes. Some of these warnings may be more serious than others; any of them can be viewed by clicking on the blue warnings text. In particular, the Transparent Huge Page (THP) setting on the nodes may have an impact on performance. See the Ambari Trouble Shooting Guide from Hortonworks for help with THP and other issues that are detected by Ambari (http://docs.hortonworks.com/HDPDocuments/Ambari-1.7.0.0/Ambari_ Trblshooting_v170/Ambari_Trblshooting_v170.pdf).

If all nodes have registered and all warnings have been reviewed, you can click Next to bring up the Choose Services window, shown in Figure 2.18.

You can install many services through Ambari. At a minimum, HDFS, YARN+MapReduce2, Nagios, Ganglia, Hive, Pig, Sqoop, Flume, Oozie, and Zookeeper should be installed. Tez and HBase are also good services to include. The other packages depend on your specific needs. When you're finished, click Next. The Assign Masters window, shown in Figure 2.19, will appear.

The Assign Masters window allows you to assign the various services to specific hosts. These choices are site specific and may require some preplanning to determine

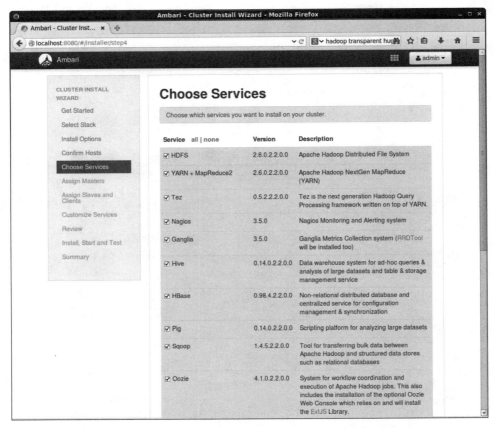

Figure 2.18 Ambari services selection screen

the best configuration. The current example simply overloads one node with all the services, which is acceptable for a small cluster. In a production installation, the NameNode and ResourceManager services may be on different nodes. If you run Zookeeper in replicated or quorum mode, you will need at least three nodes (one copy of the Zookeeper server on each node). There are no hard-and-fast rules on how to assign resources to services, however.

The four-node cluster example presented here places all the services on the main node. As shown in Figure 2.19, the host name *limulus* has been selected for all services. When you're finished with this screen, select Next to move to the Assign Slaves and Clients window, shown in Figure 2.20.

As with the nodes running Hadoop services, the roles of individual slave nodes depend on your specific needs. In this example, slaves can take on all roles (all boxes checked). In addition, the main node (*limulus*) is used as a worker node. In a production system with more nodes, this configuration is not recommended.

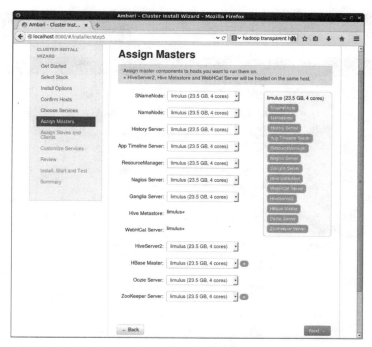

Figure 2.19   Assign the master nodes (in this case one node for everything)

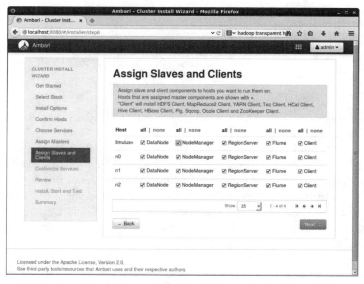

Figure 2.20   Ambari assign slaves and clients (note limulus also serves as a DataNode and NodeManager)

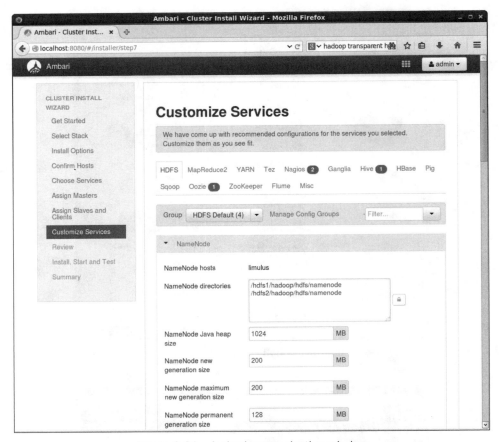

Figure 2.21   Ambari customization window

Once you're finished with this screen, click Next to bring up the Customize Services window, shown in Figure 2.21.

In this step, Hadoop services can be customized. These settings are placed in the /etc/hadoop/conf XML configuration files. Each service can be tuned to your specific needs using this screen. (As will be discussed in more detail in Chapter 9, "Managing Hadoop with Apache Ambari," you should not modify the XML files by hand.) Make sure to check the NameNode, Secondary NameNode, and DataNode directory assignments. An explanation of each setting can be obtained by placing the mouse over the text box. Settings can be undone by clicking the undo box that appears under the text box.

The services with red numbers near their names require user attention. In the case of Hive, Nagios, and Oozie, passwords need to be assigned for the service. In addition, Nagios requires a system administration email address to send alerts.

When you're finished, click Next at the bottom of the page. Note that the Next icon will be grayed out until all the required settings have been made. A Review window will be presented with all the settings listed, as shown in Figure 2.22. If you like, you can print this page for reference. If you find an issue or want to make a change, it is possible to go back and make changes at this point.

Once you are sure that the configuration is correct, click Deploy. The Install, Start and Test window, shown in Figure 2.23, will be displayed.

Depending on the size of your cluster and the network speed, the Install, Start, and Test phase can take a while. Progress bars will provide the real-time status of the installation process.

If everything goes well, the status bars will be green, as shown in Figure 2.24. There are two other possible outcomes, however. First, installation or test failures will be indicated by red bars. Orange bars (not shown) indicate warnings. Information about the error or warning can be found by clicking on the Failures encountered or

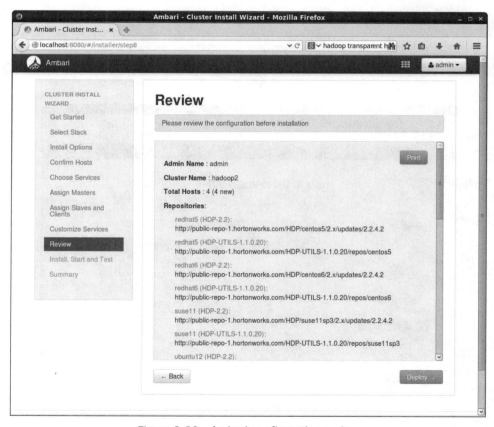

Figure 2.22   Ambari configuration review

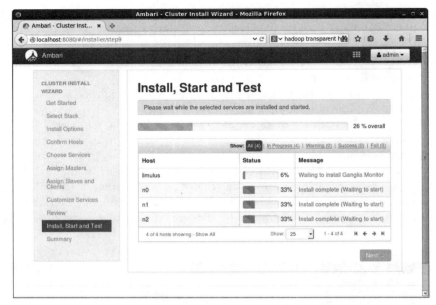

Figure 2.23   Ambari install started and test progress

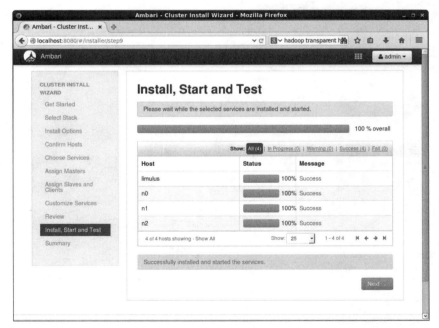

Figure 2.24   Ambari successful installation

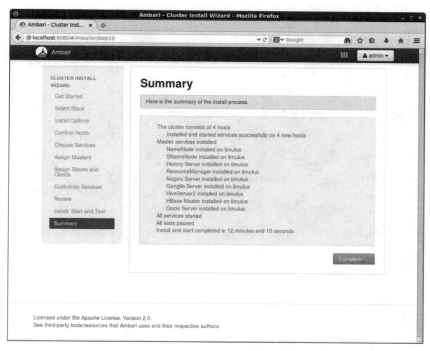

Figure 2.25   Ambari installation summary

Warnings encountered messages next to the bars. Depending on the error or warning, it may be possible to fix the issue and then click the Retry button.

The installation can proceed if installation warnings are generated. Usually these warnings are triggered by failed service tests or some other configuration issue that does not prevent the core Hadoop services from running.

At this point, the Next button will be active. Clicking it allows you to move to the Ambari Summary window, shown in Figure 2.25. After reviewing the summary information, click Complete to open the Ambari dashboard shown previously in Figure 2.11.

Undoing the Ambari Install

Although Ambari is a powerful and comprehensive installation tool, there may be times when you need to wipe the slate clean and do a reinstall. The following steps can help in this process.

To remove the installation information from the database, stop the Ambari server and issue a `reset` command. Ample warnings will be issued because `reset` completely wipes the installation.

```
# ambari-server stop
# ambari-server reset
```

At this point, it is probably a good idea to restart all the Ambari agents on the nodes. For instance, you can restart the Ambari agent for the previous installation example (on both the worker nodes and the main node):

```
# service ambari-agent restart
# pdsh -w n[0-2] "service ambari-agent restart" | sort
```

Next as was done previously, the Ambari server must be set up and restarted.

```
# ambari-server setup -j /usr/lib/jvm/java-1.7.0-openjdk.x86_64
# ambari-server start
```

If a complete cleanup is required, the HostCleanup.py tool can be used. This option can be dangerous because it performs some system-wide deletions; see the --skip option in the following example:

```
# python /usr/lib/python2.6/site-packages/ambari_agent/HostCleanup.py --help
Usage: HostCleanup.py [options]

Options:
  -h, --help            show this help message and exit
  -v, --verbose         output verbosity.
  -f FILE, --file=FILE  host check result file to read.
  -o FILE, --out=FILE   log file to store results.
  -k SKIP, --skip=SKIP  (packages|users|directories|repositories|processes|alt
                        ernatives). Use , as separator.
  -s, --silent          Silently accepts default prompt values
```

Installing Hadoop in the Cloud Using Apache Whirr

Apache Whirr is a set of libraries for running cloud services. It can be used to easily start Hadoop instances in the cloud. Whirr provides the following benefits:

- A cloud-neutral way to run services. You don't have to worry about the idiosyncrasies of each provider.

- A common service API. The details of provisioning are particular to the service (currently supported cloud services are Amazon and Rackspace).

- Smart defaults for services. You can get a properly configured system running quickly, while still being able to override settings as needed.

More information on Whirr can be found at https://whirr.apache.org. In this example we will start a four-node cluster using Amazon EC2.

To use Whirr, you will need an account on either Amazon EC2 or RackSpace Cloud Servers. In this example we use Amazon EC2 to create a four-node Hadoop cluster.

There is more to the Whirr package than what is illustrated in the following example. Please consult the Apache Whirr documentation at http://whirr.apache.org/docs/0.8.2 for more information and features.

Also, it is important to remember to take down your cluster when you are finished, as described in Step 4.

Step 1: Install Whirr

Whirr can be run from a desktop or laptop. The example assumes a Linux system is available. To use Whirr, the following is assumed:

- Java 6 or better is installed on your system.

> **Note**
>
> Some versions of the Java JDK have a bug that will cause Whirr to fail. If you get an error that looks like this:
>
> ```
> org.jclouds.rest.RestContext<org.jclouds.aws.ec2.AWSEC2Client, A> cannot be used as a key; it is not fully specified.
> ```
>
> then you may want to try a different JDK. This bug is reported to have surfaced in java 1.7u51 (java-1.7.0-openjdk-devel-1.7.0.51-2.4.4.1.el6_5.x86_64).
>
> For the example, Java 1.7u45 was used (java-1.7.0-openjdk-1.7.0.45-2.4.3.2.el6_4.x86_64).

- You have an account with a cloud provider, such as Amazon EC2 or Rackspace Cloud Servers.
- An SSH client is installed on your system.

Download the latest version of Whirr using the following command. Check whether an updated version may be available. Whirr can be run from a user account.

```
$ wget http://mirrors.ibiblio.org/apache/whirr/stable/whirr-0.8.2.tar.gz
```

Next, extract the Whirr files with the following command:

```
$ tar xvzf whirr-0.8.2.tar.gz
```

Step 2: Configure Whirr

Whirr needs a safe place to store your credentials. The following steps are intended to provide a secure file for credentials. First, make a .whirr directory in your home path:

```
$ mkdir ~/.whirr
```

Next, copy the sample credential files to the new directory:

```
$ cp whirr-0.8.2/conf/credentials.sample ~/.whirr/credentials
```

An optional step is to make sure the directory is private:

```
$ chmod -R go-rwx ~/.whirr
```

To add your credentials, edit your local credentials file (vi ~/.whirr/credentials) and change the following to match those in Table 2.1:

```
#PROVIDER=
#IDENTITY=
#CREDENTIAL=
```

That is, set the PROVIDER to either aws-ecs or cloudserver-us. Use the appropriate INDENTITY and CREDENTIAL for the provider.

For example, if using Amazon EC2, the entries should look like the following (The following INDENTITY and CREDENTIALS are fake—they will not work.)

```
PROVIDER=aws-ec2
IDENTITY=MFNNU7JETMEM7ONDASMF
CREDENTIAL=eyN3PTTAkmmlAq4CCHuRWaSDBLxcvb1ED7NKDvtq
```

Whirr comes with recipes for setting up Hadoop clusters in the cloud. We will use a basic Hadoop recipe, but the Whirr documentation offers tips on further customization. To configure a Hadoop version 2.6 cluster, copy the recipe as follows:

```
$ cp whirr-0.8.2/recipes/hadoop-yarn-ec2.properties.
```

Next, edit the hadoop-yarn-ec2.properities file to update the version of Hadoop to 2.6.0. Change the following line from

```
whirr.hadoop.version=0.23.5
```

to

```
whirr.hadoop.version=2.6.0
```

As shown in the following, comment out the following lines that set credentials (add a # in front of the lines):

```
#whirr.provider=aws-ec2
#whirr.identity=${env:AWS_ACCESS_KEY_ID}
#whirr.credential=${env:AWS_SECRET_ACCESS_KEY}
```

If you do not have a proper ssh public and private key in ~/.ssh, you will need to run ssh-keygen (i.e., you should have both id_rsa and id_rsa.pub in your ~/.ssh).

Table 2.1 Whirr Providers, Identities, and Credentials Needed for Credentials File

	PROVIDER=	IDENTITY=	CREDENTIAL=
Amazon EC2	aws-ec2	Access Key ID	Secret Access Key
Rackspace	cloudservers-us	Username	API Key

Finally, the roles of the cloud instances are set with the following line:

```
whirr.instance-templates=1 hadoop-namenode+yarn-resourcemanager+mapreduce-
historyserver,3 hadoop-datanode+yarn-nodemanager
```

This line will configure the Hadoop cluster as follows.

- One main node with:
  - `hadoop-namenode`
  - `yarn-resourcemanager`
  - `mapreduce-historyserver`

- Three worker nodes with:
  - `hadoop-datanode`
  - `yarn-nodemanager`

The number of worker nodes can be increased or decreased by changing the 3 in the code at the top of the page.

The `hadoop-yarn-ec2.properties` file also allows you to change various default properties in the Hadoop configuration files (Once the cluster is running in the cloud, these properties will be in the `/etc/hadoop/conf` directory). In particular, if you are using Hadoop version 2.2.0 or greater (recommended), you will need to change the `hadoop-yarn.yarn.nodemanager.aux-services` property from `mapreduce.shuffle` to `mapreduce_shuffle`. The updated line in the `hadoop-yarn-ec2.properties` file should read as follows:

```
hadoop-yarn.yarn.nodemanager.aux-services=mapreduce_shuffle
```

Step 3: Launch the Cluster

The Hadoop cluster can be launched by running the following command:

```
$ whirr-0.8.2/bin/whirr launch-cluster --config hadoop-yarn-ec2.properties
```

After some time, and if all goes well, you will see something similar to the following output. A large number of messages will scroll across the screen while the cluster boots; when the boot is finished, the following will be displayed (IP address will be different):

```
[hadoop-namenode+yarn-resourcemanager+mapreduce-historyserver]: ssh -i /home/
hdfs/.ssh/id_rsa -o "UserKnownHostsFile /dev/null" -o StrictHostKeyChecking=no
hdfs@54.146.139.132
[hadoop-datanode+yarn-nodemanager]: ssh -i /home/hdfs/.ssh/id_rsa -o
"UserKnownHostsFile /dev/null" -o StrictHostKeyChecking=no hdfs@54.162.70.164
[hadoop-datanode+yarn-nodemanager]: ssh -i /home/hdfs/.ssh/id_rsa -o
"UserKnownHostsFile /dev/null" -o StrictHostKeyChecking=no hdfs@54.162.8.6
[hadoop-datanode+yarn-nodemanager]: ssh -i /home/hdfs/.ssh/id_rsa -o
"UserKnownHostsFile /dev/null" -o StrictHostKeyChecking=no hdfs@54.225.50.65
To destroy cluster, run 'whirr destroy-cluster' with the same options used to
launch it.
```

There are four IP addresses—one for the main node (54.146.139.132) and three for the worker nodes. The following line will allow you to ssh to the main node without a password. Whirr also creates an account under your local user name and imports your ssh public key. (The command ssh hdfs@54.146.139.132 should work as well.)

```
$ ssh -i /home/hdfs/.ssh/id_rsa -o "UserKnownHostsFile /dev/null" -o
StrictHostKeyChecking=no hdfs@54.146.139.132
```

If the login was successful, the following prompt showing the private IP address should be available. The ip-10-234-19-148 will be different from the public IP address used to reach the main node. This IP address is for the private network that is available only within the cluster:

```
hdfs@ip-10-234-19-148:~$
```

Hadoop administration (including HDFS) must be done as user hadoop. To accomplish this change, use sudo to change to user hadoop:

```
hdfs@ip-10-234-19-148:~$ sudo su - hadoop
```

When given by user hadoop, the hdfs dfsadmin -report command shows 1.18TB of storage in the cluster. (The full output is truncated here and the native library warning removed):

```
$ hdfs dfsadmin -report
Configured Capacity: 1293682139136 (1.18 TB)
Present Capacity: 1230004011008 (1.12 TB)
DFS Remaining: 1230003863552 (1.12 TB)
DFS Used: 147456 (144 KB)
DFS Used%: 0.00%
Under replicated blocks: 0
Blocks with corrupt replicas: 0
Missing blocks: 0


-------------------------------------------------

Live datanodes (3):
...
```

The worker nodes' private IP addresses can be found using the hdfs command as follows:

```
$ hdfs dfsadmin -report|grep Name
Name: 10.12.93.252:50010 (ip-10-12-93-252.ec2.internal)
Name: 10.152.159.179:50010 (ip-10-152-159-179.ec2.internal)
Name: 10.166.54.102:50010 (ip-10-166-54-102.ec2.internal)
```

You can ssh without a password to these IP addresses from the main node when working as user hdfs. Note that this user name is the local user name from which you started your whirr cluster.

When working as user hadoop, you can give the jps command to verify that the Namenode, ResourceManager, and JobHistoryServer are running:

```
$ jps
7226 JobHistoryServer
7771 Jps
7150 ResourceManager
5703 NameNode
```

Logging into the worker nodes can be done by using the private or public IP address. For instance, you can log from the main node to a worker node:

```
hdfs@ip-10-234-19-148:~$ ssh 10.166.54.102
```

Once on the worker node, you can check which services are running by using the jps command. In this case, as specified in the properties file, the workers are running as the DataNode and NodeManager daemons:

```
hdfs@ip-10-166-54-102:~$ sudo su - hadoop
$ jps
5590 DataNode
6730 Jps
6504 NodeManager
```

Finally, you can view the HDFS web interface on your local machine by starting a browser with the following IP address and port number. (Your IP address will be different.) For Firefox:

```
$ firefox http://54.146.139.132:50070
```

Similarly, the YARN web interface can viewed by entering this command:

```
$ firefox http://54.146.139.132:8088
```

Step 4: Take Down Your Cluster

The important final step is to take down your cluster when you are finished. If you do not remove your cluster, it will continue to run and accumulate charges to your account. To take down the cluster, exit back to your local account and enter the following command. Make sure you use the same properties file that you used to start the cluster.

```
$ whirr-0.8.2/bin/whirr destroy-cluster --config hadoop-yarn-ec2.properties
```

Whirr has more features and options that can be explored by consulting the project web page located at https://whirr.apache.org.

Summary and Additional Resources

Apache Hadoop installation can span many different types of hardware and component services. In this chapter, the core Apache Hadoop services and configuration files were introduced in addition to four installation scenarios. Two single-machine recipes using a virtual Hadoop sandbox and Hadoop pseudo-distributed mode were provided as a way to help explore the examples in other chapters.

A real cluster installation was performed with Apache Ambari. Although not a large production installation, the four-node cluster example illustrated the important steps in the Ambari installation and can easily be adapted to larger systems. Finally, using the Apache Whirr toolkit, a cloud-based Hadoop cluster was created and configured using Amazon EC2. Each of the installation scenarios can serve as a launch point for further exploration of the Apache Hadoop ecosystem.

Additional information and background on the installation methods can be obtained from the following resources.

- **Apache Hadoop XML configuration files description:**
  - https://hadoop.apache.org/docs/stable/ (scroll down to the lower lefthand corner under Configuration)
- **Official Hadoop sources and supported Java versions:**
  - http://www.apache.org/dyn/closer.cgi/hadoop/common/
  - http://wiki.apache.org/hadoop/HadoopJavaVersions.
- **Oracle VirtualBox:**
  - https://www.virtualbox.org
- **Hortonworks Hadoop Sandbox (virtual machine):**
  - http://hortonworks.com/hdp/downloads.
- **Ambari project page:**
  - https://ambari.apache.org/
- **Ambari installation guide:**
  - http://docs.hortonworks.com/HDPDocuments/Ambari-1.7.0.0/Ambari_Install_v170/Ambari_Install_v170.pdf.
- **Ambari troubleshooting guide:**
  - http://docs.hortonworks.com/HDPDocuments/Ambari-1.7.0.0/Ambari_Trblshooting_v170/Ambari_Trblshooting_v170.pdf.
- **Apache Whirr cloud tools:**
  - https://whirr.apache.org

3

Hadoop Distributed
File System Basics

In This Chapter:

- The design and operation of the Hadoop Distributed File System (HDFS) are presented.
- Important HDFS topics such as block replication, Safe Mode, rack awareness, High Availability, Federation, backup, snapshots, NFS mounting, and the HDFS web GUI are discussed.
- Examples of basic HDFS user commands are provided.
- HDFS programming examples using Java and C are provided.

The Hadoop Distributed File System is the backbone of Hadoop MapReduce processing. New users and administrators often find HDFS different than most other UNIX/Linux file systems. This chapter highlights the design goals and capabilities of HDFS that make it useful for Big Data processing.

Hadoop Distributed File System Design Features

The Hadoop Distributed File System (HDFS) was designed for Big Data processing. Although capable of supporting many users simultaneously, HDFS is not designed as a true parallel file system. Rather, the design assumes a large file write-once/read-many model that enables other optimizations and relaxes many of the concurrency and coherence overhead requirements of a true parallel file system. For instance, HDFS rigorously restricts data writing to one user at a time. All additional writes are "append-only," and there is no random writing to HDFS files. Bytes are always appended to the end of a stream, and byte streams are guaranteed to be stored in the order written.

The design of HDFS is based on the design of the Google File System (GFS). A paper published by Google provides further background on GFS (http://research .google.com/archive/gfs.html).

HDFS is designed for data streaming where large amounts of data are read from disk in bulk. The HDFS block size is typically 64MB or 128MB. Thus, this approach is entirely unsuitable for standard POSIX file system use. In addition, due to the sequential nature of the data, there is no local caching mechanism. The large block and file sizes make it more efficient to reread data from HDFS than to try to cache the data.

Perhaps the most interesting aspect of HDFS—and the one that separates it from other file systems—is its data locality. A principal design aspect of Hadoop MapReduce is the emphasis on moving the computation to the data rather than moving the data to the computation. This distinction is reflected in how Hadoop clusters are implemented. In other high-performance systems, a parallel file system will exist on hardware separate from the compute hardware. Data is then moved to and from the computer components via high-speed interfaces to the parallel file system array. HDFS, in contrast, is designed to work on the same hardware as the compute portion of the cluster. That is, a single server node in the cluster is often both a computation engine and a storage engine for the application.

Finally, Hadoop clusters assume node (and even rack) failure will occur at some point. To deal with this situation, HDFS has a redundant design that can tolerate system failure and still provide the data needed by the compute part of the program.

The following points summarize the important aspects of HDFS:

- The write-once/read-many design is intended to facilitate streaming reads.
- Files may be appended, but random seeks are not permitted. There is no caching of data.
- Converged data storage and processing happen on the same server nodes.
- "Moving computation is cheaper than moving data."
- A reliable file system maintains multiple copies of data across the cluster. Consequently, failure of a single node (or even a rack in a large cluster) will not bring down the file system.
- A specialized file system is used, which is not designed for general use.

HDFS Components

The design of HDFS is based on two types of nodes: a NameNode and multiple DataNodes. In a basic design, a single NameNode manages all the metadata needed to store and retrieve the actual data from the DataNodes. No data is actually stored on the NameNode, however. For a minimal Hadoop installation, there needs to be a single NameNode daemon and a single DataNode daemon running on at least one machine (see the section "Installing Hadoop from Apache Sources" in Chapter 2, "Installation Recipes").

The design is a master/slave architecture in which the master (NameNode) manages the file system namespace and regulates access to files by clients. File system namespace operations such as opening, closing, and renaming files and directories are all managed by the NameNode. The NameNode also determines the mapping of blocks to DataNodes and handles DataNode failures.

The slaves (DataNodes) are responsible for serving read and write requests from the file system to the clients. The NameNode manages block creation, deletion, and replication.

An example of the client/NameNode/DataNode interaction is provided in Figure 3.1. When a client writes data, it first communicates with the NameNode and requests to create a file. The NameNode determines how many blocks are needed and provides the client with the DataNodes that will store the data. As part of the storage

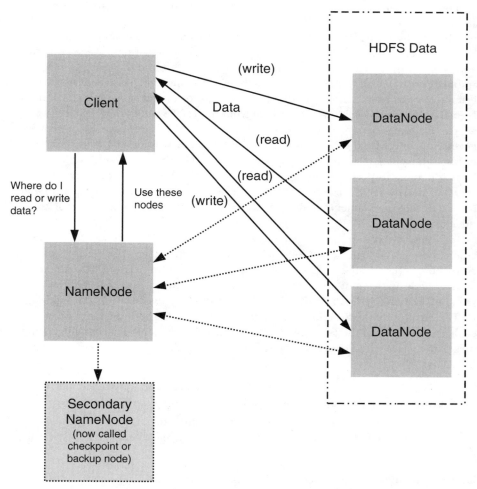

Figure 3.1   Various system roles in an HDFS deployment

process, the data blocks are replicated after they are written to the assigned node. Depending on how many nodes are in the cluster, the NameNode will attempt to write replicas of the data blocks on nodes that are in other separate racks (if possible). If there is only one rack, then the replicated blocks are written to other servers in the same rack. After the DataNode acknowledges that the file block replication is complete, the client closes the file and informs the NameNode that the operation is complete. Note that the NameNode does not write any data directly to the DataNodes. It does, however, give the client a limited amount of time to complete the operation. If it does not complete in the time period, the operation is canceled.

Reading data happens in a similar fashion. The client requests a file from the NameNode, which returns the best DataNodes from which to read the data. The client then accesses the data directly from the DataNodes.

Thus, once the metadata has been delivered to the client, the NameNode steps back and lets the conversation between the client and the DataNodes proceed. While data transfer is progressing, the NameNode also monitors the DataNodes by listening for heartbeats sent from DataNodes. The lack of a heartbeat signal indicates a potential node failure. In such a case, the NameNode will route around the failed DataNode and begin re-replicating the now-missing blocks. Because the file system is redundant, DataNodes can be taken offline (decommissioned) for maintenance by informing the NameNode of the DataNodes to exclude from the HDFS pool.

The mappings between data blocks and the physical DataNodes are not kept in persistent storage on the NameNode. For performance reasons, the NameNode stores all metadata in memory. Upon startup, each DataNode provides a block report (which it keeps in persistent storage) to the NameNode. The block reports are sent every 10 heartbeats. (The interval between reports is a configurable property.) The reports enable the NameNode to keep an up-to-date account of all data blocks in the cluster.

In almost all Hadoop deployments, there is a SecondaryNameNode. While not explicitly required by a NameNode, it is highly recommended. The term "Secondary-NameNode" (now called CheckPointNode) is somewhat misleading. It is not an active failover node and cannot replace the primary NameNode in case of its failure. (See the section "NameNode High Availability" later in this chapter for more explanation.)

The purpose of the SecondaryNameNode is to perform periodic checkpoints that evaluate the status of the NameNode. Recall that the NameNode keeps all system metadata memory for fast access. It also has two disk files that track changes to the metadata:

- An image of the file system state when the NameNode was started. This file begins with `fsimage_*` and is used only at startup by the NameNode.

- A series of modifications done to the file system after starting the NameNode. These files begin with `edit_*` and reflect the changes made after the `fsimage_*` file was read.

The location of these files is set by the `dfs.namenode.name.dir` property in the `hdfs-site.xml` file.

The SecondaryNameNode periodically downloads `fsimage` and edits files, joins them into a new `fsimage`, and uploads the new `fsimage` file to the NameNode. Thus, when the NameNode restarts, the `fsimage` file is reasonably up-to-date and requires only the edit logs to be applied since the last checkpoint. If the SecondaryNameNode were not running, a restart of the NameNode could take a prohibitively long time due to the number of changes to the file system.

Thus, the various roles in HDFS can be summarized as follows:

- HDFS uses a master/slave model designed for large file reading/streaming.
- The NameNode is a metadata server or "data traffic cop."
- HDFS provides a single namespace that is managed by the NameNode.
- Data is redundantly stored on DataNodes; there is no data on the NameNode.
- The SecondaryNameNode performs checkpoints of NameNode file system's state but is not a failover node.

HDFS Block Replication

As mentioned, when HDFS writes a file, it is replicated across the cluster. The amount of replication is based on the value of `dfs.replication` in the `hdfs-site.xml` file. This default value can be overruled with the `hdfs dfs-setrep` command. For Hadoop clusters containing more than eight DataNodes, the replication value is usually set to 3. In a Hadoop cluster of eight or fewer DataNodes but more than one DataNode, a replication factor of 2 is adequate. For a single machine, like the pseudo-distributed install in Chapter 2, the replication factor is set to 1.

If several machines must be involved in the serving of a file, then a file could be rendered unavailable by the loss of any one of those machines. HDFS combats this problem by replicating each block across a number of machines (three is the default).

In addition, the HDFS default block size is often 64MB. In a typical operating system, the block size is 4KB or 8KB. The HDFS default block size is not the minimum block size, however. If a 20KB file is written to HDFS, it will create a block that is approximately 20KB in size. (The underlying file system may have a minimal block size that increases the actual file size.) If a file of size 80MB is written to HDFS, a 64MB block and a 16MB block will be created.

As mentioned in Chapter 1, "Background and Concepts," HDFS blocks are not exactly the same as the data splits used by the MapReduce process. The HDFS blocks are based on size, while the splits are based on a logical partitioning of the data. For instance, if a file contains discrete records, the logical split ensures that a record is not split physically across two separate servers during processing. Each HDFS block may consist of one or more splits.

Figure 3.2 provides an example of how a file is broken into blocks and replicated across the cluster. In this case, a replication factor of 3 ensures that any one DataNode can fail and the replicated blocks will be available on other nodes—and then subsequently re-replicated on other DataNodes.

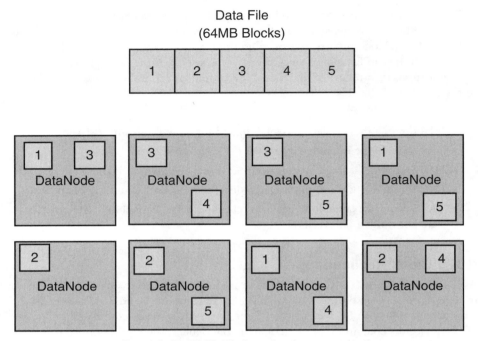

Figure 3.2   HDFS block replication example

HDFS Safe Mode

When the NameNode starts, it enters a read-only *safe mode* where blocks cannot be replicated or deleted. Safe Mode enables the NameNode to perform two important processes:

1. The previous file system state is reconstructed by loading the `fsimage` file into memory and replaying the edit log.

2. The mapping between blocks and data nodes is created by waiting for enough of the DataNodes to register so that at least one copy of the data is available. Not all DataNodes are required to register before HDFS exits from Safe Mode. The registration process may continue for some time.

HDFS may also enter Safe Mode for maintenance using the `hdfs dfsadmin-safemode` command or when there is a file system issue that must be addressed by the administrator.

Rack Awareness

Rack awareness deals with data locality. Recall that one of the main design goals of Hadoop MapReduce is to move the computation to the data. Assuming that most data center networks do not offer full bisection bandwidth, a typical Hadoop cluster will exhibit three levels of data locality:

1. Data resides on the local machine (best).
2. Data resides in the same rack (better).
3. Data resides in a different rack (good).

When the YARN scheduler is assigning MapReduce containers to work as mappers, it will try to place the container first on the local machine, then on the same rack, and finally on another rack.

In addition, the NameNode tries to place replicated data blocks on multiple racks for improved fault tolerance. In such a case, an entire rack failure will not cause data loss or stop HDFS from working. Performance may be degraded, however.

HDFS can be made rack-aware by using a user-derived script that enables the master node to map the network topology of the cluster. A default Hadoop installation assumes all the nodes belong to the same (large) rack. In that case, there is no option 3.

NameNode High Availability

With early Hadoop installations, the NameNode was a single point of failure that could bring down the entire Hadoop cluster. NameNode hardware often employed redundant power supplies and storage to guard against such problems, but it was still susceptible to other failures. The solution was to implement NameNode High Availability (HA) as a means to provide true failover service.

As shown in Figure 3.3, an HA Hadoop cluster has two (or more) separate NameNode machines. Each machine is configured with exactly the same software.

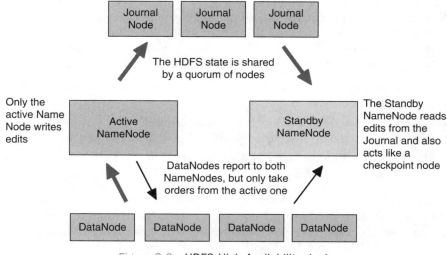

Figure 3.3   HDFS High Availability design

One of the NameNode machines is in the Active state, and the other is in the Standby state. Like a single NameNode cluster, the Active NameNode is responsible for all client HDFS operations in the cluster. The Standby NameNode maintains enough state to provide a fast failover (if required).

To guarantee the file system state is preserved, both the Active and Standby NameNodes receive block reports from the DataNodes. The Active node also sends all file system edits to a quorum of Journal nodes. At least three physically separate JournalNode daemons are required, because edit log modifications must be written to a majority of the JournalNodes. This design will enable the system to tolerate the failure of a single JournalNode machine. The Standby node continuously reads the edits from the JournalNodes to ensure its namespace is synchronized with that of the Active node. In the event of an Active NameNode failure, the Standby node reads all remaining edits from the JournalNodes before promoting itself to the Active state.

To prevent confusion between NameNodes, the JournalNodes allow only one NameNode to be a writer at a time. During failover, the NameNode that is chosen to become active takes over the role of writing to the JournalNodes. A Secondary-NameNode is not required in the HA configuration because the Standby node also performs the tasks of the Secondary NameNode.

Apache ZooKeeper is used to monitor the NameNode health. Zookeeper is a highly available service for maintaining small amounts of coordination data, notifying clients of changes in that data, and monitoring clients for failures. HDFS failover relies on ZooKeeper for failure detection and for Standby to Active NameNode election. The Zookeeper components are not depicted in Figure 3.3.

HDFS NameNode Federation

Another important feature of HDFS is NameNode Federation. Older versions of HDFS provided a single namespace for the entire cluster managed by a single NameNode. Thus, the resources of a single NameNode determined the size of the namespace. Federation addresses this limitation by adding support for multiple NameNodes/namespaces to the HDFS file system. The key benefits are as follows:

- *Namespace scalability.* HDFS cluster storage scales horizontally without placing a burden on the NameNode.
- *Better performance.* Adding more NameNodes to the cluster scales the file system read/write operations throughput by separating the total namespace.
- *System isolation.* Multiple NameNodes enable different categories of applications to be distinguished, and users can be isolated to different namespaces.

Figure 3.4 illustrates how HDFS NameNode Federation is accomplished. NameNode1 manages the /research and /marketing namespaces, and NameNode2 manages the /data and /project namespaces. The NameNodes do not communicate with each other and the DataNodes "just store data block" as directed by either NameNode.

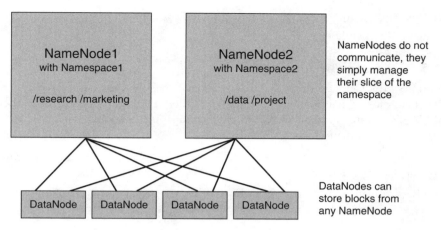

Figure 3.4   HDFS NameNode Federation example

HDFS Checkpoints and Backups

As mentioned earlier, the NameNode stores the metadata of the HDFS file system in a file called `fsimage`. File systems modifications are written to an edits log file, and at startup the NameNode merges the edits into a new `fsimage`. The Secondary-NameNode or CheckpointNode periodically fetches edits from the NameNode, merges them, and returns an updated `fsimage` to the NameNode.

An HDFS BackupNode is similar, but also maintains an up-to-date copy of the file system namespace both in memory and on disk. Unlike a CheckpointNode, the BackupNode does not need to download the `fsimage` and edits files from the active NameNode because it already has an up-to-date namespace state in memory. A NameNode supports one BackupNode at a time. No CheckpointNodes may be registered if a Backup node is in use.

HDFS Snapshots

HDFS snapshots are similar to backups, but are created by administrators using the `hdfs dfs -snapshot` command. HDFS snapshots are read-only point-in-time copies of the file system. They offer the following features:

- Snapshots can be taken of a sub-tree of the file system or the entire file system.
- Snapshots can be used for data backup, protection against user errors, and disaster recovery.
- Snapshot creation is instantaneous.
- Blocks on the DataNodes are not copied, because the snapshot files record the block list and the file size. There is no data copying, although it appears to the user that there are duplicate files.
- Snapshots do not adversely affect regular HDFS operations.

See Chapter 10, "Basic Hadoop Administration Procedures," for information on creating HDFS snapshots.

HDFS NFS Gateway

The HDFS NFS Gateway supports NFSv3 and enables HDFS to be mounted as part of the client's local file system. Users can browse the HDFS file system through their local file systems that provide an NFSv3 client compatible operating system. This feature offers users the following capabilities:

- Users can easily download/upload files from/to the HDFS file system to/from their local file system.
- Users can stream data directly to HDFS through the mount point. Appending to a file is supported, but random write capability is not supported.

Mounting a HDFS over NFS is explained in Chapter 10, "Basic Hadoop Administration Procedures."

HDFS User Commands

The following is a brief command reference that will facilitate navigation within HDFS. Be aware that there are alternative options for each command and that the examples given here are simple use-cases. What follows is by no means a full description of HDFS functionality. For more information, see the section "Summary and Additional Resources" at the end of the chapter.

Brief HDFS Command Reference

The preferred way to interact with HDFS in Hadoop version 2 is through the `hdfs` command. Previously, in version 1 and subsequently in many Hadoop examples, the `hadoop dfs` command was used to manage files in HDFS. The `hadoop dfs` command will still work in version 2, but its use will cause a message to be displayed indicating that the use of `hadoop dfs` is deprecated.

The following listing presents the full range of options that are available for the `hdfs` command. In the next section, only portions of the `dfs` and `hdfsadmin` options are explored. Chapter 10, "Basic Hadoop Administration Procedures," provides examples of administration with the `hdfs` command.

```
Usage: hdfs [--config confdir] COMMAND
       where COMMAND is one of:
  dfs                  run a file system command on the file systems
                       supported in Hadoop.
  namenode -format     format the DFS file system
  secondarynamenode    run the DFS secondary namenode
  namenode             run the DFS namenode
  journalnode          run the DFS journalnode
  zkfc                 run the ZK Failover Controller daemon
```

```
datanode              run a DFS datanode
dfsadmin              run a DFS admin client
haadmin               run a DFS HA admin client
fsck                  run a DFS file system checking utility
balancer              run a cluster balancing utility
jmxget                get JMX exported values from NameNode or DataNode.
mover                 run a utility to move block replicas across
                      storage types
oiv                   apply the offline fsimage viewer to an fsimage
oiv_legacy            apply the offline fsimage viewer to an legacy
                      fsimage
oev                   apply the offline edits viewer to an edits file
fetchdt               fetch a delegation token from the NameNode
getconf               get config values from configuration
groups                get the groups which users belong to
snapshotDiff          diff two snapshots of a directory or diff the
                      current directory contents with a snapshot
lsSnapshottableDir    list all snapshottable dirs owned by the current
                      user Use -help to see options
portmap               run a portmap service
nfs3                  run an NFS version 3 gateway
cacheadmin            configure the HDFS cache
crypto                configure HDFS encryption zones
storagepolicies       get all the existing block storage policies
version               print the version
```

Most commands print help when invoked w/o parameters.

General HDFS Commands

The version of HDFS can be found from the version option. Examples in this section are run on the HDFS version shown here:

```
$ hdfs version
Hadoop 2.6.0.2.2.4.2-2
Subversion git@github.com:hortonworks/hadoop.git -r
22a563ebe448969d07902aed869ac13c652b2872
Compiled by jenkins on 2015-03-31T19:49Z
Compiled with protoc 2.5.0
From source with checksum b3481c2cdbe2d181f2621331926e267
This command was run using /usr/hdp/2.2.4.2-2/hadoop/hadoop-
common-2.6.0.2.2.4.2-2.jar
```

HDFS provides a series of commands similar to those found in a standard POSIX file system. A list of those commands can be obtained by issuing the following command. Several of these commands will be highlighted here under the user account `hdfs`.

```
$ hdfs dfs
Usage: hadoop fs [generic options]
        [-appendToFile <localsrc> ... <dst>]
```

```
[-cat [-ignoreCrc] <src> ...]
[-checksum <src> ...]
[-chgrp [-R] GROUP PATH...]
[-chmod [-R] <MODE[,MODE]... | OCTALMODE> PATH...]
[-chown [-R] [OWNER][:[GROUP]] PATH...]
[-copyFromLocal [-f] [-p] [-l] <localsrc> ... <dst>]
[-copyToLocal [-p] [-ignoreCrc] [-crc] <src> ... <localdst>]
[-count [-q] [-h] <path> ...]
[-cp [-f] [-p | -p[topax]] <src> ... <dst>]
[-createSnapshot <snapshotDir> [<snapshotName>]]
[-deleteSnapshot <snapshotDir> <snapshotName>]
[-df [-h] [<path> ...]]
[-du [-s] [-h] <path> ...]
[-expunge]
[-get [-p] [-ignoreCrc] [-crc] <src> ... <localdst>]
[-getfacl [-R] <path>]
[-getfattr [-R] {-n name | -d} [-e en] <path>]
[-getmerge [-nl] <src> <localdst>]
[-help [cmd ...]]
[-ls [-d] [-h] [-R] [<path> ...]]
[-mkdir [-p] <path> ...]
[-moveFromLocal <localsrc> ... <dst>]
[-moveToLocal <src> <localdst>]
[-mv <src> ... <dst>]
[-put [-f] [-p] [-l] <localsrc> ... <dst>]
[-renameSnapshot <snapshotDir> <oldName> <newName>]
[-rm [-f] [-r|-R] [-skipTrash] <src> ...]
[-rmdir [--ignore-fail-on-non-empty] <dir> ...]
[-setfacl [-R] [{-b|-k} {-m|-x <acl_spec>} <path>]|[--set
  <acl_spec> <path>]]
[-setfattr {-n name [-v value] | -x name} <path>]
[-setrep [-R] [-w] <rep> <path> ...]
[-stat [format] <path> ...]
[-tail [-f] <file>]
[-test -[defsz] <path>]
[-text [-ignoreCrc] <src> ...]
[-touchz <path> ...]
[-truncate [-w] <length> <path> ...]
[-usage [cmd ...]]

Generic options supported are
-conf <configuration file>      specify an application configuration file
-D <property=value>             use value for given property
-fs <local|namenode:port>       specify a namenode
-jt <local|resourcemanager:port>   specify a ResourceManager
-files <comma separated list of files>   specify comma separated files to
                                   be copied to the map reduce cluster
```

```
-libjars <comma separated list of jars>    specify comma separated jar
                                   files to include in the classpath.
-archives <comma separated list of archives>   specify comma separated
                                        archives to be unarchived
                                          on the compute machines.


The general command line syntax is
bin/hadoop command [genericOptions] [commandOptions]
```

List Files in HDFS

To list the files in the root HDFS directory, enter the following command:

```
$ hdfs dfs -ls /

Found 10 items
drwxrwxrwx   - yarn   hadoop          0 2015-04-29 16:52 /app-logs
drwxr-xr-x   - hdfs   hdfs            0 2015-04-21 14:28 /apps
drwxr-xr-x   - hdfs   hdfs            0 2015-05-14 10:53 /benchmarks
drwxr-xr-x   - hdfs   hdfs            0 2015-04-21 15:18 /hdp
drwxr-xr-x   - mapred hdfs            0 2015-04-21 14:26 /mapred
drwxr-xr-x   - hdfs   hdfs            0 2015-04-21 14:26 /mr-history
drwxr-xr-x   - hdfs   hdfs            0 2015-04-21 14:27 /system
drwxrwxrwx   - hdfs   hdfs            0 2015-05-07 13:29 /tmp
drwxr-xr-x   - hdfs   hdfs            0 2015-04-27 16:00 /user
drwx-wx-wx   - hdfs   hdfs            0 2015-05-27 09:01 /var
```

To list files in your home directory, enter the following command:

```
$ hdfs dfs -ls

Found 13 items
drwx------   - hdfs hdfs          0 2015-05-27 20:00 .Trash
drwx------   - hdfs hdfs          0 2015-05-26 15:43 .staging
drwxr-xr-x   - hdfs hdfs          0 2015-05-28 13:03 DistributedShell
drwxr-xr-x   - hdfs hdfs          0 2015-05-14 09:19 TeraGen-50GB
drwxr-xr-x   - hdfs hdfs          0 2015-05-14 10:11 TeraSort-50GB
drwxr-xr-x   - hdfs hdfs          0 2015-05-24 20:06 bin
drwxr-xr-x   - hdfs hdfs          0 2015-04-29 16:52 examples
drwxr-xr-x   - hdfs hdfs          0 2015-04-27 16:00 flume-channel
drwxr-xr-x   - hdfs hdfs          0 2015-04-29 14:33 oozie-4.1.0
drwxr-xr-x   - hdfs hdfs          0 2015-04-30 10:35 oozie-examples
drwxr-xr-x   - hdfs hdfs          0 2015-04-29 20:35 oozie-oozi
drwxr-xr-x   - hdfs hdfs          0 2015-05-24 18:11 war-and-peace-input
drwxr-xr-x   - hdfs hdfs          0 2015-05-25 15:22 war-and-peace-output
```

The same result can be obtained by issuing the following command:

```
$ hdfs dfs -ls /user/hdfs
```

Make a Directory in HDFS

To make a directory in HDFS, use the following command. As with the -ls command, when no path is supplied, the user's home directory is used (e.g., /users/hdfs).

```
$ hdfs dfs -mkdir stuff
```

Copy Files to HDFS

To copy a file from your current local directory into HDFS, use the following command. If a full path is not supplied, your home directory is assumed. In this case, the file test is placed in the directory stuff that was created previously.

```
$ hdfs dfs -put test stuff
```

The file transfer can be confirmed by using the -ls command:

```
$ hdfs dfs -ls stuff
```

```
Found 1 items
-rw-r--r--   2 hdfs hdfs      12857 2015-05-29 13:12 stuff/test
```

Copy Files from HDFS

Files can be copied back to your local file system using the following command. In this case, the file we copied into HDFS, test, will be copied back to the current local directory with the name test-local.

```
$ hdfs dfs -get stuff/test test-local
```

Copy Files within HDFS

The following command will copy a file in HDFS:

```
$ hdfs dfs -cp stuff/test test.hdfs
```

Delete a File within HDFS

The following command will delete the HDFS file test.dhfs that was created previously:

```
$ hdfs dfs -rm test.hdfs
```

```
Moved: 'hdfs://limulus:8020/user/hdfs/stuff/test' to trash at: hdfs://
limulus:8020/user/hdfs/.Trash/Current
```

Note that when the fs.trash.interval option is set to a non-zero value in core-site.xml, all deleted files are moved to the user's .Trash directory. This can be avoided by including the -skipTrash option.

```
$ hdfs dfs -rm -skipTrash stuff/test
```

```
Deleted stuff/test
```

Delete a Directory in HDFS

The following command will delete the HDFS directory stuff and all its contents:

```
$ hdfs dfs -rm -r -skipTrash stuff
Deleted stuff
```

Get an HDFS Status Report

Regular users can get an abbreviated HDFS status report using the following command. Those with HDFS administrator privileges will get a full (and potentially long) report. Also, this command uses dfsadmin instead of dfs to invoke administrative commands. The status report is similar to the data presented in the HDFS web GUI (see the section "HDFS Web GUI").

```
$ hdfs dfsadmin -report

Configured Capacity: 1503409881088 (1.37 TB)
Present Capacity: 1407945981952 (1.28 TB)
DFS Remaining: 1255510564864 (1.14 TB)
DFS Used: 152435417088 (141.97 GB)
DFS Used%: 10.83%
Under replicated blocks: 54
Blocks with corrupt replicas: 0
Missing blocks: 0


-------------------------------------------------
report: Access denied for user deadline. Superuser privilege is required
```

HDFS Web GUI

HDFS provides an informational web interface. Starting the interface is described in Chapter 2, "Installation Recipes," in the section "Install Hadoop from Apache Sources." The interface can also be started from inside the Ambari management interface (see Chapter 9, "Managing Hadoop with Apache Ambari"). HDFS must be started and running on the cluster before the GUI can be used. It may be helpful to examine the information reported by the GUI as a way to explore some of the HDFS concepts presented in this chapter. The HDFS web GUI is described further in Chapter 10, "Basic Hadoop Administration Procedures."

Using HDFS in Programs

This section describes two methods for writing user applications that can use HDFS from within programs.

HDFS Java Application Example

When using Java, reading from and writing to Hadoop DFS is no different from the corresponding operations with other file systems. The code in Listing 3.1 is an example of reading, writing, and deleting files from HDFS, as well as making directories. The example is available from the book download page (see Appendix A, "Book Webpage and Code Download") or from http://wiki.apache.org/hadoop/HadoopDfsReadWriteExample.

To be able to read from or write to HDFS, you need to create a Configuration object and pass configuration parameters to it using Hadoop configuration files. The example in Listing 3.1 assumes the Hadoop configuration files are in /etc/hadoop/conf. If you do not assign the configuration objects to the local Hadoop XML files, your HDFS operation will be performed on the local file system and not on the HDFS.

Listing 3.1   **HadoopDFSFileReadWrite.java**

```java
package org.myorg;
import java.io.BufferedInputStream;
import java.io.BufferedOutputStream;
import java.io.File;
import java.io.FileInputStream;
import java.io.FileOutputStream;
import java.io.IOException;
import java.io.InputStream;
import java.io.OutputStream;

import org.apache.hadoop.conf.Configuration;
import org.apache.hadoop.fs.FSDataInputStream;
import org.apache.hadoop.fs.FSDataOutputStream;
import org.apache.hadoop.fs.FileSystem;
import org.apache.hadoop.fs.Path;

public class HDFSClient {
    public HDFSClient() {
    }
    public void addFile(String source, String dest) throws IOException {
        Configuration conf = new Configuration();
        // Conf object will read the HDFS configuration parameters from
        // these XML files.
        conf.addResource(new Path("/etc/hadoop/conf/core-site.xml"));
        conf.addResource(new Path("/etc/hadoop/conf/hdfs-site.xml"));
        FileSystem fileSystem = FileSystem.get(conf);
        // Get the filename out of the file path
        String filename = source.substring(source.lastIndexOf('/') + 1,
            source.length());
        // Create the destination path including the filename.
        if (dest.charAt(dest.length() - 1) != '/') {
            dest = dest + "/" + filename;
```

```
        } else {
            dest = dest + filename;
        }
        // System.out.println("Adding file to " + destination);
        // Check if the file already exists
        Path path = new Path(dest);
        if (fileSystem.exists(path)) {
            System.out.println("File " + dest + " already exists");
            return;
        }
        // Create a new file and write data to it.
        FSDataOutputStream out = fileSystem.create(path);
        InputStream in = new BufferedInputStream(new FileInputStream(
            new File(source)));
        byte[] b = new byte[1024];
        int numBytes = 0;
        while ((numBytes = in.read(b)) > 0) {
            out.write(b, 0, numBytes);
        }
        // Close all the file descripters
        in.close();
        out.close();
        fileSystem.close();
    }

    public void readFile(String file) throws IOException {
        Configuration conf = new Configuration();
        conf.addResource(new Path("/etc/hadoop/conf/core-site.xml"));
        FileSystem fileSystem = FileSystem.get(conf);
        Path path = new Path(file);
        if (!fileSystem.exists(path)) {
            System.out.println("File " + file + " does not exists");
            return;
        }
        FSDataInputStream in = fileSystem.open(path);
        String filename = file.substring(file.lastIndexOf('/') + 1,
            file.length());
        OutputStream out = new BufferedOutputStream(new FileOutputStream(
            new File(filename)));
        byte[] b = new byte[1024];
        int numBytes = 0;
        while ((numBytes = in.read(b)) > 0) {
            out.write(b, 0, numBytes);
        }
        in.close();
        out.close();
        fileSystem.close();
    }
```

```java
public void deleteFile(String file) throws IOException {
    Configuration conf = new Configuration();
    conf.addResource(new Path("/etc/hadoop/conf/core-site.xml"));
    FileSystem fileSystem = FileSystem.get(conf);
    Path path = new Path(file);
    if (!fileSystem.exists(path)) {
        System.out.println("File " + file + " does not exists");
        return;
    }
    fileSystem.delete(new Path(file), true);
    fileSystem.close();
}

public void mkdir(String dir) throws IOException {
    Configuration conf = new Configuration();
    conf.addResource(new Path("/etc/hadoop/conf/core-site.xml"));
    FileSystem fileSystem = FileSystem.get(conf);
    Path path = new Path(dir);
    if (fileSystem.exists(path)) {
        System.out.println("Dir " + dir + " already not exists");
        return;
    }
    fileSystem.mkdirs(path);
    fileSystem.close();
}

public static void main(String[] args) throws IOException {
    if (args.length < 1) {
        System.out.println("Usage: hdfsclient add/read/delete/mkdir" +
            " [<local_path> <hdfs_path>]");
        System.exit(1);
    }
    HDFSClient client = new HDFSClient();
    if (args[0].equals("add")) {
        if (args.length < 3) {
            System.out.println("Usage: hdfsclient add <local_path> " +
            "<hdfs_path>");
            System.exit(1);
        }
        client.addFile(args[1], args[2]);
    } else if (args[0].equals("read")) {
        if (args.length < 2) {
            System.out.println("Usage: hdfsclient read <hdfs_path>");
            System.exit(1);
        }
        client.readFile(args[1]);
    } else if (args[0].equals("delete")) {
```

```
            if (args.length < 2) {
                System.out.println("Usage: hdfsclient delete <hdfs_path>");
                System.exit(1);
            }
            client.deleteFile(args[1]);
        } else if (args[0].equals("mkdir")) {
            if (args.length < 2) {
                System.out.println("Usage: hdfsclient mkdir <hdfs_path>");
                System.exit(1);
            }
            client.mkdir(args[1]);
        } else {
            System.out.println("Usage: hdfsclient add/read/delete/mkdir" +
                " [<local_path> <hdfs_path>]");
            System.exit(1);
        }
        System.out.println("Done!");
    }
}
```

The `HadoopDFSFileReadWrite.java` example in Listing 3.1 can be compiled on Linux systems using the following steps. First, create a directory to hold the classes:

```
$ mkdir  HDFSClient-classes
```

Next, compile the program using `'hadoop classpath'` to ensure all the class paths are available:

```
$ javac -cp 'hadoop classpath' -d HDFSClient-classes HDFSClient.java
```

Finally, create a Java archive file:

```
$ jar -cvfe HDFSClient.jar org/myorg.HDFSClient -C HDFSClient-classes/ .
```

The program can be run to check for available options as follows:

```
$ hadoop jar ./HDFSClient.jar
Usage: hdfsclient add/read/delete/mkdir [<local_path> <hdfs_path>]
```

A simple file copy from the local system to HDFS can be accomplished using the following command:

```
$ hadoop jar ./HDFSClient.jar add ./NOTES.txt /user/hdfs
```

The file can be seen in HDFS by using the `hdfs dfs -ls` command:

```
$ hdfs dfs -ls NOTES.txt
-rw-r--r--   2 hdfs hdfs         502 2015-06-03 15:43 NOTES.txt
```

HDFS C Application Example

HDFS can be used in C programs by incorporating the Java Native Interface (JNI)–based C application programming interface (API) for Hadoop HDFS. The library, libhdfs, provides a simple C API to manipulate HDFS files and the file system. libhdfs is normally available as part of the Hadoop installation. More information about the API can be found on the Apache webpage, http://wiki.apache.org/hadoop/LibHDFS.

Listing 3.2 is small example program that illustrates use of the API. This example is available from the book download page; see Appendix A, "Book Webpage and Code Download."

Listing 3.2   **hdfs-simple-test.c**

```c
#include  <stdio.h>
#include <stdlib.h>
#include <string.h>
#include "hdfs.h"

int main(int argc, char **argv) {

    hdfsFS fs = hdfsConnect("default", 0);
    const char* writePath = "/tmp/testfile.txt";
    hdfsFile writeFile = hdfsOpenFile(fs, writePath, WRONGLY|O_CREAT, 0, 0, 0);
    if(!writeFile) {
         fprintf(stderr, "Failed to open %s for writing!\n", writePath);
         exit(-1);
    }
    char* buffer = "Hello, World!\n";
    tSize num_written_bytes = hdfsWrite(fs, writeFile, (void*)buffer,
strlen(buffer)+1);
    if (hdfsFlush(fs, writeFile)) {
          fprintf(stderr, "Failed to 'flush' %s\n", writePath);
          exit(-1);
    }
   hdfsCloseFile(fs, writeFile);
}
```

The example can be built using the following steps. The following software environment is assumed:

- Operating system: Linux
- Platform: RHEL 6.6
- Hortonworks HDP 2.2 with Hadoop Version: 2.6

The first step loads the Hadoop environment paths. In particular, the $HADOOP_LIB path is needed for the compiler.

```
$ . /etc/hadoop/conf/hadoop-env.sh
```

The program is compiled using gcc and the following command line. In addition to $HADOOP_LIB, the $JAVA_HOME path is assumed to be in the local environment. If the compiler issues errors or warnings, confirm that all paths are correct for the Hadoop and Java environment.

```
$ gcc hdfs-simple-test.c -I$HADOOP_LIB/include -I$JAVA_HOME/include
➥ -L$HADOOP_LIB/lib -L$JAVA_HOME/jre/lib/amd64/server -ljvm -lhdfs
➥ -o hdfs-simple-test
```

The location of the run-time library path needs to be set with the following command:

```
$ export LD_LIBRARY_PATH=
➥ $LD_LIBRARY_PATH:$JAVA_HOME/jre/lib/amd64/server:$HADOOP_LIB/lib
```

The Hadoop class path needs to be set with the following command. The --glob option is required because Hadoop version 2 uses a wildcard syntax in the output of the hadoop classpath command. Hadoop version 1 used the full path to every jar file without wildcards. Unfortunately, Java does not expand the wildcards automatically when launching an embedded JVM via JNI, so older scripts may not work. The --glob option expands the wildcards.

```
$ export CLASSPATH='hadoop classpath -glob'
```

The program can be run using the following. There may be some warnings that can be ignored.

```
$ /hdfs-simple-test
```

The new file contents can be inspected using the hdfs dfs -cat command:

```
$ hdfs dfs -cat /tmp/testfile.txt
Hello, World!
```

Summary and Additional Resources

Apache Hadoop HDFS has become a mature, high-performance, Big Data file system. Its design is fundamentally different from many conventional file systems and provides many important capabilities needed by Hadoop applications—including data locality. The two key components, the NameNode and DataNodes, combine to offer a scalable and robust distributed storage solution that operates on commodity servers. The NameNode can be augmented by secondary or checkpoint nodes to improve performance and robustness. Advanced features like High Availability, NameNode Federation, snapshots, and NFSv3 mounts are also available to HDFS administrators.

Users interact with HDFS using a command interface that is similar to traditional POSIX-style file systems. A small subset of HDFS user commands is all that is needed to gain immediate use of HDFS. In addition, HDFS presents a web interface for easy navigation of file system information. Finally, HDFS can be easily used in end-user applications written using the Java or C languages.

Additional information and background on HDFS can be obtained from the following resources:

- **HDFS background**
  - http://hadoop.apache.org/docs/stable1/hdfs_design.html
  - http://developer.yahoo.com/hadoop/tutorial/module2.html
  - http://hadoop.apache.org/docs/stable/hdfs_user_guide.html
- **HDFS user commands**
  - http://hadoop.apache.org/docs/stable/hadoop-project-dist/hadoop-hdfs/HDFSCommands.html
- **HDFS Java programming**
  - http://wiki.apache.org/hadoop/HadoopDfsReadWriteExample
- **HDFS libhdfs programming in C**
  - http://hadoop.apache.org/docs/stable/hadoop-project-dist/hadoop-hdfs/LibHdfs.html

4

Running Example Programs and Benchmarks

When using new or updated hardware or software, simple examples and benchmarks help confirm proper operation. Apache Hadoop includes many examples and benchmarks to aid in this task. This chapter provides instructions on how to run, monitor, and manage some basic MapReduce examples and benchmarks.

Running MapReduce Examples

All Hadoop releases come with MapReduce example applications. Running the existing MapReduce examples is a simple process—once the example files are located, that is. For example, if you installed Hadoop version 2.6.0 from the Apache sources under /opt, the examples will be in the following directory:

```
/opt/hadoop-2.6.0/share/hadoop/mapreduce/
```

In other versions, the examples may be in /usr/lib/hadoop-mapreduce/ or some other location. The exact location of the example jar file can be found using the find command:

```
$ find / -name "hadoop-mapreduce-examples*.jar" -print
```

For this chapter the following software environment will be used:

- OS: Linux
- Platform: RHEL 6.6
- Hortonworks HDP 2.2 with Hadoop Version: 2.6

In this environment, the location of the examples is /usr/hdp/2.2.4.2-2/hadoop-mapreduce. For the purposes of this example, an environment variable called HADOOP_EXAMPLES can be defined as follows:

```
$ export HADOOP_EXAMPLES=/usr/hdp/2.2.4.2-2/hadoop-mapreduce
```

Once you define the examples path, you can run the Hadoop examples using the commands discussed in the following sections.

Listing Available Examples

A list of the available examples can be found by running the following command. In some cases, the version number may be part of the jar file (e.g., in the version 2.6 Apache sources, the file is named hadoop-mapreduce-examples-2.6.0.jar).

```
$ yarn jar $HADOOP_EXAMPLES/hadoop-mapreduce-examples.jar
```

> **Note**
> In previous versions of Hadoop, the command hadoop jar ... was used to run MapReduce programs. Newer versions provide the yarn command, which offers more capabilities. Both commands will work for these examples.

The possible examples are as follows:

```
An example program must be given as the first argument.
Valid program names are:
  aggregatewordcount: An Aggregate based map/reduce program that counts
  the words in the input files.
  aggregatewordhist: An Aggregate based map/reduce program that computes
  the histogram of the words in the input files.
  bbp: A map/reduce program that uses Bailey-Borwein-Plouffe to compute
  exact digits of Pi.
  dbcount: An example job that count the pageview counts from a database.
  distbbp: A map/reduce program that uses a BBP-type formula to compute
  exact bits of Pi.
  grep: A map/reduce program that counts the matches of a regex in the
  input.
  join: A job that effects a join over sorted, equally partitioned
  datasets
  multifilewc: A job that counts words from several files.
  pentomino: A map/reduce tile laying program to find solutions to
  pentomino problems.
```

```
pi: A map/reduce program that estimates Pi using a quasi-Monte
Carlo method.
randomtextwriter: A map/reduce program that writes 10GB of random
textual data per node.
randomwriter: A map/reduce program that writes 10GB of random data
per node.
secondarysort: An example defining a secondary sort to the reduce.
sort: A map/reduce program that sorts the data written by the
random writer.
sudoku: A sudoku solver.
teragen: Generate data for the terasort
terasort: Run the terasort
teravalidate: Checking results of terasort
wordcount: A map/reduce program that counts the words in the
input files.
wordmean: A map/reduce program that counts the average length of
the words in the input files.
wordmedian: A map/reduce program that counts the median length of
the words in the input files.
wordstandarddeviation: A map/reduce program that counts the standard
deviation of the length of the words in the input files.
```

To illustrate several features of Hadoop and the YARN ResourceManager service GUI, the pi and terasort examples are presented next. To find help for running the other examples, enter the example name without any arguments. Chapter 6, "MapReduce Programming," covers one of the other popular examples called wordcount.

Running the Pi Example

The pi example calculates the digits of π using a quasi-Monte Carlo method. If you have not added users to HDFS (see Chapter 10, "Basic Hadoop Administration Procedures"), run these tests as user hdfs. To run the pi example with 16 maps and 1,000,000 samples per map, enter the following command:

```
$ yarn jar $HADOOP_EXAMPLES/hadoop-mapreduce-examples.jar pi 16 1000000
```

If the program runs correctly, you should see output similar to the following. (Some of the Hadoop INFO messages have been removed for clarity.)

```
Number of Maps  = 16
Samples per Map = 1000000
Wrote input for Map #0
Wrote input for Map #1
Wrote input for Map #2
Wrote input for Map #3
Wrote input for Map #4
Wrote input for Map #5
Wrote input for Map #6
```

```
Wrote input for Map #7
Wrote input for Map #8
Wrote input for Map #9
Wrote input for Map #10
Wrote input for Map #11
Wrote input for Map #12
Wrote input for Map #13
Wrote input for Map #14
Wrote input for Map #15
Starting Job
...
15/05/13 20:10:30 INFO mapreduce.Job:  map 0% reduce 0%
15/05/13 20:10:37 INFO mapreduce.Job:  map 19% reduce 0%
15/05/13 20:10:39 INFO mapreduce.Job:  map 50% reduce 0%
15/05/13 20:10:46 INFO mapreduce.Job:  map 56% reduce 0%
15/05/13 20:10:47 INFO mapreduce.Job:  map 94% reduce 0%
15/05/13 20:10:48 INFO mapreduce.Job:  map 100% reduce 100%
15/05/13 20:10:48 INFO mapreduce.Job: Job job_1429912013449_0047 completed
successfully
15/05/13 20:10:48 INFO mapreduce.Job: Counters: 49
        File System Counters
                FILE: Number of bytes read=358
                FILE: Number of bytes written=1949395
                FILE: Number of read operations=0
                FILE: Number of large read operations=0
                FILE: Number of write operations=0
                HDFS: Number of bytes read=4198
                HDFS: Number of bytes written=215
                HDFS: Number of read operations=67
                HDFS: Number of large read operations=0
                HDFS: Number of write operations=3
        Job Counters
                Launched map tasks=16
                Launched reduce tasks=1
                Data-local map tasks=16
                Total time spent by all maps in occupied slots (ms)=158378
                Total time spent by all reduces in occupied slots (ms)=8462
                Total time spent by all map tasks (ms)=158378
                Total time spent by all reduce tasks (ms)=8462
                Total vcore-seconds taken by all map tasks=158378
                Total vcore-seconds taken by all reduce tasks=8462
                Total megabyte-seconds taken by all map tasks=243268608
                Total megabyte-seconds taken by all reduce tasks=12997632
        Map-Reduce Framework
                Map input records=16
                Map output records=32
                Map output bytes=288
                Map output materialized bytes=448
```

```
        Input split bytes=2310
        Combine input records=0
        Combine output records=0
        Reduce input groups=2
        Reduce shuffle bytes=448
        Reduce input records=32
        Reduce output records=0
        Spilled Records=64
        Shuffled Maps=16
        Failed Shuffles=0
        Merged Map outputs=16
        GC time elapsed (ms)=1842
        CPU time spent (ms)=11420
        Physical memory (bytes) snapshot=13405769728
        Virtual memory (bytes) snapshot=33911930880
        Total committed heap usage (bytes)=17026777088
    Shuffle Errors
        BAD_ID=0
        CONNECTION=0
        IO_ERROR=0
        WRONG_LENGTH=0
        WRONG_MAP=0
        WRONG_REDUCE=0
    File Input Format Counters
        Bytes Read=1888
    File Output Format Counters
        Bytes Written=97
Job Finished in 23.718 seconds
Estimated value of Pi is 3.14159125000000000000
```

Notice that the MapReduce progress is shown in the same way as Hadoop version 1, but the application statistics are different. Most of the statistics are self-explanatory. The one important item to note is that the YARN MapReduce framework is used to run the program. (See Chapter 1, "Background and Concepts," and Chapter 8, "Hadoop YARN Applications," for more information about YARN frameworks.)

Using the Web GUI to Monitor Examples

This section provides an illustration of using the YARN ResourceManager web GUI to monitor and find information about YARN jobs. The Hadoop version 2 YARN ResourceManager web GUI differs significantly from the MapReduce web GUI found in Hadoop version 1. Figure 4.1 shows the main YARN web interface. The cluster metrics are displayed in the top row, while the running applications are displayed in the main table. A menu on the left provides navigation to the nodes table, various job categories (e.g., New, Accepted, Running, Finished, Failed), and the Capacity Scheduler (covered in Chapter 10, "Basic Hadoop Administration Procedures"). This interface can be opened directly from the Ambari YARN service Quick Links menu or by

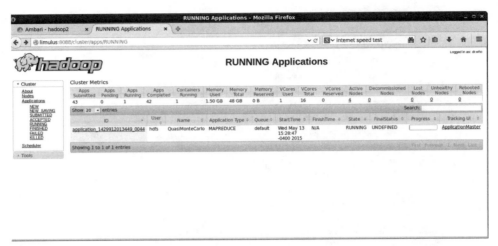

Figure 4.1   Hadoop RUNNING Applications web GUI for the pi example

directly entering http://hostname:8088 into a local web browser. For this example, the pi application is used. Note that the application can run quickly and may finish before you have fully explored the GUI. A longer-running application, such as terasort, may be helpful when exploring all the various links in the GUI.

For those readers who have used or read about Hadoop version 1, if you look at the Cluster Metrics table, you will see some new information. First, you will notice that the "Map/Reduce Task Capacity" has been replaced by the number of running containers. If YARN is running a MapReduce job, these containers can be used for both map and reduce tasks. Unlike in Hadoop version 1, the number of mappers and reducers is not fixed. There are also memory metrics and links to node status. If you click on the Nodes link (left menu under About), you can get a summary of the node activity and state. For example, Figure 4.2 is a snapshot of the node activity while the pi application is running. Notice the number of containers, which are used by the MapReduce framework as either mappers or reducers.

Going back to the main Applications/Running window (Figure 4.1), if you click on the application_14299… link, the Application status window in Figure 4.3 will appear. This window provides an application overview and metrics, including the cluster node on which the ApplicationMaster container is running.

Clicking the ApplicationMaster link next to "Tracking URL:" in Figure 4.3 leads to the window shown in Figure 4.4. Note that the link to the application's ApplicationMaster is also found in the last column on the main Running Applications screen shown in Figure 4.1.

In the MapReduce Application window, you can see the details of the MapReduce application and the overall progress of mappers and reducers. Instead of containers, the MapReduce application now refers to maps and reducers. Clicking job_14299… brings up the window shown in Figure 4.5. This window displays more detail about the

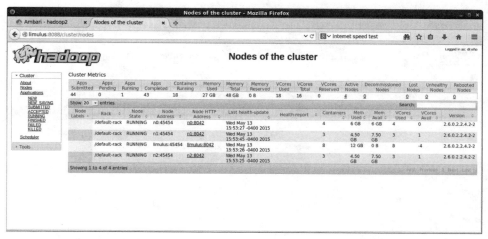

Figure 4.2 Hadoop YARN ResourceManager nodes status window

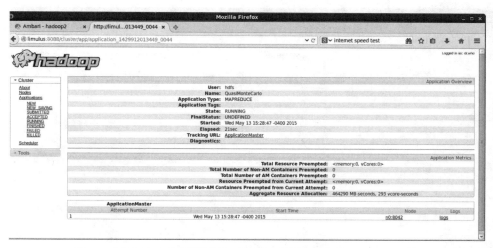

Figure 4.3 Hadoop YARN application status for the `pi` example

number of pending, running, completed, and failed mappers and reducers, including the elapsed time since the job started.

The status of the job in Figure 4.5 will be updated as the job progresses (the window needs to be refreshed manually). The ApplicationMaster collects and reports the progress of each mapper and reducer task. When the job is finished, the window is updated to that shown in Figure 4.6. It reports the overall run time and provides a breakdown of the timing of the key phases of the MapReduce job (map, shuffle, merge, reduce).

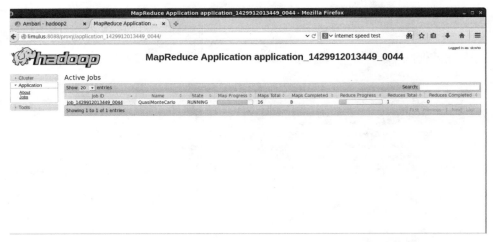

Figure 4.4   Hadoop YARN ApplicationMaster for MapReduce application

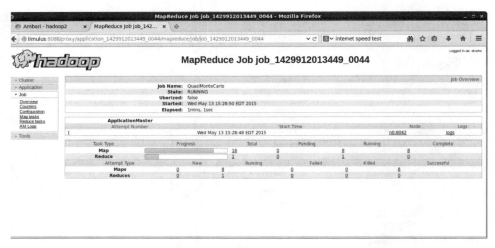

Figure 4.5   Hadoop YARN MapReduce job progress

If you click the node used to run the ApplicationMaster (n0:8042 in Figure 4.6), the window in Figure 4.7 opens and provides a summary from the NodeManager on node n0. Again, the NodeManager tracks only containers; the actual tasks running in the containers are determined by the ApplicationMaster.

Going back to the job summary page (Figure 4.6), you can also examine the logs for the ApplicationMaster by clicking the "logs" link. To find information about the mappers and reducers, click the numbers under the Failed, Killed, and Successful columns. In this example, there were 16 successful mappers and

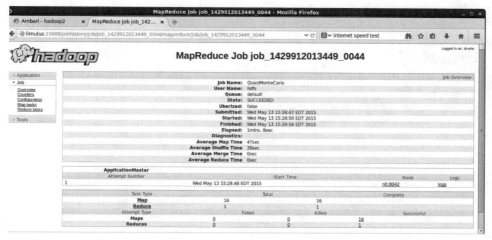

Figure 4.6   Hadoop YARN completed MapReduce job summary

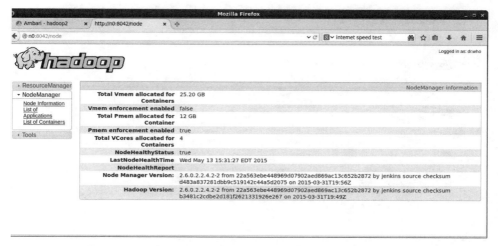

Figure 4.7   Hadoop YARN NodeManager for n0 job summary

one successful reducer. All the numbers in these columns lead to more information about individual map or reduce process. For instance, clicking the "16" under
"Successful" in Figure 4.6 displays the table of map tasks in Figure 4.8. The metrics
for the Application Master container are displayed in table form. There is also a
link to the log file for each process (in this case, a map process). Viewing the logs
requires that the yarn.log.aggregation-enable variable in the yarn-site.xml file
be set. For more on changing Hadoop settings, see Chapter 9, "Managing Hadoop
with Apache Ambari."

Figure 4.8   Hadoop YARN MapReduce logs available for browsing

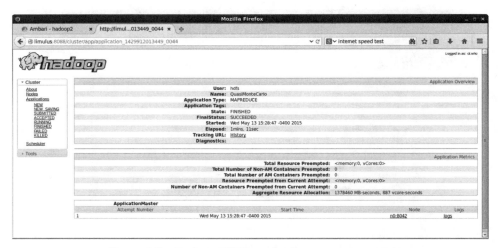

Figure 4.9   Hadoop YARN application summary page

If you return to the main cluster window (Figure 4.1), choose Applications/ Finished, and then select our application, you will see the summary page shown in Figure 4.9.

There are a few things to notice in the previous windows. First, because YARN manages applications, all information reported by the ResourceManager concerns the resources provided and the application type (in this case, MAPREDUCE). In Figure 4.1 and Figure 4.4, the YARN ResourceManager refers to the pi example by its application-id (`application_1429912013449_0044`). YARN has no data about the actual application other than the fact that it is a MapReduce job. Data from the actual MapReduce job are provided by the MapReduce framework and referenced by a job-id (`job_1429912013449_0044`) in Figure 4.6. Thus, two clearly different data streams are combined in the web GUI: YARN *applications* and MapReduce framework *jobs*. If the framework does not provide job information, then certain parts of the web GUI will not have anything to display.

Another interesting aspect of the previous windows is the dynamic nature of the mapper and reducer tasks. These tasks are executed as YARN containers, and their number will change as the application runs. Users may request specific numbers of mappers and reducers, but the ApplicationMaster uses them in a dynamic fashion. As mappers complete, the ApplicationMaster will return the containers to the Resource-Manager and request a smaller number of reducer containers. This feature provides for much better cluster utilization because mappers and reducers are dynamic—rather than fixed—resources.

Running Basic Hadoop Benchmarks

Many Hadoop benchmarks can provide insight into cluster performance. The best benchmarks are always those that reflect real application performance. The two benchmarks discussed in this section, `terasort` and `TestDFSIO`, provide a good sense of how well your Hadoop installation is operating and can be compared with public data published for other Hadoop systems. The results, however, should not be taken as a single indicator for system-wide performance on all applications.

The following benchmarks are designed for full Hadoop cluster installations. These tests assume a multi-disk HDFS environment. Running these benchmarks in the Hortonworks Sandbox or in the pseudo-distributed single-node install from Chapter 2 is not recommended because all input and output (I/O) are done using a single system disk drive.

Running the Terasort Test

The `terasort` benchmark sorts a specified amount of randomly generated data. This benchmark provides combined testing of the HDFS and MapReduce layers of a Hadoop cluster. A full `terasort` benchmark run consists of the following three steps:

1. Generating the input data via `teragen` program.
2. Running the actual `terasort` benchmark on the input data.
3. Validating the sorted output data via the `teravalidate` program.

In general, each row is 100 bytes long; thus the total amount of data written is 100 times the number of rows specified as part of the benchmark (i.e., to write 100GB of data, use 1 billion rows). The input and output directories need to be specified in HDFS. The following sequence of commands will run the benchmark for 50GB of data as user `hdfs`. Make sure the `/user/hdfs` directory exists in HDFS before running the benchmarks.

1. Run `teragen` to generate rows of random data to sort.

```
$ yarn jar $HADOOP_EXAMPLES/hadoop-mapreduce-examples.jar teragen 500000000
➥/user/hdfs/TeraGen-50GB
```

2. Run `terasort` to sort the database.

```
$ yarn jar $HADOOP_EXAMPLES/hadoop-mapreduce-examples.jar terasort
➥/user/hdfs/TeraGen-50GB /user/hdfs/TeraSort-50GB
```

3. Run `teravalidate` to validate the sort.

```
$ yarn jar $HADOOP_EXAMPLES/hadoop-mapreduce-examples.jar teravalidate
➥/user/hdfs/TeraSort-50GB /user/hdfs/TeraValid-50GB
```

To report results, the time for the actual sort (`terasort`) is measured and the benchmark rate in megabytes/second (MB/s) is calculated. For best performance, the actual `terasort` benchmark should be run with a replication factor of 1. In addition, the default number of `terasort` reducer tasks is set to 1. Increasing the number of reducers often helps with benchmark performance. For example, the following command will instruct `terasort` to use four reducer tasks:

```
$ yarn jar $HADOOP_EXAMPLES/hadoop-mapreduce-examples.jar terasort
➥ -Dmapred.reduce.tasks=4 /user/hdfs/TeraGen-50GB /user/hdfs/TeraSort-50GB
```

Also, do not forget to clean up the `terasort` data between runs (and after testing is finished). The following command will perform the cleanup for the previous example:

```
$ hdfs dfs -rm -r -skipTrash Tera*
```

Running the TestDFSIO Benchmark

Hadoop also includes an HDFS benchmark application called `TestDFSIO`. The `TestDFSIO` benchmark is a read and write test for HDFS. That is, it will write or read a number of files to and from HDFS and is designed in such a way that it will use one map task per file. The file size and number of files are specified as command-line arguments. Similar to the `terasort` benchmark, you should run this test as user `hdfs`.

Similar to `terasort`, `TestDFSIO` has several steps. In the following example, 16 files of size 1GB are specified. Note that the `TestDFSIO` benchmark is part of the `hadoop-mapreduce-client-jobclient.jar`. Other benchmarks are also available as part of this jar file. Running it with no arguments will yield a list. In addition to `TestDFSIO`, `NNBench` (load testing the NameNode) and `MRBench` (load testing the MapReduce framework) are commonly used Hadoop benchmarks. Nevertheless, `TestDFSIO` is perhaps the most widely reported of these benchmarks. The steps to run `TestDFSIO` are as follows:

1. Run `TestDFSIO` in write mode and create data.

```
$ yarn jar $HADOOP_EXAMPLES/hadoop-mapreduce-client-jobclient-tests.jar
➥ TestDFSIO -write  -nrFiles 16 -fileSize 1000
```

Example results are as follows (date and time prefix removed).

```
fs.TestDFSIO: ----- TestDFSIO ----- : write
fs.TestDFSIO:            Date & time: Thu May 14 10:39:33 EDT 2015
fs.TestDFSIO:        Number of files: 16
fs.TestDFSIO: Total MBytes processed: 16000.0
fs.TestDFSIO:       Throughput mb/sec: 14.890106361891005
fs.TestDFSIO: Average IO rate mb/sec: 15.690713882446289
fs.TestDFSIO:  IO rate std deviation: 4.0227035201665595
fs.TestDFSIO:      Test exec time sec: 105.631
```

2. Run `TestDFSIO` in read mode.

```
$ yarn jar $HADOOP_EXAMPLES/hadoop-mapreduce-client-jobclient-tests.jar
➥ TestDFSIO -read -nrFiles 16 -fileSize 1000
```

Example results are as follows (date and time prefix removed). The large standard deviation is due to the placement of tasks in the cluster on a small four-node cluster.

```
fs.TestDFSIO: ----- TestDFSIO ----- : read
fs.TestDFSIO:            Date & time: Thu May 14 10:44:09 EDT 2015
fs.TestDFSIO:        Number of files: 16
fs.TestDFSIO: Total MBytes processed: 16000.0
fs.TestDFSIO:       Throughput mb/sec: 32.38643494172466
fs.TestDFSIO: Average IO rate mb/sec: 58.72880554199219
fs.TestDFSIO:  IO rate std deviation: 64.60017624360337
fs.TestDFSIO:      Test exec time sec: 62.798
```

3. Clean up the TestDFSIO data.

```
$ yarn jar $HADOOP_EXAMPLES/hadoop-mapreduce-client-jobclient-tests.jar
➥ TestDFSIO -clean
```

Running the `TestDFSIO` and `terasort` benchmarks help you gain confidence in a Hadoop installation and detect any potential problems. It is also instructive to view the Ambari dashboard and the YARN web GUI (as described previously) as the tests run.

Managing Hadoop MapReduce Jobs

Hadoop MapReduce jobs can be managed using the `mapred job` command. The most important options for this command in terms of the examples and benchmarks are `-list`, `-kill`, and `-status`. In particular, if you need to kill one of the examples or benchmarks, you can use the `mapred job -list` command to find the `job-id` and then use `mapred job -kill <job-id>` to kill the job across the cluster. MapReduce jobs can also be controlled at the application level with the `yarn application` command (see Chapter 10, "Basic Hadoop Administration Procedures"). The possible options for `mapred job` are as follows:

```
$ mapred job
Usage: CLI <command> <args>
        [-submit <job-file>]
```

```
[-status <job-id>]
[-counter <job-id> <group-name> <counter-name>]
[-kill <job-id>]
[-set-priority <job-id> <priority>]. Valid values for priorities
 are: VERY_HIGH HIGH NORMAL LOW VERY_LOW
[-events <job-id> <from-event-#> <#-of-events>]
[-history <jobHistoryFile>]
[-list [all]]
[-list-active-trackers]
[-list-blacklisted-trackers]
[-list-attempt-ids <job-id> <task-type> <task-state>]. Valid values
 for <task-type> are REDUCE MAP. Valid values for <task-state> are
 running, completed
[-kill-task <task-attempt-id>]
[-fail-task <task-attempt-id>]
[-logs <job-id> <task-attempt-id>]
```

```
Generic options supported are
-conf <configuration file>      specify an application configuration file
-D <property=value>             use value for given property
-fs <local|namenode:port>       specify a namenode
-jt <local|resourcemanager:port>    specify a ResourceManager
-files <comma separated list of files>    specify comma separated files to
  be copied to the map reduce cluster
-libjars <comma separated list of jars>    specify comma separated jar
  files to include in the classpath.
-archives <comma separated list of archives>    specify comma separated
  archives to be unarchived on the compute machines.
```

```
The general command line syntax is
bin/hadoop command [genericOptions] [commandOptions]
```

Summary and Additional Resources

No matter what the size of the Hadoop cluster, confirming and measuring the
MapReduce performance of that cluster is an important first step. Hadoop includes
some simple applications and benchmarks that can be used for this purpose. The
YARN ResourceManager web GUI is a good way to monitor the progress of any
application. Jobs that run under the MapReduce framework report a large number
of run-time metrics directly (including logs) back to the GUI; these metrics are then
presented to the user in a clear and coherent fashion. Should issues arise when running the examples and benchmarks, the mapred job command can be used to kill a
MapReduce job.

Additional information and background on each of the examples and benchmarks can be found from the following resources:

- **Pi Benchmark**
  - https://hadoop.apache.org/docs/current/api/org/apache/hadoop/examples/pi/package-summary.html
- **Terasort Benchmark**
  - https://hadoop.apache.org/docs/current/api/org/apache/hadoop/examples/terasort/package-summary.html
- **Benchmarking and Stress Testing an Hadoop Cluster**
  - http://www.michael-noll.com/blog/2011/04/09/benchmarking-and-stress-testing-an-hadoop-cluster-with-terasort-testdfsio-nnbench-mrbench (uses Hadoop V1, will work with V2)

## 5

Hadoop MapReduce Framework

In This Chapter:

- The MapReduce computation model is presented using simple examples.
- The Apache Hadoop MapReduce framework data flow is explained.
- MapReduce fault tolerance, speculative execution, and hardware are discussed.

The MapReduce programming model is conceptually simple. Based on two simple steps—applying a mapping process and then reducing (condensing/collecting) the results—it can be applied to many real-world problems. In this chapter, we examine the MapReduce process using basic command-line tools. We then expand this concept into a parallel MapReduce model.

The MapReduce Model

Apache Hadoop is often associated with MapReduce computing. Prior to Hadoop version 2, this assumption was certainly true. Hadoop version 2 maintained the MapReduce capability and also made other processing models available to users. Virtually all the tools developed for Hadoop, such as Pig and Hive, will work seamlessly on top of the Hadoop version 2 MapReduce.

The MapReduce computation model provides a very powerful tool for many applications and is more common than most users realize. Its underlying idea is very simple. There are two stages: a mapping stage and a reducing stage. In the mapping stage, a *mapping procedure* is applied to input data. The map is usually some kind of filter or sorting process.

For instance, assume you need to count how many times the name "Kutuzov" appears in the novel *War and Peace*. One solution is to gather 20 friends and give them each a section of the book to search. This step is the map stage. The reduce phase happens when everyone is done counting and you sum the total as your friends tell you their counts.

Now consider how this same process could be accomplished using simple *nix command-line tools. The following `grep` command applies a specific map to a text file:

```
$ grep " Kutuzov " war-and-peace.txt
```

This command searches for the word `Kutuzov` (with leading and trailing spaces) in a text file called `war-and-peace.txt`. Each match is reported as a single line of text that contains the search term. The actual text file is a 3.2MB text dump of the novel *War and Peace* and is available from the book download page (see Appendix A, "Book Webpage and Code Download"). The search term, `Kutuzov`, is a character in the book. If we ignore the `grep` count (`-c`) option for the moment, we can reduce the number of instances to a single number (257) by sending (piping) the results of `grep` into `wc -l`. (`wc -l` or "word count" reports the number of lines it receives.)

```
$ grep " Kutuzov " war-and-peace.txt|wc -l
257
```

Though not strictly a MapReduce process, this idea is quite similar to and much faster than the manual process of counting the instances of Kutuzov in the printed book. The analogy can be taken a bit further by using the two simple (and naive) shell scripts shown in Listing 5.1 and Listing 5.2. The shell scripts are available from the book download page (see Appendix A). We can perform the same operation (much more slowly) and tokenize both the `Kutuzov` and `Petersburg` strings in the text:

```
$ cat war-and-peace.txt |./mapper.sh |./reducer.sh
Kutuzov,315
Petersburg,128
```

Notice that more instances of Kutuzov have been found (the first `grep` command ignored instances like "Kutuzov." or "Kutuzov,"). The mapper inputs a text file and then outputs data in a (key, value) pair (token-name, count) format. Strictly speaking, the input to the script is the file and the keys are `Kutuzov` and `Petersburg`. The reducer script takes these key–value pairs and combines the similar tokens and counts the total number of instances. The result is a new key–value pair (token-name, sum).

Listing 5.1   Simple Mapper Script

```bash
#!/bin/bash
while read line ; do
  for token in $line; do
  if [ "$token" = "Kutuzov" ] ; then
    echo "Kutuzov,1"
  elif [ "$token" = "Petersburg" ] ; then
    echo "Petersburg,1"
  fi
  done
done
```

Listing 5.2 **Simple Reducer Script**

```
#!/bin/bash
kcount=0
pcount=0
while read line ; do
  if [ "$line" = "Kutuzov,1" ] ; then
   let kcount=kcount+1
  elif [ "$line" = "Petersburg,1" ] ; then
   let pcount=pcount+1
  fi
done
echo "Kutuzov,$kcount"
echo "Petersburg,$pcount"
```

Formally, the MapReduce process can be described as follows. The mapper and reducer functions are both defined with respect to data structured in (key, value) pairs. The mapper takes one pair of data with a type in one data domain, and returns a list of pairs in a different domain:

```
Map(key1,value1) → list(key2,value2)
```

The reducer function is then applied to each key–value pair, which in turn produces a collection of values in the same domain:

```
Reduce(key2, list (value2)) → list(value3)
```

Each reducer call typically produces either one value (value3) or an empty response. Thus, the MapReduce framework transforms a list of (key, value) pairs into a list of values.

The MapReduce model is inspired by the map and reduce functions commonly used in many functional programming languages. The functional nature of MapReduce has some important properties:

- Data flow is in one direction (map to reduce). It is possible to use the output of a reduce step as the input to another MapReduce process.

- As with functional programing, the input data are not changed. By applying the mapping and reduction functions to the input data, new data are produced. In effect, the original state of the Hadoop data lake is always preserved (see Chapter 1, "Background and Concepts").

- Because there is no dependency on how the mapping and reducing functions are applied to the data, the mapper and reducer data flow can be implemented in any number of ways to provide better performance.

Distributed (parallel) implementations of MapReduce enable large amounts of data to be analyzed quickly. In general, the mapper process is fully scalable and can be applied to any subset of the input data. Results from multiple parallel mapping functions are then combined in the reducer phase.

As mentioned in Chapter 1, Hadoop accomplishes parallelism by using a distributed file system (HDFS) to slice and spread data over multiple servers. Apache Hadoop MapReduce will try to move the mapping tasks to the server that contains the data slice. Results from each data slice are then combined in the reducer step. This process is explained in more detail in the next section.

HDFS is not required for Hadoop MapReduce, however. A sufficiently fast parallel file system can be used in its place. In these designs, each server in the cluster has access to a high-performance parallel file system that can rapidly provide any data slice. These designs are typically more expensive than the commodity servers used for many Hadoop clusters.

MapReduce Parallel Data Flow

From a programmer's perspective, the MapReduce algorithm is fairly simple. The programmer must provide a mapping function and a reducing function. Operationally, however, the Apache Hadoop parallel MapReduce data flow can be quite complex. Parallel execution of MapReduce requires other steps in addition to the mapper and reducer processes. The basic steps are as follows:

1. **Input Splits.** As mentioned, HDFS distributes and replicates data over multiple servers. The default data chunk or block size is 64MB. Thus, a 500MB file would be broken into 8 blocks and written to different machines in the cluster. The data are also replicated on multiple machines (typically three machines). These data slices are physical boundaries determined by HDFS and have nothing to do with the data in the file. Also, while not considered part of the MapReduce process, the time required to load and distribute data throughout HDFS servers can be considered part of the total processing time.

   The input splits used by MapReduce are logical boundaries based on the input data. For example, the split size can be based on the number of records in a file (if the data exist as records) or an actual size in bytes. Splits are almost always smaller than the HDFS block size. The number of splits corresponds to the number of mapping processes used in the map stage.

2. **Map Step.** The mapping process is where the parallel nature of Hadoop comes into play. For large amounts of data, many mappers can be operating at the same time. The user provides the specific mapping process. MapReduce will try to execute the mapper on the machines where the block resides. Because the file is replicated in HDFS, the least busy node with the data will be chosen. If all nodes holding the data are too busy, MapReduce will try to pick a node that is closest to the node that hosts the data block (a characteristic called rack-awareness). The last choice is any node in the cluster that has access to HDFS.

3. **Combiner Step.** It is possible to provide an optimization or pre-reduction as part of the map stage where key–value pairs are combined prior to the next stage. The combiner stage is optional.

4. **Shuffle Step.** Before the parallel reduction stage can complete, all similar keys must be combined and counted by the same reducer process. Therefore, results of the map stage must be collected by key–value pairs and shuffled to the same reducer process. If only a single reducer process is used, the shuffle stage is not needed.

5. **Reduce Step.** The final step is the actual reduction. In this stage, the data reduction is performed as per the programmer's design. The reduce step is also optional. The results are written to HDFS. Each reducer will write an output file. For example, a MapReduce job running four reducers will create files called `part-0000`, `part-0001`, `part-0002`, and `part-0003`.

Figure 5.1 is an example of a simple Hadoop MapReduce data flow for a word count program. The map process counts the words in the split, and the reduce process calculates the total for each word. As mentioned earlier, the actual computation of the map and reduce stages are up to the programmer. The MapReduce data flow shown in Figure 5.1 is the same regardless of the specific map and reduce tasks.

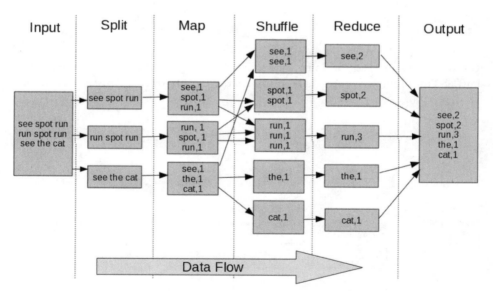

Figure 5.1   Apache Hadoop parallel MapReduce data flow

The input to the MapReduce application is the following file in HDFS with three lines of text. The goal is to count the number of times each word is used.

```
see spot run
run spot run
see the cat
```

The first thing MapReduce will do is create the data splits. For simplicity, each line will be one split. Since each split will require a map task, there are three mapper processes that count the number of words in the split. On a cluster, the results of each map task are written to local disk and not to HDFS. Next, similar keys need to be collected and sent to a reducer process. The shuffle step requires data movement and can be expensive in terms of processing time. Depending on the nature of the application, the amount of data that must be shuffled throughout the cluster can vary from small to large.

Once the data have been collected and sorted by key, the reduction step can begin (even if only partial results are available). It is not necessary—and not normally recommended—to have a reducer for each key–value pair as shown in Figure 5.1. In some cases, a single reducer will provide adequate performance; in other cases, multiple reducers may be required to speed up the reduce phase. The number of reducers is a tunable option for many applications. The final step is to write the output to HDFS.

As mentioned, a combiner step enables some pre-reduction of the map output data. For instance, in the previous example, one map produced the following counts:

```
(run,1)
(spot,1)
(run,1)
```

As shown in Figure 5.2, the count for run can be combined into (run,2) before the shuffle. This optimization can help minimize the amount of data transfer needed for the shuffle phase.

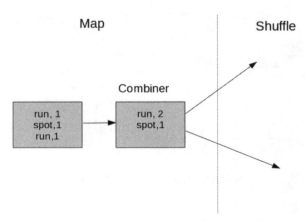

Figure 5.2   Adding a combiner process to the map step in MapReduce

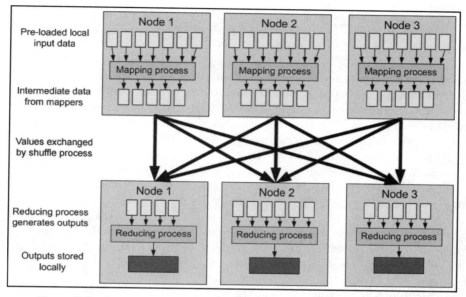

Figure 5.3   Process placement during MapReduce (Adapted from Yahoo
Hadoop Documentation)

The Hadoop YARN resource manager and the MapReduce framework determine the actual placement of mappers and reducers. As mentioned earlier, the MapReduce framework will try to place the map task as close to the data as possible. It will request the placement from the YARN scheduler but may not get the best placement due to the load on the cluster. In general, nodes can run both mapper and reducer tasks. Indeed, the dynamic nature of YARN enables the work containers used by completed map tasks to be returned to the pool of available resources.

Figure 5.3 shows a simple three-node MapReduce process. Once the mapping is complete, the same nodes begin the reduce process. The shuffle stage makes sure the necessary data are sent to each mapper. Also note that there is no requirement that all the mappers complete at the same time or that the mapper on a specific node be complete before a reducer is started. Reducers can be set to start shuffling based on a threshold of percentage of mappers that have finished.

Finally, although the examples are simple in nature, the parallel MapReduce algorithm can be scaled up to extremely large data sizes. For instance, the Hadoop word count sample application (see Chapter 6, "MapReduce Programming") can be run on the three lines given earlier or on a 3TB file. The application requires no changes to account for the scale of the problem—a feature that is one of the remarkable advantages of MapReduce processing.

Fault Tolerance and Speculative Execution

One of the most interesting aspects of parallel MapReduce operation is the strict control of data flow throughout the execution of the program. For example, mapper processes do not exchange data with other mapper processes, and data can only go from mappers to reducers—not the other direction. The confined data flow enables MapReduce to operate in a fault-tolerant fashion.

The design of MapReduce makes it possible to easily recover from the failure of one or many map processes. For example, should a server fail, the map tasks that were running on that machine could easily be restarted on another working server because there is no dependence on any other map task. In functional language terms, the map tasks "do not share state" with other mappers. Of course, the application will run more slowly because work needs to be redone, but it will complete.

In a similar fashion, failed reducers can be restarted. However, there may be additional work that has to be redone in such a case. Recall that a completed reduce task writes results to HDFS. If a node fails after this point, the data should still be available due to the redundancy in HDFS. If reduce tasks remain to be completed on a down node, the MapReduce ApplicationMaster will need to restart the reducer tasks. If the mapper output is not available for the newly restarted reducer, then these map tasks will need to be restarted. This process is totally transparent to the user and provides a fault-tolerant system to run applications.

Speculative Execution

One of the challenges with many large clusters is the inability to predict or manage unexpected system bottlenecks or failures. In theory, it is possible to control and monitor resources so that network traffic and processor load can be evenly balanced; in practice, however, this problem represents a difficult challenge for large systems. Thus, it is possible that a congested network, slow disk controller, failing disk, high processor load, or some other similar problem might lead to slow performance without anyone noticing.

When one part of a MapReduce process runs slowly, it ultimately slows down everything else because the application cannot complete until all processes are finished. The nature of the parallel MapReduce model provides an interesting solution to this problem. Recall that input data are immutable in the MapReduce process. Therefore, it is possible to start a copy of a running map process without disturbing any other running mapper processes. For example, suppose that as most of the map tasks are coming to a close, the ApplicationMaster notices that some are still running and schedules redundant copies of the remaining jobs on less busy or free servers. Should the secondary processes finish first, the other first processes are then terminated (or vice versa). This process is known as *speculative execution*. The same approach can be applied to reducer processes that seem to be taking a long time. Speculative execution can reduce cluster efficiency because redundant resources are assigned to applications that seem to have a slow spot. It can also be turned off and on in the `mapred-site.xml` configuration file (see Chapter 9, "Managing Hadoop with Apache Ambari").

Hadoop MapReduce Hardware

The capability of Hadoop MapReduce and HDFS to tolerate server—or even whole rack—failures can influence hardware designs. The use of commodity (typically x86_64) servers for Hadoop clusters has made low-cost, high-availability implementations of Hadoop possible for many data centers. Indeed, the Apache Hadoop philosophy seems to assume servers will always fail and takes steps to keep failure from stopping application progress on a cluster.

The use of server nodes for both storage (HDFS) and processing (mappers, reducers) is somewhat different from the traditional separation of these two tasks in the data center. It is possible to build Hadoop systems and separate the roles (discrete storage and processing nodes). However, a majority of Hadoop systems use the general approach where servers enact both roles. Another interesting feature of dynamic MapReduce execution is the capability to tolerate dissimilar servers. That is, old and new hardware can be used together. Of course, large disparities in performance will limit the faster systems, but the dynamic nature of MapReduce execution will still work effectively on such systems.

Summary and Additional Resources

The Apache Hadoop MapReduce framework is a powerful yet simple computation model that can be scaled from one to thousands of processors. The functional nature of MapReduce enables scalable operation without the need to modify the user's application. In essence, the programmer can focus on the application requirements and not the parallel execution methodology.

Parallel MapReduce data flow is easily understood by examining the various component steps and identifying how key–value pairs traverse the cluster. The Hadoop MapReduce design also makes possible transparent fault tolerance and possible optimizations through speculative execution. Further information on Apache Hadoop MapReduce can be found from the following sources:

- https://developer.yahoo.com/hadoop/tutorial/module4.html (based on Hadoop version 1, but still a good MapReduce background)
- http://en.wikipedia.org/wiki/MapReduce
- http://research.google.com/pubs/pub36249.html

## 6

MapReduce Programming

In This Chapter:

- The classic Java WordCount program for Hadoop is compiled and run.
- A Python WordCount application using the Hadoop streaming interface is introduced.
- The Hadoop Pipes interface is used to run a C++ version of WordCount.
- An example of MapReduce chaining is presented using the Hadoop Grep example.
- Strategies for MapReduce debugging are presented.

At the base level, Hadoop provides a platform for Java-based MapReduce programming. These applications run natively on most Hadoop installations. To offer more variability, a streaming interface is provided that enables almost any programming language to take advantage of the Hadoop MapReduce engine. In addition, a pipes C++ interface is provided that can work directly with the MapReduce components. This chapter provides programming examples of these interfaces and presents some debugging strategies.

Compiling and Running the Hadoop WordCount Example

The Apache Hadoop `WordCount.java` program for Hadoop version 2, shown in Listing 6.1, is the equivalent of the C programing language `hello-world.c` example. It should be noted that two versions of this program can be found on the Internet. The Hadoop version 1 example uses the older `org.apache.hadoop.mapred` API, while the Hadoop version 2 example, shown here in Listing 6.1, uses the newer `org.apache.hadoop.mapreduce` API. If you experience errors compiling `WordCount.java`, double-check the source code and Hadoop versions.

Listing 6.1   **WordCount.java**

```java
import java.io.IOException;
import java.util.StringTokenizer;

import org.apache.hadoop.conf.Configuration;
import org.apache.hadoop.fs.Path;
import org.apache.hadoop.io.IntWritable;
import org.apache.hadoop.io.Text;
import org.apache.hadoop.mapreduce.Job;
import org.apache.hadoop.mapreduce.Mapper;
import org.apache.hadoop.mapreduce.Reducer;
import org.apache.hadoop.mapreduce.lib.input.FileInputFormat;
import org.apache.hadoop.mapreduce.lib.output.FileOutputFormat;

public class WordCount {

  public static class TokenizerMapper
       extends Mapper<Object, Text, Text, IntWritable>{

    private final static IntWritable one = new IntWritable(1);
    private Text word = new Text();

    public void map(Object key, Text value, Context context
                    ) throws IOException, InterruptedException {
      StringTokenizer itr = new StringTokenizer(value.toString());
      while (itr.hasMoreTokens()) {
        word.set(itr.nextToken());
        context.write(word, one);
      }
    }
  }

  public static class IntSumReducer
       extends Reducer<Text,IntWritable,Text,IntWritable> {
    private IntWritable result = new IntWritable();

    public void reduce(Text key, Iterable<IntWritable> values,
                       Context context
                       ) throws IOException, InterruptedException {
      int sum = 0;
      for (IntWritable val : values) {
        sum += val.get();
      }
      result.set(sum);
      context.write(key, result);
    }
  }
```

```
public static void main(String[] args) throws Exception {
    Configuration conf = new Configuration();
    Job job = Job.getInstance(conf, "word count");
    job.setJarByClass(WordCount.class);
    job.setMapperClass(TokenizerMapper.class);
    job.setCombinerClass(IntSumReducer.class);
    job.setReducerClass(IntSumReducer.class);
    job.setOutputKeyClass(Text.class);
    job.setOutputValueClass(IntWritable.class);
    FileInputFormat.addInputPath(job, new Path(args[0]));
    FileOutputFormat.setOutputPath(job, new Path(args[1]));
    System.exit(job.waitForCompletion(true) ? 0 : 1);
  }
}
```

WordCount is a simple application that counts the number of occurrences of each word in a given input set. The example will work with all installation methods presented in Chapter 2, "Installation Recipes" (i.e., HDP Sandbox, pseudo-distributed, full cluster, or cloud).

As discussed in Chapter 5, the MapReduce framework operates exclusively on key–value pairs; that is, the framework views the input to the job as a set of key–value pairs and produces a set of key–value pairs of different types. The MapReduce job proceeds as follows:

```
(input) <k1, v1> -> map -> <k2, v2> -> combine -> <k2, v2> -> reduce -> <k3, v3>
(output)
```

The mapper implementation, via the map method, processes one line at a time as provided by the specified TextInputFormat class. It then splits the line into tokens separated by whitespaces using the StringTokenizer and emits a key–value pair of <word, 1>. The relevant code section is as follows:

```
public void map(Object key, Text value, Context context
                ) throws IOException, InterruptedException {
    StringTokenizer itr = new StringTokenizer(value.toString());
    while (itr.hasMoreTokens()) {
      word.set(itr.nextToken());
      context.write(word, one);
    }
  }
```

Given two input files with contents Hello World Bye World and Hello Hadoop Goodbye Hadoop, the WordCount mapper will produce two maps:

```
< Hello, 1>
< World, 1>
```

```
< Bye, 1>
< World, 1>

< Hello, 1>
< Hadoop, 1>
< Goodbye, 1>
< Hadoop, 1>
```

As can be seen in Listing 6.1, WordCount sets a mapper

```
job.setMapperClass(TokenizerMapper.class);
```

a combiner

```
job.setCombinerClass(IntSumReducer.class);
```

and a reducer

```
job.setReducerClass(IntSumReducer.class);
```

Hence, the output of each map is passed through the local combiner (which sums the values in the same way as the reducer) for local aggregation and then sends the data on to the final reducer. Thus, each map above the combiner performs the following pre-reductions:

```
< Bye, 1>
< Hello, 1>
< World, 2>

< Goodbye, 1>
< Hadoop, 2>
< Hello, 1>
```

The reducer implementation, via the reduce method, simply sums the values, which are the occurrence counts for each key. The relevant code section is as follows:

```
public void reduce(Text key, Iterable<IntWritable> values,
                     Context context
                     ) throws IOException, InterruptedException {
    int sum = 0;
    for (IntWritable val : values) {
      sum += val.get();
    }
    result.set(sum);
    context.write(key, result);
  }
```

The final output of the reducer is the following:

```
< Bye, 1>
< Goodbye, 1>
```

```
< Hadoop, 2>
< Hello, 2>
< World, 2>`
```

The source code for WordCount.java is available from the book download page
(see Appendix A, "Book Webpage and Code Download"). To compile and run the
program from the command line, perform the following steps:

1. Make a local wordcount_classes directory.

   ```
   $ mkdir wordcount_classes
   ```

2. Compile the WordCount.java program using the 'hadoop classpath'
   command to include all the available Hadoop class paths.

   ```
   $ javac -cp `hadoop classpath` -d wordcount_classes WordCount.java
   ```

3. The jar file can be created using the following command:

   ```
   $ jar -cvf wordcount.jar -C wordcount_classes/
   ```

4. To run the example, create an input directory in HDFS and place a text file in
   the new directory. For this example, we will use the war-and-peace.txt file
   (available from the book download page; see Appendix A):

   ```
   $ hdfs dfs -mkdir war-and-peace-input
   $ hdfs dfs -put war-and-peace.txt war-and-peace-input
   ```

5. Run the WordCount application using the following command:

   ```
   $ hadoop jar wordcount.jar WordCount war-and-peace-input
   ➥ war-and-peace-output
   ```

If everything is working correctly, Hadoop messages for the job should look like
the following (abbreviated version):

```
15/05/24 18:13:26 INFO impl.TimelineClientImpl: Timeline service address:
http://limulus:8188/ws/v1/timeline/
15/05/24 18:13:26 INFO client.RMProxy: Connecting to ResourceManager at
limulus/10.0.0.1:8050
15/05/24 18:13:26 WARN mapreduce.JobSubmitter: Hadoop command-line option parsing
not performed. Implement the Tool interface and execute your application with
ToolRunner to remedy this.
15/05/24 18:13:26 INFO input.FileInputFormat: Total input paths to process : 1
15/05/24 18:13:27 INFO mapreduce.JobSubmitter: number of splits:1
[...]
File Input Format Counters
               Bytes Read=3288746
File Output Format Counters
               Bytes Written=467839
```

In addition, the following files should be in the war-and-peace-output directory.
The actual file name may be slightly different depending on your Hadoop version.

```
$ hdfs dfs -ls war-and-peace-output
Found 2 items
-rw-r--r--   2 hdfs hdfs            0 2015-05-24 11:14 war-and-peace-output/_SUCCESS
-rw-r--r--   2 hdfs hdfs       467839 2015-05-24 11:14 war-and-peace-output/
part-r-00000
```

The complete list of word counts can be copied from HDFS to the working directory with the following command:

```
$ hdfs dfs -get war-and-peace-output/part-r-00000.
```

If the WordCount program is run again using the same outputs, it will fail when it tries to overwrite the war-and-peace-output directory. The output directory and all contents can be removed with the following command:

```
$ hdfs dfs -rm -r -skipTrash war-and-peace-output
```

Using the Streaming Interface

The Apache Hadoop steaming interface enables almost any program to use the MapReduce engine. The streams interface will work with any program that can read and write to stdin and stdout.

When working in the Hadoop streaming mode, only the mapper and the reducer are created by the user. This approach does have the advantage that the mapper and the reducer can be easily tested from the command line. In this example, a Python mapper and reducer, shown in Listings 6.2 and 6.3, will be used. The source code can be found on the book download page (see Appendix A) or at http://www.michael-noll.com/tutorials/writing-an-hadoop-mapreduce-program-in-python.

Listing 6.2   **Python Mapper Script (mapper.py)**

```
#!/usr/bin/env python

import sys

# input comes from STDIN (standard input)
for line in sys.stdin:
    # remove leading and trailing whitespace
    line = line.strip()
    # split the line into words
    words = line.split()
    # increase counters
    for word in words:
        # write the results to STDOUT (standard output);
        # what we output here will be the input for the
        # Reduce step, i.e. the input for reducer.py
        #
        # tab-delimited; the trivial word count is 1
        print '%s\t%s' % (word, 1)
```

Listing 6.3 **Python Reducer Script (reducer.py)**

```python
#!/usr/bin/env python

from operator import itemgetter
import sys

current_word = None
current_count = 0
word = None

# input comes from STDIN
for line in sys.stdin:
    # remove leading and trailing whitespace
    line = line.strip()
    # parse the input we got from mapper.py
    word, count = line.split('\t', 1)
    # convert count (currently a string) to int
    try:
        count = int(count)
    except ValueError:
        # count was not a number, so silently
        # ignore/discard this line
        continue

    # this IF-switch only works because Hadoop sorts map output
    # by key (here: word) before it is passed to the reducer
    if current_word == word:
        current_count += count
    else:
        if current_word:
            # write result to STDOUT
            print '%s\t%s' % (current_word, current_count)
        current_count = count
        current_word = word

# do not forget to output the last word if needed!
if current_word == word:
    print '%s\t%s' % (current_word, current_count)
```

The operation of the mapper.py script can be observed by running the command as shown in the following:

```
$ echo "foo foo quux labs foo bar quux" | ./mapper.py
Foo     1
Foo     1
Quux    1
Labs    1
Foo     1
```

```
Bar      1
Quux     1
```

Piping the results of the map into the sort command can create a simulated shuffle phase:

```
$ echo "foo foo quux labs foo bar quux" | ./mapper.py|sort -k1,1
Bar      1
Foo      1
Foo      1
Foo      1
Labs     1
Quux     1
Quux     1
```

Finally, the full MapReduce process can be simulated by adding the reducer.py script to the following command pipeline:

```
$ echo "foo foo quux labs foo bar quux" | ./mapper.py|sort
➥ -k1,1|./reducer.py
Bar      1
Foo      3
Labs     1
Quux     2
```

To run this application using a Hadoop installation, create, if needed, a directory and move the war-and-peace.txt input file into HDFS:

```
$ hdfs dfs -mkdir war-and-peace-input
$ hdfs dfs -put war-and-peace.txt war-and-peace-input
```

Make sure the output directory is removed from any previous test runs:

```
$ hdfs dfs -rm -r -skipTrash war-and-peace-output
```

Locate the hadoop-streaming.jar file in your distribution. The location may vary, and it may contain a version tag. In this example, the Hortonworks HDP 2.2 distribution was used. The following command line will use the mapper.py and reducer.py to do a word count on the input file.

```
$ hadoop jar /usr/hdp/current/hadoop-mapreduce-client/hadoop-streaming.jar
➥ \
-file ./mapper.py \
-mapper ./mapper.py \
-file ./reducer.py -reducer ./reducer.py \
-input war-and-peace-input/war-and-peace.txt \
-output war-and-peace-output
```

The output will be the familiar (_SUCCESS and part-00000) in the war-and-peace-output directory. The actual file name may be slightly different depending on your Hadoop version. Also note that the Python scripts used in this example could be Bash, Perl, Tcl, Awk, compiled C code, or any language that can read and write from stdin and stdout.

Although the streaming interface is rather simple, it does have some disadvantages over using Java directly. In particular, not all applications are string and character based, and it would be awkward to try to use stdin and stdout as a way to transmit binary data. Another disadvantage is that many tuning parameters available through the full Java Hadoop API are not available in streaming.

Using the Pipes Interface

Pipes is a library that allows C++ source code to be used for mapper and reducer code. Applications that require high performance when crunching numbers may achieve better throughput if written in C++ and used through the Pipes interface.

Both key and value inputs to pipes programs are provided as STL strings (std::string). As shown in Listing 6.4, the program must define an instance of a mapper and an instance of a reducer. A program to use with Pipes is defined by writing classes extending Mapper and Reducer. Hadoop must then be informed as to which classes to use to run the job.

The Pipes framework on each machine assigned to your job will start an instance of your C++ program. Therefore, the executable must be placed in HDFS prior to use.

Listing 6.4 **wordcount.cpp and Example of Hadoop Pipes Interface Using C++**

```
#include <algorithm>
#include <limits>
#include <string>
#include "stdint.h"  // <--- to prevent uint64_t errors!
#include "Pipes.hh"
#include "TemplateFactory.hh"
#include "StringUtils.hh"

using namespace std;
class WordCountMapper : public HadoopPipes::Mapper {
public:
  // constructor: does nothing
  WordCountMapper( HadoopPipes::TaskContext& context ) {
  }
  // map function: receives a line, outputs (word,"1")
  // to reducer.
  void map( HadoopPipes::MapContext& context ) {
    //--- get line of text ---
    string line = context.getInputValue();
```

```
    //--- split it into words ---
    vector< string > words =
      HadoopUtils::splitString( line, " " );
    //--- emit each word tuple (word, "1" ) ---
    for ( unsigned int i=0; i < words.size(); i++ ) {
      context.emit( words[i], HadoopUtils::toString( 1 ) );
    }
  }
};
class WordCountReducer : public HadoopPipes::Reducer {
public:
  // constructor: does nothing
  WordCountReducer(HadoopPipes::TaskContext& context) {
  }
  // reduce function
  void reduce( HadoopPipes::ReduceContext& context ) {
    int count = 0;
    //--- get all tuples with the same key, and count their numbers ---
    while ( context.nextValue() ) {
      count += HadoopUtils::toInt( context.getInputValue() );
    }
//--- emit (word, count) ---
    context.emit(context.getInputKey(), HadoopUtils::toString( count ));
  }
};
int main(int argc, char *argv[]) {
  return HadoopPipes::runTask(HadoopPipes::TemplateFactory<
                              WordCountMapper,
                              WordCountReducer >() );
}
```

The wordcount.cpp source is available from the book download page (see Appendix A) or from http://wiki.apache.org/hadoop/C++WordCount. The location of the Hadoop include files and libraries may need to be specified when compiling the code. If $HADOOP_HOME is defined, the following options should provide the correct path. Check to make sure the paths are correct for your installation.

```
-L$HADOOP_HOME/lib/native/ -I$HADOOP_HOME/include
```

Additionally, the original source code may need to be changed depending on where the include files are located (i.e., some distributions may not use the hadoop prefix). In Listing 6.4, the following lines (from the original program) had the hadoop prefix removed:

```
#include "hadoop/Pipes.hh"
#include "hadoop/TemplateFactory.hh"
#include "hadoop/StringUtils.hh"
```

The program can be compiled with the following line (adjusted for `include` file and library locations). In this example, use of Hortonworks HDP 2.2 is assumed.

```
$ g++ wordcount.cpp -o wordcount -L$HADOOP_HOME/lib/native/
➥ -I$HADOOP_HOME/../usr/include -lhadooppipes -lhadooputils
➥ -lpthread -lcrypto
```

If needed, create the `war-and-peace-input` directory and move the file into HDFS:

```
$ hdfs dfs -mkdir war-and-peace-input
$ hdfs dfs -put war-and-peace.txt war-and-peace-input
```

As mentioned, the executable must be placed into HDFS so YARN can find the program. Also, the output directory must be removed before running the program:

```
$ hdfs dfs -put wordcount bin
$ hdfs dfs -rm -r -skipTrash war-and-peace-output
```

To run the program, enter the following line (shown in multiple lines for clarity). The lines specifying the `recordreader` and `recordwriter` indicate that the default Java text versions should be used. Also note that the location of the program in HDFS must be specified.

```
$ mapred pipes \
-D hadoop.pipes.java.recordreader=true  \
-D hadoop.pipes.java.recordwriter=true \
-input war-and-peace-input     \
-output war-and-peace-output  \
-program bin/wordcount
```

When run, the program will produce the familiar output (`_SUCCESS` and `part-00000`) in the `war-and-peace-output` directory. The `part-00000` file should be identical to the Java WordCount version.

Compiling and Running the Hadoop Grep Chaining Example

The Hadoop `Grep.java` example extracts matching strings from text files and counts how many times they occurred. The command works differently from the *nix `grep` command in that it does not display the complete matching line, only the matching string. If matching lines are needed for the string `foo`, use `.*foo.*` as a regular expression.

The program runs two map/reduce jobs in sequence and is an example of *MapReduce chaining*. The first job counts how many times a matching string occurs in the input, and the second job sorts matching strings by their frequency and stores the output in a single file. Listing 6.5 displays the source code for Grep.java. It is also available from the book download page (see Appendix A) or directly from the Hadoop examples source jar file.

Note that all the Hadoop example source files can be extracted by locating the hadoop-mapreduce-examples-*-sources.jar either from a Hadoop distribution or from the Apache Hadoop website (as part of a full Hadoop package) and then extracting the files using the following command (your version tag may be different):

```
$ jar xf hadoop-mapreduce-examples-2.6.0-sources.jar
```

Listing 6.5   **Hadoop Grep.java Example**

```java
package org.apache.hadoop.examples;

import java.util.Random;
import org.apache.hadoop.conf.Configuration;
import org.apache.hadoop.conf.Configured;
import org.apache.hadoop.fs.FileSystem;
import org.apache.hadoop.fs.Path;
import org.apache.hadoop.io.LongWritable;
import org.apache.hadoop.io.Text;
import org.apache.hadoop.mapreduce.*;
import org.apache.hadoop.mapreduce.lib.input.FileInputFormat;
import org.apache.hadoop.mapreduce.lib.input.SequenceFileInputFormat;
import org.apache.hadoop.mapreduce.lib.map.InverseMapper;
import org.apache.hadoop.mapreduce.lib.map.RegexMapper;
import org.apache.hadoop.mapreduce.lib.output.FileOutputFormat;
import org.apache.hadoop.mapreduce.lib.output.SequenceFileOutputFormat;
import org.apache.hadoop.mapreduce.lib.reduce.LongSumReducer;
import org.apache.hadoop.util.Tool;
import org.apache.hadoop.util.ToolRunner;

/* Extracts matching regexs from input files and counts them. */
public class Grep extends Configured implements Tool {
  private Grep() {}                              // singleton
  public int run(String[] args) throws Exception {
    if (args.length < 3) {
      System.out.println("Grep <inDir> <outDir> <regex> [<group>]");
      ToolRunner.printGenericCommandUsage(System.out);
      return 2;
    }
    Path tempDir =
      new Path("grep-temp-"+
          Integer.toString(new Random().nextInt(Integer.MAX_VALUE)));
    Configuration conf = getConf();
```

```
      conf.set(RegexMapper.PATTERN, args[2]);
      if (args.length == 4)
        conf.set(RegexMapper.GROUP, args[3]);

      Job grepJob = new Job(conf);
      try {
        grepJob.setJobName("grep-search");
        FileInputFormat.setInputPaths(grepJob, args[0]);
        grepJob.setMapperClass(RegexMapper.class);
        grepJob.setCombinerClass(LongSumReducer.class);
        grepJob.setReducerClass(LongSumReducer.class);
        FileOutputFormat.setOutputPath(grepJob, tempDir);
        grepJob.setOutputFormatClass(SequenceFileOutputFormat.class);
        grepJob.setOutputKeyClass(Text.class);
        grepJob.setOutputValueClass(LongWritable.class);
        grepJob.waitForCompletion(true);

        Job sortJob = new Job(conf);
        sortJob.setJobName("grep-sort");
        FileInputFormat.setInputPaths(sortJob, tempDir);
        sortJob.setInputFormatClass(SequenceFileInputFormat.class);
        sortJob.setMapperClass(InverseMapper.class);
        sortJob.setNumReduceTasks(1);                 // write a single file
        FileOutputFormat.setOutputPath(sortJob, new Path(args[1]));
        sortJob.setSortComparatorClass(          // sort by decreasing freq
          LongWritable.DecreasingComparator.class);
        sortJob.waitForCompletion(true);
      }
      finally {
        FileSystem.get(conf).delete(tempDir, true);
      }
      return 0;
  }
  public static void main(String[] args) throws Exception {
    int res = ToolRunner.run(new Configuration(), new Grep(), args);
    System.exit(res);
  }
}
```

In the preceding code, each mapper of the first job takes a line as input and matches the user-provided regular expression against the line. The RegexMapper class is used to perform this task and extracts text matching using the given regular expression. The matching strings are output as <matching string, 1> pairs. As in the previous Word-Count example, each reducer sums up the number of matching strings and employs a combiner to do local sums. The actual reducer uses the LongSumReducer class that outputs the sum of long values per reducer input key.

The second job takes the output of the first job as its input. The mapper is an inverse map that reverses (or swaps) its input <key , value> pairs into <value, key>. There is no reduction step, so the `IdentityReducer` class is used by default. All input is simply passed to the output. (Note: There is also an `IdentityMapper` class.) The number of reducers is set to 1, so the output is stored in one file and it is sorted by count in descending order. The output text file contains a count and a string per line.

The example also demonstrates how to pass a command-line parameter to a mapper or a reducer.

The following discussion describes how to compile and run the `Grep.java` example. The steps are similar to the previous WordCount example:

1. Create a directory for the application classes as follows:

   ```
   $ mkdir Grep_classes
   ```

2. Compile the `WordCount.java` program using the following line:

   ```
   $ javac -cp `hadoop classpath`  -d Grep_classes Grep.java
   ```

3. Create a Java archive using the following command:

   ```
   $ jar -cvf Grep.jar -C Grep_classes/ .
   ```

If needed, create a directory and move the `war-and-peace.txt` file into HDFS:

```
$ hdfs dfs -mkdir war-and-peace-input
$ hdfs dfs -put war-and-peace.txt war-and-peace-input
```

As always, make sure the output directory has been removed by issuing the following command:

```
$ hdfs dfs -rm -r -skipTrash war-and-peace-output
```

Entering the following command will run the Grep program:

```
$ hadoop jar Grep.jar org.apache.hadoop.examples.Grep war-and-peace-input
➥ war-and-peace-output Kutuzov
```

As the example runs, two stages will be evident. Each stage is easily recognizable in the program output. The results can be found by examining the resultant output file.

```
$ hdfs dfs -cat war-and-peace-output/part-r-00000
530    Kutuzov
```

Debugging MapReduce

The best advice for debugging *parallel* MapReduce applications is this: Don't. The key word here is *parallel*. Debugging on a distributed system is hard and should be avoided at all costs.

The best approach is to make sure applications run on a simpler system (i.e., the HDP Sandbox or the pseudo-distributed single-machine install) with smaller data sets. Errors on these systems are much easier to locate and track. In addition, unit testing applications before running at scale is important. If applications can run successfully on a single system with a subset of real data, then running in parallel should be a simple task because the MapReduce algorithm is transparently scalable. Note that many higher-level tools (e.g., Pig and Hive) enable local mode development for this reason. Should errors occur at scale, the issue can be tracked from the log file (see the section "Hadoop Log Management") and may stem from a systems issue rather than a program artifact.

When investigating program behavior at scale, the best approach is to use the application logs to inspect the actual MapReduce progress. The time-tested debug print statements are also visible in the logs.

Listing, Killing, and Job Status

As mentioned in Chapter 4, "Running Example Programs and Benchmarks," jobs can be managed using the `mapred job` command. The most import options are `-list`, `-kill`, and `-status`. In addition, the `yarn application` command can be used to control all applications running on the cluster (See Chapter 10, "Basic Hadoop Administration Procedures").

Hadoop Log Management

The MapReduce logs provide a comprehensive listing of both mappers and reducers. The actual log output consists of three files—`stdout`, `stderr`, and `syslog` (Hadoop system messages)—for the application. There are two modes for log storage. The first (and best) method is to use log aggregation. In this mode, logs are aggregated in HDFS and can be displayed in the YARN ResourceManager user interface (see Figure 6.1) or examined with the `yarn logs` command (see the section "Command-Line Log Viewing").

If log aggregation is not enabled, the logs will be placed locally on the cluster nodes on which the mapper or reducer ran. The location of the unaggregated local logs is given by the `yarn.nodemanager.log-dirs` property in the `yarn-site.xml` file. Without log aggregation, the cluster nodes used by the job must be noted, and then the log files must be obtained directly from the nodes. Log aggregation is *highly recommended*.

Enabling YARN Log Aggregation

If Apache Hadoop was installed from the official Apache Hadoop sources, the following settings will ensure log aggregation is turned on for the system.

If you are using Ambari or some other management tool, change the setting using that tool (see Chapter 9, "Managing Hadoop with Apache Ambari"). Do not hand-modify the configuration files. For example, if you are using Apache Ambari, check under the YARN Service Configs tab for `yarn.log-aggregation-enable`. The default setting is enabled.

Figure 6.1   Log information for map process (stdout, stderr, and syslog)

> **Note**
> Log aggregation is disabled in the pseudo-distributed installation presented in Chapter 2.

To manually enable log aggregation, follows these steps:

1. As the HDFS superuser administrator (usually user `hdfs`), create the following directory in HDFS:

```
$ hdfs dfs -mkdir -p /yarn/logs
$ hdfs dfs -chown -R yarn:hadoop /yarn/logs
$ hdfs dfs -chmod -R g+rw /yarn/logs
```

2. Add the following properties in the yarn-site.xml (on all nodes) and restart all YARN services on all nodes (the ResourceManager, NodeManagers, and JobHistoryServer).

```
<property>
  <name>yarn.nodemanager.remote-app-log-dir</name>
  <value>/yarn/logs</value>
</property>
<property>
  <name>yarn.log-aggregation-enable</name>
  <value>true</value>
</property>
```

Web Interface Log View

The most convenient way to view logs is to use the YARN ResourceManager web user interface. In Chapter 4, a list of mapper tasks is shown in Figure 4.8. Each task has a link to the logs for that task. If log aggregation is enabled, clicking on the log link will show a window similar to Figure 6.1.

In the figure, the contents of stdout, stderr, and syslog are displayed on a single page. If log aggregation is not enabled, a message stating that the logs are not available will be displayed.

Command-Line Log Viewing

MapReduce logs can also be viewed from the command line. The yarn logs command enables the logs to be easily viewed together without having to hunt for individual log files on the cluster nodes. As before, log aggregation is required for use. The options to yarn logs are as follows:

```
$ yarn logs
Retrieve logs for completed YARN applications.
usage: yarn logs -applicationId <application ID> [OPTIONS]

general options are:
 -appOwner <Application Owner>    AppOwner (assumed to be current user if
                                  not specified)
 -containerId <Container ID>      ContainerId (must be specified if node
                                  address is specified)
 -nodeAddress <Node Address>      NodeAddress in the format nodename:port
                                  (must be specified if container id is
                                  specified)
```

For example, after running the pi example program (discussed in Chapter 4), the logs can be examined as follows:

```
$ hadoop jar $HADOOP_EXAMPLES/hadoop-mapreduce-examples.jar pi 16 100000
```

After the pi example completes, note the applicationId, which can be found either from the application output or by using the yarn application command. The applicationId will start with application_ and appear under the Application-Id column.

```
$ yarn application -list -appStates FINISHED
```

Next, run the following command to produce a dump of all the logs for that application. Note that the output can be long and is best saved to a file.

```
$ yarn logs -applicationId application_1432667013445_0001 > AppOut
```

The AppOut file can be inspected using a text editor. Note that for each container, stdout, stderr, and syslog are provided (the same as the GUI version in Figure 6.1). The list of actual containers can be found by using the following command:

```
$ grep -B 1 ===== AppOut
```

For example (output truncated):

```
[...]

Container: container_1432667013445_0001_01_000008 on limulus_45454
======================================================================
--
Container: container_1432667013445_0001_01_000010 on limulus_45454
======================================================================
--
Container: container_1432667013445_0001_01_000001 on n0_45454
=================================================================
--
Container: container_1432667013445_0001_01_000023 on n1_45454
=================================================================

[...]
```

A specific container can be examined by using the containerId and the nodeAddress from the preceding output. For example, container_1432667013445_0001_01_000023 can be examined by entering the command following this paragraph. Note that the node name (n1) and port number are written as n1_45454 in the command output. To get the nodeAddress, simply replace the _ with a : (i.e., -nodeAddress n1:45454). Thus, the results for a single container can be found by entering this line:

```
$ yarn logs -applicationId application_1432667013445_0001 -containerId
➥ container_1432667013445_0001_01_000023 -nodeAddress n1:45454|more
```

Summary and Additional Resources

Writing MapReduce programs for Hadoop can be done in a variety of ways. The most direct method uses Java and the current MapReduce API. The WordCount.java example is a good starting point from which to explore this process.

Apache Hadoop also offers a streaming interface that enables the user to write mappers and reducers in any language that supports the stdin and stdout interfaces. These text-based applications can be written in almost any programming language.

The Hadoop Pipes interface enables MapReduce applications to be written in C++ and run directly on the cluster. The Hadoop Grep.java application provides an example of cascading MapReduce and can be used as a starting point for further exploration.

Finally, the need to debug MapReduce applications can be minimized by careful testing and staging of those applications before they are run at scale (over many servers in the cluster). Hadoop log analysis provides plenty of information to assist with debugging and is available both in the web YARN ResourceManager GUI and from the command line.

Additional information and background on the MapReduce programming methods can be found from the following resources:

- **Apache Hadoop Java MapReduce example**
  - http://hadoop.apache.org/docs/current/hadoop-mapreduce-client/hadoop-mapreduce-client-core/MapReduceTutorial.html#Example:_WordCount_v1.0

- **Apache Hadoop streaming example**
  - http://hadoop.apache.org/docs/r1.2.1/streaming.html
  - http://www.michael-noll.com/tutorials/writing-an-hadoop-mapreduce-program-in-python

- **Apache Hadoop pipes example**
  - http://wiki.apache.org/hadoop/C++WordCount
  - https://developer.yahoo.com/hadoop/tutorial/module4.html#pipes

- **Apache Hadoop grep example**
  - http://wiki.apache.org/hadoop/Grep
  - https://developer.yahoo.com/hadoop/tutorial/module4.html#chaining

- **Debugging MapReduce**
  - http://wiki.apache.org/hadoop/HowToDebugMapReducePrograms
  - http://hadoop.apache.org/docs/current/hadoop-mapreduce-client/hadoop-mapreduce-client-core/MapReduceTutorial.html#Debugging

7

Essential Hadoop Tools

In This Chapter:

- The Pig scripting tool is introduced as a way to quickly examine data both locally and on a Hadoop cluster.
- The Hive SQL-like query tool is explained using two examples.
- The Sqoop RDBMS tool is used to import and export data from MySQL to/from HDFS.
- The Flume streaming data transport utility is configured to capture weblog data into HDFS.
- The Oozie workflow manager is used to run basic and complex Hadoop workflows.
- The distributed HBase database is used to store and access data on a Hadoop cluster.

The Hadoop ecosystem offers many tools to help with data input, high-level processing, workflow management, and creation of huge databases. Each tool is managed as a separate Apache Software foundation project, but is designed to operate with the core Hadoop services including HDFS, YARN, and MapReduce. Background on each tool is provided in this chapter, along with a *start to finish* example.

Using Apache Pig

Apache Pig is a high-level language that enables programmers to write complex MapReduce transformations using a simple scripting language. Pig Latin (the actual language) defines a set of transformations on a data set such as aggregate, join, and sort. Pig is often used to extract, transform, and load (ETL) data pipelines, quick research on raw data, and iterative data processing.

Apache Pig has several usage modes. The first is a local mode in which all processing is done on the local machine. The non-local (cluster) modes are MapReduce and Tez. These modes execute the job on the cluster using either

Table 7.1 **Apache Pig Usage Modes**

	Local Mode	Tez Local Mode	MapReduce Mode	Tez Mode
Interactive Mode	Yes	Experimental	Yes	Yes
Batch Mode	Yes	Experimental	Yes	Yes

the MapReduce engine or the optimized Tez engine. (Tez, which is Hindi for "speed," optimizes multistep Hadoop jobs such as those found in many Pig queries.) There are also interactive and batch modes available; they enable Pig applications to be developed locally in interactive modes, using small amounts of data, and then run at scale on the cluster in a production mode. The modes are summarized in Table 7.1.

Pig Example Walk-Through

For this example, the following software environment is assumed. Other environments should work in a similar fashion.

- OS: Linux
- Platform: RHEL 6.6
- Hortonworks HDP 2.2 with Hadoop version: 2.6
- Pig version: 0.14.0

If you are using the pseudo-distributed installation from Chapter 2, "Installation Recipes," instructions for installing Pig are provided in that chapter. More information on installing Pig by hand can be found on the Pig website: http://pig.apache. org/#Getting+Started. Apache Pig is also installed as part of the Hortonworks HDP Sandbox.

In this simple example, Pig is used to extract user names from the /etc/passwd file. A full description of the Pig Latin language is beyond the scope of this introduction, but more information about Pig can be found at http://pig.apache.org/docs/r0.14.0/ start.html. The following example assumes the user is hdfs, but any valid user with access to HDFS can run the example.

To begin the example, copy the passwd file to a working directory for local Pig operation:

```
$ cp /etc/passwd .
```

Next, copy the data file into HDFS for Hadoop MapReduce operation:

```
$ hdfs dfs -put passwd passwd
```

You can confirm the file is in HDFS by entering the following command:

```
hdfs dfs -ls passwd
-rw-r--r--   2 hdfs hdfs        2526 2015-03-17 11:08 passwd
```

In the following example of local Pig operation, all processing is done on the local machine (Hadoop is not used). First, the interactive command line is started:

```
$ pig -x local
```

If Pig starts correctly, you will see a grunt> prompt. You may also see a bunch of INFO messages, which you can ignore. Next, enter the following commands to load the passwd file and then grab the user name and dump it to the terminal. Note that Pig commands must end with a semicolon (;).

```
grunt> A = load 'passwd' using PigStorage(':');
grunt> B = foreach A generate $0 as id;
grunt> dump B;
```

The processing will start and a list of user names will be printed to the screen. To exit the interactive session, enter the command quit.

```
$ grunt> quit
```

To use Hadoop MapReduce, start Pig as follows (or just enter pig):

```
$ pig -x mapreduce
```

The same sequence of commands can be entered at the grunt> prompt. You may wish to change the $0 argument to pull out other items in the passwd file. In the case of this simple script, you will notice that the MapReduce version takes much longer. Also, because we are running this application under Hadoop, make sure the file is placed in HDFS.

If you are using the Hortonworks HDP distribution with tez installed, the tez engine can be used as follows:

```
$ pig -x tez
```

Pig can also be run from a script. An example script (id.pig) is available from the example code download (see Appendix A, "Book Webpage and Code Download"). This script, which is repeated here, is designed to do the same things as the interactive version:

```
/* id.pig */
A = load 'passwd' using PigStorage(':');   -- load the passwd file
B = foreach A generate $0 as id;  -- extract the user IDs
dump B;
store B into 'id.out'; -- write the results to a directory name id.out
```

Comments are delineated by /* */ and -- at the end of a line. The script will create a directory called id.out for the results. First, ensure that the id.out directory is not in your local directory, and then start Pig with the script on the command line:

```
$ /bin/rm -r id.out/
$ pig -x local id.pig
```

If the script worked correctly, you should see at least one data file with the results and a zero-length file with the name _SUCCESS. To run the MapReduce version, use the same procedure; the only difference is that now all reading and writing takes place in HDFS.

```
$ hdfs dfs -rm -r id.out
$ pig id.pig
```

If Apache tez is installed, you can run the example script using the -x tez option. You can learn more about writing Pig scripts at http://pig.apache.org/docs/r0.14.0/start.html.

Using Apache Hive

Apache Hive is a data warehouse infrastructure built on top of Hadoop for providing data summarization, ad hoc queries, and the analysis of large data sets using a SQL-like language called HiveQL. Hive is considered the de facto standard for interactive SQL queries over petabytes of data using Hadoop and offers the following features:

- Tools to enable easy data extraction, transformation, and loading (ETL)
- A mechanism to impose structure on a variety of data formats
- Access to files stored either directly in HDFS or in other data storage systems such as HBase
- Query execution via MapReduce and Tez (optimized MapReduce)

Hive provides users who are already familiar with SQL the capability to query the data on Hadoop clusters. At the same time, Hive makes it possible for programmers who are familiar with the MapReduce framework to add their custom mappers and reducers to Hive queries. Hive queries can also be dramatically accelerated using the Apache Tez framework under YARN in Hadoop version 2.

Hive Example Walk-Through

For this example, the following software environment is assumed. Other environments should work in a similar fashion.

- OS: Linux
- Platform: RHEL 6.6
- Hortonworks HDP 2.2 with Hadoop version: 2.6
- Hive version: 0.14.0

If you are using the pseudo-distributed installation from Chapter 2, instructions for installing Hive are provided in that chapter. More information on installation can be found on the Hive website: http://hive.apache.org. Hive is also installed as part of the Hortonworks HDP Sandbox. Although the following example assumes the user is hdfs, any valid user with access to HDFS can run the example.

To start Hive, simply enter the hive command. If Hive starts correctly, you should get a hive> prompt.

```
$ hive
(some messages may show up here)
hive>
```

As a simple test, create and drop a table. Note that Hive commands must end with a semicolon (;).

```
hive> CREATE TABLE pokes (foo INT, bar STRING);
OK
Time taken: 1.705 seconds
hive> SHOW TABLES;
OK
pokes
Time taken: 0.174 seconds, Fetched: 1 row(s)
hive> DROP TABLE pokes;
OK
Time taken: 4.038 seconds
```

A more detailed example can be developed using a web server log file to summarize message types. First, create a table using the following command:

```
hive> CREATE TABLE logs(t1 string, t2 string, t3 string, t4 string,
➥ t5 string, t6 string, t7 string) ROW FORMAT DELIMITED FIELDS
➥ TERMINATED BY ' ';
OK
Time taken: 0.129 seconds
```

Next, load the data—in this case, from the sample.log file. This file is available from the example code download (see Appendix A). Note that the file is found in the local directory and not in HDFS.

```
hive> LOAD DATA LOCAL INPATH 'sample.log' OVERWRITE INTO TABLE logs;
Loading data to table default.logs
Table default.logs stats: [numFiles=1, numRows=0, totalSize=99271, rawDataSize=0]
OK
Time taken: 0.953 seconds
```

Finally, apply the select step to the file. Note that this invokes a Hadoop MapReduce operation. The results appear at the end of the output (e.g., totals for the message types DEBUG, ERROR, and so on).

```
hive> SELECT t4 AS sev, COUNT(*) AS cnt FROM logs WHERE t4 LIKE '[%' GROUP BY t4;
Query ID = hdfs_20150327130000_d1e1a265-a5d7-4ed8-b785-2c6569791368
Total jobs = 1
Launching Job 1 out of 1
Number of reduce tasks not specified. Estimated from input data size: 1
In order to change the average load for a reducer (in bytes):
  set hive.exec.reducers.bytes.per.reducer=<number>
In order to limit the maximum number of reducers:
  set hive.exec.reducers.max=<number>
In order to set a constant number of reducers:
  set mapreduce.job.reduces=<number>
Starting Job = job_1427397392757_0001, Tracking URL = http://norbert:8088/proxy/
application_1427397392757_0001/
Kill Command = /opt/hadoop-2.6.0/bin/hadoop job  -kill job_1427397392757_0001
Hadoop job information for Stage-1: number of mappers: 1; number of reducers: 1
2015-03-27 13:00:17,399 Stage-1 map = 0%,  reduce = 0%
2015-03-27 13:00:26,100 Stage-1 map = 100%,  reduce = 0%, Cumulative CPU 2.14 sec
2015-03-27 13:00:34,979 Stage-1 map = 100%,  reduce = 100%, Cumulative CPU 4.07 sec
MapReduce Total cumulative CPU time: 4 seconds 70 msec
Ended Job = job_1427397392757_0001
MapReduce Jobs Launched:
Stage-Stage-1: Map: 1  Reduce: 1   Cumulative CPU: 4.07 sec    HDFS Read: 106384
HDFS Write: 63 SUCCESS
Total MapReduce CPU Time Spent: 4 seconds 70 msec
OK
[DEBUG]  434
[ERROR]  3
[FATAL]  1
[INFO]   96
[TRACE]  816
[WARN]   4
Time taken: 32.624 seconds, Fetched: 6 row(s)
```

To exit Hive, simply type exit;:

```
hive> exit;
```

A More Advanced Hive Example

A more advanced usage case from the Hive documentation can be developed using the movie rating data files obtained from the GroupLens Research (http://group-lens.org/datasets/movielens) webpage. The data files are collected from Movie-Lens website (http://movielens.org). The files contain various numbers of movie reviews, starting at 100,000 and going up to 20 million entries. The data file and queries used in the following example are available from the book website (see Appendix A).

In this example, 100,000 records will be transformed from userid, movieid, rating, unixtime to userid, movieid, rating, and weekday using Apache Hive and a

Python program (i.e., the UNIX time notation will be transformed to the day of the week). The first step is to download and extract the data:

```
$ wget http://files.grouplens.org/datasets/movielens/ml-100k.zip
$ unzip ml-100k.zip
$ cd ml-100k
```

Before we use Hive, we will create a short Python program called weekday_mapper.py with following contents:

```
import sys
import datetime

for line in sys.stdin:
  line = line.strip()
  userid, movieid, rating, unixtime = line.split('\t')
  weekday = datetime.datetime.fromtimestamp(float(unixtime)).isoweekday()
  print '\t'.join([userid, movieid, rating, str(weekday)])LOAD DATA LOCAL INPATH
'./u.data' OVERWRITE INTO TABLE u_data;
```

Next, start Hive and create the data table (u_data) by entering the following at the hive> prompt:

```
CREATE TABLE u_data (
  userid INT,
  movieid INT,
  rating INT,
  unixtime STRING)
ROW FORMAT DELIMITED
FIELDS TERMINATED BY '\t'
STORED AS TEXTFILE;
```

Load the movie data into the table with the following command:

```
hive> LOAD DATA LOCAL INPATH './u.data' OVERWRITE INTO TABLE u_data;
```

The number of rows in the table can be reported by entering the following command:

```
hive > SELECT COUNT(*) FROM u_data;
```

This command will start a single MapReduce job and should finish with the following lines:

```
...
MapReduce Jobs Launched:
Stage-Stage-1: Map: 1  Reduce: 1   Cumulative CPU: 2.26 sec   HDFS Read: 1979380
HDFS Write: 7 SUCCESS
Total MapReduce CPU Time Spent: 2 seconds 260 msec
OK
100000
Time taken: 28.366 seconds, Fetched: 1 row(s)
```

Now that the table data are loaded, use the following command to make the new table (u_data_new):

```
hive> CREATE TABLE u_data_new (
  userid INT,
  movieid INT,
  rating INT,
  weekday INT)
ROW FORMAT DELIMITED
FIELDS TERMINATED BY '\t';
```

The next command adds the weekday_mapper.py to Hive resources:

```
hive> add FILE weekday_mapper.py;
```

Once weekday_mapper.py is successfully loaded, we can enter the transformation query:

```
hive> INSERT OVERWRITE TABLE u_data_new
SELECT
  TRANSFORM (userid, movieid, rating, unixtime)
  USING 'python weekday_mapper.py'
  AS (userid, movieid, rating, weekday)
FROM u_data;
```

If the transformation was successful, the following final portion of the output should be displayed:

```
...
Table default.u_data_new stats: [numFiles=1, numRows=100000, totalSize=1179173,
rawDataSize=1079173]
MapReduce Jobs Launched:
Stage-Stage-1: Map: 1    Cumulative CPU: 3.44 sec    HDFS Read: 1979380 HDFS Write:
1179256 SUCCESS
Total MapReduce CPU Time Spent: 3 seconds 440 msec
OK
Time taken: 24.06 seconds
```

The final query will sort and group the reviews by weekday:

```
hive> SELECT weekday, COUNT(*) FROM u_data_new GROUP BY weekday;
```

Final output for the review counts by weekday should look like the following:

```
...
MapReduce Jobs Launched:
Stage-Stage-1: Map: 1 Reduce: 1    Cumulative CPU: 2.39 sec    HDFS Read: 1179386
HDFS Write: 56 SUCCESS
Total MapReduce CPU Time Spent: 2 seconds 390 msec
OK
1       13278
2       14816
```

```
3        15426
4        13774
5        17964
6        12318
7        12424
Time taken: 22.645 seconds, Fetched: 7 row(s)
```

As shown previously, you can remove the tables used in this example with the
DROP TABLE command. In this case, we are also using the -e command-line option.
Note that queries can be loaded from files using the -f option as well.

```
$ hive -e 'drop table u_data_new'
$ hive -e 'drop table u_data'
```

Using Apache Sqoop to Acquire Relational Data

Sqoop is a tool designed to transfer data between Hadoop and relational databases.
You can use Sqoop to import data from a relational database management system
(RDBMS) into the Hadoop Distributed File System (HDFS), transform the data in
Hadoop, and then export the data back into an RDBMS.

Sqoop can be used with any Java Database Connectivity (JDBC)–compliant
database and has been tested on Microsoft SQL Server, PostgresSQL, MySQL,
and Oracle. In version 1 of Sqoop, data were accessed using connectors written for
specific databases. Version 2 (in beta) does not support connectors or version 1 data
transfer from a RDBMS directly to Hive or HBase, or data transfer from Hive or
HBase to your RDBMS. Instead, version 2 offers more generalized ways to accomplish
these tasks.

The remainder of this section provides a brief overview of how Sqoop works with
Hadoop. In addition, a basic Sqoop example walk-through is demonstrated. To fully
explore Sqoop, more information can found by consulting the Sqoop project website:
http://sqoop.apache.org

Apache Sqoop Import and Export Methods

Figure 7.1 describes the Sqoop data import (to HDFS) process. The data import
is done in two steps. In the first step, shown in the figure, Sqoop examines the
database to gather the necessary metadata for the data to be imported. The second
step is a map-only (no reduce step) Hadoop job that Sqoop submits to the cluster.
This job does the actual data transfer using the metadata captured in the
previous step. Note that each node doing the import must have access to the
database.

The imported data are saved in an HDFS directory. Sqoop will use the database
name for the directory, or the user can specify any alternative directory where the files
should be populated. By default, these files contain comma-delimited fields, with new
lines separating different records. You can easily override the format in which data are
copied over by explicitly specifying the field separator and record terminator charac-
ters. Once placed in HDFS, the data are ready for processing.

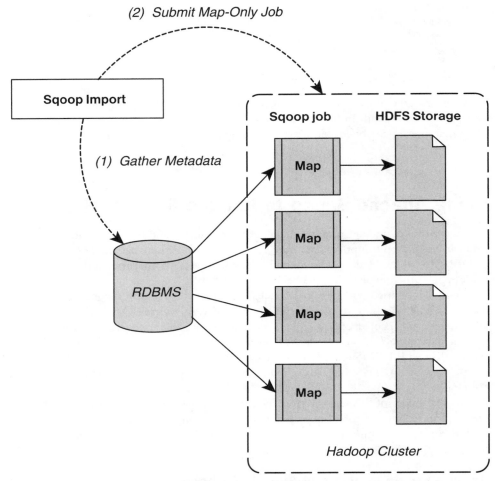

Figure 7.1 Two-step Apache Sqoop data import method (Adapted from Apache Sqoop Documentation)

Data export from the cluster works in a similar fashion. The export is done in two steps, as shown in Figure 7.2. As in the import process, the first step is to examine the database for metadata. The export step again uses a map-only Hadoop job to write the data to the database. Sqoop divides the input data set into splits, then uses individual map tasks to push the splits to the database. Again, this process assumes the map tasks have access to the database.

Apache Sqoop Version Changes

Sqoop Version 1 uses specialized connectors to access external systems. These connectors are often optimized for various RDBMSs or for systems that do not support

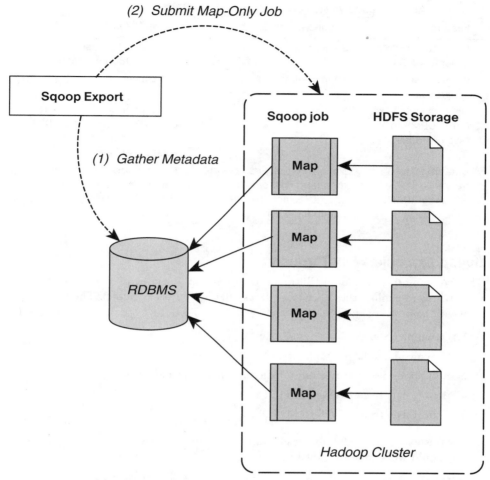

Figure 7.2   Two-step Sqoop data export method (Adapted from Apache Sqoop Documentation)

JDBC. Connectors are plug-in components based on Sqoop's extension framework and can be added to any existing Sqoop installation. Once a connector is installed, Sqoop can use it to efficiently transfer data between Hadoop and the external store supported by the connector. By default, Sqoop version 1 includes connectors for popular databases such as MySQL, PostgreSQL, Oracle, SQL Server, and DB2. It also supports direct transfer to and from the RDBMS to HBase or Hive.

In contrast, to streamline the Sqoop input methods, Sqoop version 2 no longer supports specialized connectors or direct import into HBase or Hive. All imports and exports are done through the JDBC interface. Table 7.2 summarizes the changes from version 1 to version 2. Due to these changes, any new development should be done with Sqoop version 2.

Table 7.2 **Apache Sqoop Version Comparison**

Feature	Sqoop Version 1	Sqoop Version 2
Connectors for all major RDBMSs	Supported.	Not supported. Use the generic JDBC connector.
Kerberos security integration	Supported.	Not supported.
Data transfer from RDBMS to Hive or HBase	Supported.	Not supported. First import data from RDBMS into HDFS, then load data into Hive or HBase manually.
Data transfer from Hive or HBase to RDBMS	Not supported. First export data from Hive or HBase into HDFS, and then use Sqoop for export.	Not supported. First export data from Hive or HBase into HDFS, then use Sqoop for export.

Sqoop Example Walk-Through

The following simple example illustrates use of Sqoop. It can be used as a foundation from which to explore the other capabilities offered by Apache Sqoop. The following steps will be performed:

1. Download Sqoop.
2. Download and load sample MySQL data.
3. Add Sqoop user permissions for the local machine and cluster.
4. Import data from MySQL to HDFS.
5. Export data from HDFS to MySQL.

For this example, the following software environment is assumed. Other environments should work in a similar fashion.

- OS: Linux
- Platform: RHEL 6.6
- Hortonworks HDP 2.2 with Hadoop version: 2.6
- Sqoop version: 1.4.5
- A working installation of MySQL on the host

If you are using the pseudo-distributed installation from Chapter 2 or want to install Sqoop by hand, see the installation instructions on the Sqoop website: http://sqoop.apache.org. Sqoop is also installed as part of the Hortonworks HDP Sandbox.

Step 1: Download Sqoop and Load Sample MySQL Database

If you have not done so already, make sure Sqoop is installed on your cluster. Sqoop is needed on only a single node in your cluster. This Sqoop node will then serve as an entry point for all connecting Sqoop clients. Because the Sqoop node is a Hadoop MapReduce client, it requires both a Hadoop installation and access to HDFS.

To install Sqoop using the HDP distribution RPM files, simply enter:

```
# yum install sqoop sqoop-metastore
```

For this example, we will use the world example database from the MySQL site (http://dev.mysql.com/doc/world-setup/en/index.html). This database has three tables:

- Country: information about countries of the world
- City: information about some of the cities in those countries
- CountryLanguage: languages spoken in each country

To get the database, use wget to download and then extract the file:

```
$ wget http://downloads.mysql.com/docs/world_innodb.sql.gz
$ gunzip world_innodb.sql.gz
```

Next, log into MySQL (assumes you have privileges to create a database) and import the desired database by following these steps:

```
$ mysql -u root -p
mysql> CREATE DATABASE world;
mysql> USE world;
mysql> SOURCE world_innodb.sql;
mysql> SHOW TABLES;
+-----------------+
| Tables_in_world |
+-----------------+
| City            |
| Country         |
| CountryLanguage |
+-----------------+
3 rows in set (0.01 sec)
```

The following MySQL command will let you see the table details (output omitted for clarity):

```
mysql> SHOW CREATE TABLE Country;
mysql> SHOW CREATE TABLE City;
mysql> SHOW CREATE TABLE CountryLanguage;
```

Step 2: Add Sqoop User Permissions for the Local Machine and Cluster

In MySQL, add the following privileges for user sqoop to MySQL. Note that you must use both the local host name and the cluster subnet for Sqoop to work properly. Also, for the purposes of this example, the sqoop password is sqoop.

```
mysql> GRANT ALL PRIVILEGES ON world.* To 'sqoop'@'limulus' IDENTIFIED BY 'sqoop';
mysql> GRANT ALL PRIVILEGES ON world.* To 'sqoop'@'10.0.0.%' IDENTIFIED BY 'sqoop';
mysql> quit
```

Next, log in as sqoop to test the permissions:

```
$ mysql -u sqoop -p
mysql> USE world;
   mysql> SHOW TABLES;
   +-----------------+
   | Tables_in_world |
   +-----------------+
   | City            |
   | Country         |
   | CountryLanguage |
   +-----------------+
   3 rows in set (0.01 sec)

   mysql> quit
```

Step 3: Import Data Using Sqoop

As a test, we can use Sqoop to list databases in MySQL. The results appear after the
warnings at the end of the output. Note the use of local host name (limulus) in the
JDBC statement.

```
$ sqoop list-databases --connect jdbc:mysql://limulus/world --username sqoop
➥ --password sqoop
   Warning: /usr/lib/sqoop/../accumulo does not exist! Accumulo imports will fail.
   Please set $ACCUMULO_HOME to the root of your Accumulo installation.
   14/08/18 14:38:55 INFO sqoop.Sqoop: Running Sqoop version: 1.4.4.2.1.2.1-471
   14/08/18 14:38:55 WARN tool.BaseSqoopTool: Setting your password on the
command-line is insecure. Consider using -P instead.
   14/08/18 14:38:55 INFO manager.MySQLManager: Preparing to use a MySQL streaming
resultset.
   information_schema
   test
   world
```

In a similar fashion, you can use Sqoop to connect to MySQL and list the tables in
the world database:

```
   sqoop list-tables --connect jdbc:mysql://limulus/world --username sqoop
➥ --password sqoop
   ...
   14/08/18 14:39:43 INFO sqoop.Sqoop: Running Sqoop version: 1.4.4.2.1.2.1-471
   14/08/18 14:39:43 WARN tool.BaseSqoopTool: Setting your password on the
command-line is insecure. Consider using -P instead.
   14/08/18 14:39:43 INFO manager.MySQLManager: Preparing to use a MySQL streaming
resultset.
   City
   Country
   CountryLanguage
```

To import data, we need to make a directory in HDFS:

```
$ hdfs dfs -mkdir sqoop-mysql-import
```

The following command imports the Country table into HDFS. The option -table signifies the table to import, --target-dir is the directory created previously, and -m 1 tells Sqoop to use one map task to import the data.

```
$ sqoop import --connect jdbc:mysql://limulus/world  --username sqoop
➡ --password sqoop --table Country  -m 1 --target-dir
➡ /user/hdfs/sqoop-mysql-import/country
   ...
   14/08/18 16:47:15 INFO mapreduce.ImportJobBase: Transferred 30.752 KB in
12.7348 seconds
   (2.4148 KB/sec)
   14/08/18 16:47:15 INFO mapreduce.ImportJobBase: Retrieved 239 records.
```

The import can be confirmed by examining HDFS:

```
$ hdfs dfs -ls sqoop-mysql-import/country
   Found 2 items
   -rw-r--r--    2 hdfs hdfs             0 2014-08-18 16:47 sqoop-mysql-import/
world/_SUCCESS
   -rw-r--r--    2 hdfs hdfs         31490 2014-08-18 16:47 sqoop-mysql-import/world/
part-m-00000
```

The file can be viewed using the hdfs dfs -cat command:

```
$ hdfs dfs -cat sqoop-mysql-import/country/part-m-00000
   ABW,Aruba,North America,Caribbean,193.0,null,103000,78.4,828.0,793.0,Aruba,
Nonmetropolitan
   Territory of The Netherlands,Beatrix,129,AW
   ...
   ZWE,Zimbabwe,Africa,Eastern Africa,390757.0,1980,11669000,37.8,5951.0,8670.0,
Zimbabwe,
   Republic,Robert G. Mugabe,4068,ZW
```

To make the Sqoop command more convenient, you can create an options file and use it on the command line. Such a file enables you to avoid having to rewrite the same options. For example, a file called world-options.txt with the following contents will include the import command, --connect, --username, and --password options:

```
import
--connect
jdbc:mysql://limulus/world
--username
sqoop
--password
sqoop
```

The same import command can be performed with the following shorter line:

```
$ sqoop  --options-file world-options.txt --table City  -m 1 --target-dir
➥ /user/hdfs/sqoop-mysql-import/city
```

It is also possible to include an SQL Query in the import step. For example, suppose we want just cities in Canada:

```
SELECT ID,Name from City WHERE CountryCode='CAN'
```

In such a case, we can include the --query option in the Sqoop import request. The --query option also needs a variable called $CONDITIONS, which will be explained next. In the following query example, a single mapper task is designated with the -m 1 option:

```
sqoop  --options-file world-options.txt -m 1 --target-dir
➥/user/hdfs/sqoop-mysql-import/canada-city --query "SELECT ID,Name
➥ from City WHERE CountryCode='CAN' AND \$CONDITIONS"
```

Inspecting the results confirms that only cities from Canada have been imported:

```
$ hdfs dfs -cat sqoop-mysql-import/canada-city/part-m-00000
```

```
1810,Montréal
1811,Calgary
1812,Toronto

. . .

1856,Sudbury
1857,Kelowna
1858,Barrie
```

Since there was only one mapper process, only one copy of the query needed to be run on the database. The results are also reported in a single file (part-m-0000).

Multiple mappers can be used to process the query if the --split-by option is used. The split-by option is used to parallelize the SQL query. Each parallel task runs a subset of the main query, with the results of each sub-query being partitioned by bounding conditions inferred by Sqoop. Your query must include the token $CONDITIONS that each Sqoop process will replace with a unique condition expression based on the --split-by option. Note that $CONDITIONS is not an environment variable. Although Sqoop will try to create balanced sub-queries based on the range of your primary key, it may be necessary to split on another column if your primary key is not uniformly distributed.

The following example illustrates the use of the --split-by option. First, remove the results of the previous query:

```
$ hdfs dfs -rm -r -skipTrash  sqoop-mysql-import/canada-city
```

Next, run the query using four mappers (-m 4), where we split by the ID number (--split-by ID):

```
sqoop  --options-file world-options.txt -m 4 --target-dir
➥ /user/hdfs/sqoop-mysql-import/canada-city --query "SELECT ID,Name
➥ from City WHERE CountryCode='CAN' AND \$CONDITIONS" --split-by ID
```

If we look at the number of results files, we find four files corresponding to the four mappers we requested in the command:

```
$ hdfs dfs -ls  sqoop-mysql-import/canada-city
Found 5 items
-rw-r--r--   2 hdfs hdfs        0 2014-08-18 21:31 sqoop-mysql-import/
canada-city/_SUCCESS
-rw-r--r--   2 hdfs hdfs      175 2014-08-18 21:31 sqoop-mysql-import/canada-city/
part-m-00000
-rw-r--r--   2 hdfs hdfs      153 2014-08-18 21:31 sqoop-mysql-import/canada-city/
part-m-00001
-rw-r--r--   2 hdfs hdfs      186 2014-08-18 21:31 sqoop-mysql-import/canada-city/
part-m-00002
-rw-r--r--   2 hdfs hdfs      182 2014-08-18 21:31 sqoop-mysql-import/canada-city/
part-m-00003
```

Step 4: Export Data from HDFS to MySQL

Sqoop can also be used to export data from HDFS. The first step is to create tables for exported data. There are actually two tables needed for each exported table. The first table holds the exported data (CityExport), and the second is used for staging the exported data (CityExportStaging). Enter the following MySQL commands to create these tables:

```
mysql> CREATE TABLE 'CityExport' (
          'ID' int(11) NOT NULL AUTO_INCREMENT,
          'Name' char(35) NOT NULL DEFAULT '',
          'CountryCode' char(3) NOT NULL DEFAULT '',
          'District' char(20) NOT NULL DEFAULT '',
          'Population' int(11) NOT NULL DEFAULT '0',
          PRIMARY KEY ('ID'));
mysql> CREATE TABLE 'CityExportStaging' (
          'ID' int(11) NOT NULL AUTO_INCREMENT,
          'Name' char(35) NOT NULL DEFAULT '',
          'CountryCode' char(3) NOT NULL DEFAULT '',
          'District' char(20) NOT NULL DEFAULT '',
          'Population' int(11) NOT NULL DEFAULT '0',
          PRIMARY KEY ('ID'));
```

Next, create a cities-export-options.txt file similar to the world-options.txt created previously, but use the export command instead of the import command.

The following command will export the cities data we previously imported back into MySQL:

```
sqoop --options-file cities-export-options.txt --table CityExport
➥   --staging-table CityExportStaging  --clear-staging-table -m 4
➥ --export-dir /user/hdfs/sqoop-mysql-import/city
```

Finally, to make sure everything worked correctly, check the table in MySQL to see if the cities are in the table:

```
$ mysql> select * from CityExport limit 10;
+----+---------------+-------------+---------------+------------+
| ID | Name          | CountryCode | District      | Population |
+----+---------------+-------------+---------------+------------+
|  1 | Kabul         | AFG         | Kabol         |    1780000 |
|  2 | Qandahar      | AFG         | Qandahar      |     237500 |
|  3 | Herat         | AFG         | Herat         |     186800 |
|  4 | Mazar-e-Sharif | AFG        | Balkh         |     127800 |
|  5 | Amsterdam     | NLD         | Noord-Holland |     731200 |
|  6 | Rotterdam     | NLD         | Zuid-Holland  |     593321 |
|  7 | Haag          | NLD         | Zuid-Holland  |     440900 |
|  8 | Utrecht       | NLD         | Utrecht       |     234323 |
|  9 | Eindhoven     | NLD         | Noord-Brabant |     201843 |
| 10 | Tilburg       | NLD         | Noord-Brabant |     193238 |
+----+---------------+-------------+---------------+------------+
10 rows in set (0.00 sec)
```

Some Handy Cleanup Commands

If you are not especially familiar with MySQL, the following commands may be helpful to clean up the examples. To remove the table in MySQL, enter the following command:

```
mysql> drop table 'CityExportStaging';
```

To remove the data in a table, enter this command:

```
mysql> delete from CityExportStaging;
```

To clean up imported files, enter this command:

```
$ hdfs dfs -rm -r  -skipTrash sqoop-mysql-import/{country,city, canada-city}
```

Using Apache Flume to Acquire Data Streams

Apache Flume is an independent agent designed to collect, transport, and store data into HDFS. Often data transport involves a number of Flume agents that may traverse a series of machines and locations. Flume is often used for log files, social media-generated data, email messages, and just about any continuous data source.

As shown in Figure 7.3, a Flume agent is composed of three components.

- *Source.* The source component receives data and sends it to a channel. It can send the data to more than one channel. The input data can be from a real-time source (e.g., weblog) or another Flume agent.
- *Channel.* A channel is a data queue that forwards the source data to the sink destination. It can be thought of as a buffer that manages input (source) and output (sink) flow rates.
- *Sink.* The sink delivers data to destination such as HDFS, a local file, or another Flume agent.

A Flume agent must have all three of these components defined. A Flume agent can have several sources, channels, and sinks. Sources can write to multiple channels, but a sink can take data from only a single channel. Data written to a channel remain in the channel until a sink removes the data. By default, the data in a channel are kept in memory but may be optionally stored on disk to prevent data loss in the event of a network failure.

As shown in Figure 7.4, Sqoop agents may be placed in a pipeline, possibly to traverse several machines or domains. This configuration is normally used when data are

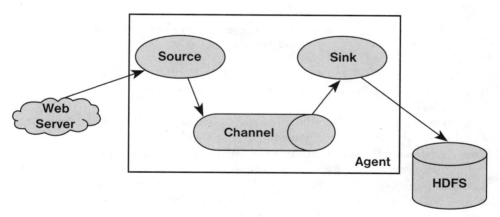

Figure 7.3   Flume agent with source, channel, and sink (Adapted from Apache Flume Documentation)

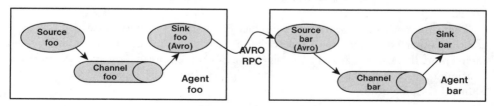

Figure 7.4   Pipeline created by connecting Flume agents (Adapted from Apache Flume Sqoop Documentation)

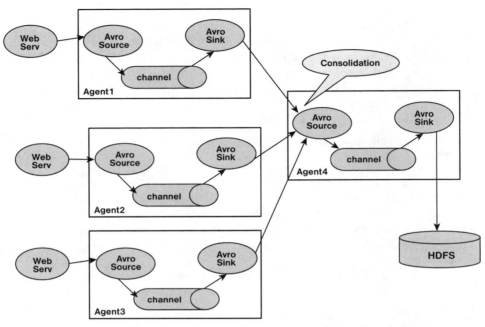

Figure 7.5   A Flume consolidation network (Adapted from Apache Flume Documentation)

collected on one machine (e.g., a web server) and sent to another machine that has access to HDFS.

In a Flume pipeline, the sink from one agent is connected to the source of another. The data transfer format normally used by Flume, which is called Apache Avro, provides several useful features. First, Avro is a data serialization/deserialization system that uses a compact binary format. The schema is sent as part of the data exchange and is defined using JSON (JavaScript Object Notation). Avro also uses remote procedure calls (RPCs) to send data. That is, an Avro sink will contact an Avro source to send data.

Another useful Flume configuration is shown in Figure 7.5. In this configuration, Flume is used to consolidate several data sources before committing them to HDFS.

There are many possible ways to construct Flume transport networks. In addition, other Flume features not described in depth here include plug-ins and interceptors that can enhance Flume pipelines. For more information and example configurations, see the Flume User Guide at https://flume.apache.org/FlumeUserGuide.html.

Flume Example Walk-Through

Follow these steps to walk through a Flume example.

Step 1: Download and Install Apache Flume

For this example, the following software environment is assumed. Other environments should work in a similar fashion.

- OS: Linux
- Platform: RHEL 6.6
- Hortonworks HDP 2.2 with Hadoop version: 2.6
- Flume version: 1.5.2

Flume can be installed by hand if you are using the pseudo-distributed installation from Chapter 2. Consult the installation instructions on the Flume website: https://flume.apache.org. Flume is also installed as part of the Hortonworks HDP Sandbox. If Flume is not installed and you are using the Hortonworks HDP repository, you can add Flume with the following command:

```
# yum install flume flume-agent
```

In addition, for the simple example, telnet will be needed:

```
# yum install telnet
```

The following examples will also require some configuration files. See Appendix A for download instructions.

Step 2: Simple Test

A simple test of Flume can be done on a single machine. To start the Flume agent, enter the flume-ng command shown here. This command uses the simple-example.conf file to configure the agent.

```
$ flume-ng agent --conf conf --conf-file simple-example.conf --name simple_agent
➥ -Dflume.root.logger=INFO,console
```

In another terminal window, use telnet to contact the agent:

```
$ telnet localhost 44444
  Trying ::1...
  telnet: connect to address ::1: Connection refused
  Trying 127.0.0.1...
  Connected to localhost.
  Escape character is '^]'.
  testing  1 2 3
  OK
```

If Flume is working correctly, the window where the Flume agent was started will
show the testing message entered in the telnet window:

```
14/08/14 16:20:58 INFO sink.LoggerSink: Event: { headers:{} body: 74 65 73 74 69
6E 67 20 20 31 20 32 20 33 0D    testing  1 2 3. }
```

Step 3: Weblog Example

In this example, a record from the weblogs from the local machine (Ambari output)
will be placed into HDFS using Flume. This example is easily modified to use other
weblogs from different machines. Two files are needed to configure Flume. (See the
sidebar and Appendix A for file downloading instructions.)

- web-server-target-agent.conf—the target Flume agent that writes the data to
  HDFS
- web-server-source-agent.conf—the source Flume agent that captures the
  weblog data

The weblog is also mirrored on the local file system by the agent that writes to
HDFS. To run the example, create the directory as root:

```
# mkdir /var/log/flume-hdfs
# chown hdfs:hadoop /var/log/flume-hdfs/
```

Next, as user hdfs, make a Flume data directory in HDFS:

```
$ hdfs dfs -mkdir /user/hdfs/flume-channel/
```

Now that you have created the data directories, you can start the Flume target
agent (execute as user hdfs):

```
$ flume-ng agent -c conf -f web-server-target-agent.conf -n collector
```

This agent writes the data into HDFS and should be started before the source agent.
(The source reads the weblogs.) This configuration enables automatic use of the Flume
agent. The /etc/flume/conf/{flume.conf, flume-env.sh.template} files need to
be configured for this purpose. For this example, the /etc/flume/conf/flume.conf
file can be the same as the web-server-target.conf file (modified for your
environment).

> **Note**
>
> With the HDP distribution, Flume can be started as a service when the system boots
> (e.g., service start flume).

In this example, the source agent is started as root, which will start to feed the
weblog data to the target agent. Alternatively, the source agent can be on another
machine if desired.

```
# flume-ng agent -c conf -f web-server-source-agent.conf -n source_agent
```

To see if Flume is working correctly, check the local log by using the `tail` command. Also confirm that the `flume-ng` agents are not reporting any errors (the file name will vary).

```
$ tail -f /var/log/flume-hdfs/1430164482581-1
```

The contents of the local log under `flume-hdfs` should be identical to that written into HDFS. You can inspect this file by using the `hdfs -tail` command (the file name will vary). Note that while running Flume, the most recent file in HDFS may have the extension `.tmp` appended to it. The `.tmp` indicates that the file is still being written by Flume. The target agent can be configured to write the file (and start another `.tmp` file) by setting some or all of the `rollCount`, `rollSize`, `rollInterval`, `idleTimeout`, and `batchSize` options in the configuration file.

```
$ hdfs dfs -tail flume-channel/apache_access_combined/150427/FlumeData.
➥ 1430164801381
```

Both files should contain the same data. For instance, the preceding example had the following data in both files:

```
10.0.0.1 - - [27/Apr/2015:16:04:21 -0400] "GET /ambarinagios/nagios/
nagios_alerts.php?q1=alerts&alert_type=all HTTP/1.1" 200 30801 "-" "Java/1.7.0_65"
10.0.0.1 - - [27/Apr/2015:16:04:25 -0400] "POST /cgi-bin/rrd.py HTTP/1.1" 200 784
"-" "Java/1.7.0_65"
10.0.0.1 - - [27/Apr/2015:16:04:25 -0400] "POST /cgi-bin/rrd.py HTTP/1.1" 200 508
"-" "Java/1.7.0_65"
```

You can modify both the target and source files to suit your system.

Flume Configuration Files

A compete explanation of Flume configuration is beyond the scope of this chapter. The Flume website has additional information on Flume configuration: http://flume.apache. org/FlumeUserGuide.html#configuration. The configurations used previously also have links to help explain the settings. Some of the important settings used in the preceding example follow.

In `web-server-source-agent.conf`, the following lines set the source. Note that the weblog is acquired by using the `tail` command to record the log file.

```
source_agent.sources = apache_server
source_agent.sources.apache_server.type = exec
source_agent.sources.apache_server.command = tail -f /etc/httpd/
logs/access_log
```

Further down in the file, the sink is defined. The `source_agent.sinks.avro_sink.hostname` is used to assign the Flume node that will write to HDFS. The port number is also set in the target configuration file.

```
source_agent.sinks = avro_sink
source_agent.sinks.avro_sink.type = avro
source_agent.sinks.avro_sink.channel = memoryChannel
source_agent.sinks.avro_sink.hostname =  192.168.93.24
source_agent.sinks.avro_sink.port = 4545
```

The HDFS settings are placed in the `web-server-target-agent.conf` file. Note the path that was used in the previous example and the data specification.

```
collector.sinks.HadoopOut.type = hdfs
collector.sinks.HadoopOut.channel = mc2
collector.sinks.HadoopOut.hdfs.path = /user/hdfs/flume-channel/%{log_type}/
%y%m%d
collector.sinks.HadoopOut.hdfs.fileType = DataStream
```

The target file also defines the port and two channels (mc1 and mc2). One of these channels writes the data to the local file system, and the other writes to HDFS. The relevant lines are shown here:

```
collector.sources.AvroIn.port = 4545
collector.sources.AvroIn.channels = mc1 mc2
collector.sinks.LocalOut.sink.directory = /var/log/flume-hdfs
collector.sinks.LocalOut.channel = mc1
```

The HDFS file rollover counts create a new file when a threshold is exceeded. In this example, that threshold is defined to allow any file size and write a new file after 10,000 events or 600 seconds.

```
collector.sinks.HadoopOut.hdfs.rollSize = 0
collector.sinks.HadoopOut.hdfs.rollCount = 10000
collector.sinks.HadoopOut.hdfs.rollInterval = 600
```

A full discussion of Flume can be found on the Flume website.

Manage Hadoop Workflows with Apache Oozie

Oozie is a workflow director system designed to run and manage multiple related Apache Hadoop jobs. For instance, complete data input and analysis may require several discrete Hadoop jobs to be run as a workflow in which the output of one job serves as the input for a successive job. Oozie is designed to construct and manage these workflows. Oozie is not a substitute for the YARN scheduler. That is, YARN manages resources for individual Hadoop jobs, and Oozie provides a way to connect and control Hadoop jobs on the cluster.

Oozie workflow jobs are represented as directed acyclic graphs (DAGs) of actions. (DAGs are basically graphs that cannot have directed loops.) Three types of Oozie jobs are permitted:

- Workflow—a specified sequence of Hadoop jobs with outcome-based decision points and control dependency. Progress from one action to another cannot happen until the first action is complete.

- Coordinator—a scheduled workflow job that can run at various time intervals or when data become available.

- Bundle—a higher-level Oozie abstraction that will batch a set of coordinator jobs.

Oozie is integrated with the rest of the Hadoop stack, supporting several types of Hadoop jobs out of the box (e.g., Java MapReduce, Streaming MapReduce, Pig, Hive, and Sqoop) as well as system-specific jobs (e.g., Java programs and shell scripts). Oozie also provides a CLI and a web UI for monitoring jobs.

Figure 7.6 depicts a simple Oozie workflow. In this case, Oozie runs a basic MapReduce operation. If the application was successful, the job ends; if an error occurred, the job is killed.

Oozie workflow definitions are written in hPDL (an XML Process Definition Language). Such workflows contain several types of nodes:

- **Control flow nodes** define the beginning and the end of a workflow. They include start, end, and optional fail nodes.

- **Action nodes** are where the actual processing tasks are defined. When an action node finishes, the remote systems notify Oozie and the next node in the workflow is executed. Action nodes can also include HDFS commands.

- **Fork/join nodes** enable parallel execution of tasks in the workflow. The fork node enables two or more tasks to run at the same time. A join node represents a rendezvous point that must wait until all forked tasks complete.

- **Control flow nodes** enable decisions to be made about the previous task. Control decisions are based on the results of the previous action (e.g., file size or file existence). Decision nodes are essentially switch-case statements that use JSP EL (Java Server Pages—Expression Language) that evaluate to either true or false.

Figure 7.7 depicts a more complex workflow that uses all of these node types. More information on Oozie can be found at http://oozie.apache.org/docs/4.1.0/index.html.

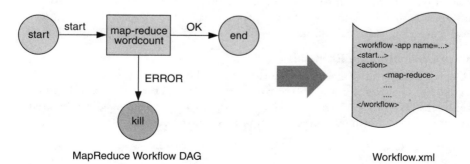

MapReduce Workflow DAG   Workflow.xml

Figure 7.6   A simple Oozie DAG workflow (Adapted from Apache Oozie Documentation)

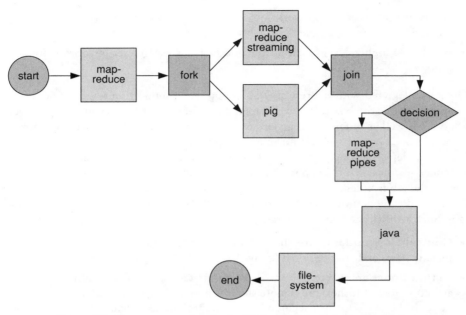

Figure 7.7   A more complex Oozie DAG workflow (Adapted from Apache
Oozie Documentation)

Oozie Example Walk-Through

For this example, the following software environment is assumed. Other environments
should work in a similar fashion.

- OS: Linux
- Platform: CentOS 6.6
- Hortonworks HDP 2.2 with Hadoop version: 2.6
- Oozie version: 4.1.0

If you are using the pseudo-distributed installation from Chapter 2 or want to
install Oozie by hand, see the installation instructions on the Ozzie website: http://
oozie.apache.org. Oozie is also installed as part of the Hortonworks HDP Sandbox.

Step 1: Download Oozie Examples

The Oozie examples used in this section can be found on the book website (see
Appendix A). They are also available as part of the `oozie-client.noarch` RPM in the
Hortonworks HDP 2.x packages. For HDP 2.1, the following command can be used
to extract the files into the working directory used for the demo:

```
$ tar xvzf /usr/share/doc/oozie-4.0.0.2.1.2.1/oozie-examples.tar.gz
```

For HDP 2.2, the following command will extract the files:

```
$ tar xvzf /usr/hdp/2.2.4.2-2/oozie/doc/oozie-examples.tar.gz
```

Once extracted, rename the examples directory to oozie-examples so that you will not confuse it with the other examples directories.

```
$ mv examples oozie-examples
```

The examples must also be placed in HDFS. Enter the following command to move the example files into HDFS:

```
$ hdfs dfs -put oozie-examples/ oozie-examples
```

The Oozie shared library must be installed in HDFS. If you are using the Ambari installation of HDP 2.x, this library is already found in HDFS: /user/oozie/share/lib.

> **Note**
>
> In HDP 2.2+, some additional version-tagged directories may appear below this path. If you installed and built Oozie by hand, then make sure /user/oozie exists in HDFS and put the oozie-sharelib files in this directory as user oozie and group hadoop.

The example applications are found under the oozie-examples/app directory, one directory per example. Each directory contains at least workflow.xml and job.properties files. Other files needed for each example are also in its directory. The inputs for all examples are in the oozie-examples/input-data directory. The examples will create output under the examples/output-data directory in HDFS.

Step 2: Run the Simple MapReduce Example

Move to the simple MapReduce example directory:

```
$ cd oozie-examples/apps/map-reduce/
```

This directory contains two files and a lib directory. The files are:

- The job.properties file defines parameters (e.g., path names, ports) for a job. This file may change per job.
- The workflow.xml file provides the actual workflow for the job. In this case, it is a simple MapReduce (pass/fail). This file usually stays the same between jobs.

The job.properties file included in the examples requires a few edits to work properly. Using a text editor, change the following lines by adding the host name of the NameNode and ResourceManager (indicated by jobTracker in the file).

```
nameNode=hdfs://localhost:8020
jobTracker=localhost:8032
```

to the following (note the port change for `jobTracker`):

```
nameNode=hdfs://_HOSTNAME_:8020
jobTracker=_HOSTNAME_:8050
```

For example, for the cluster created with Ambari in Chapter 2, the lines were changed to

```
nameNode=hdfs://limulus:8020
jobTracker=limulus:8050
```

The `examplesRoot` variable must also be changed to `oozie-examples`, reflecting the change made previously:

```
examplesRoot=oozie-examples
```

These changes must be done for the all the `job.properties` files in the Oozie examples that you choose to run.

The DAG for the simple MapReduce example is shown in Figure 7.6. The `workflow.xml` file describes these simple steps and has the following workflow nodes:

```
<start to="mr-node"/>
<action name="mr-node">
<kill name="fail">
<end name="end"/>
```

A complete description of Oozie workflows is beyond the scope of this chapter. However, in the simple case described here, basic aspects of the file can be highlighted. First, under the `<action name="mr-node">` tag, the MapReduce process is set with a `<map-reduce>` tag. As part of this description, the `<prepare>` and `<configuration>` tags set up the job. Note that the `mapred.{mapper,reducer}.class` refer to the local `lib` directory. As shown in Figure 7.6, this simple workflow runs an example MapReduce job and prints an error message if it fails.

To run the Oozie MapReduce example job from the `oozie-examples/apps` `/map-reduce` directory, enter the following line:

```
$ oozie job -run -oozie http://limulus:11000/oozie -config job.properties
```

When Oozie accepts the job, a job ID will be printed:

```
job: 0000001-150424174853048-oozie-oozi-W
```

You will need to change the "limulus" host name to match the name of the node running your Oozie server. The job ID can be used to track and control job progress.

The "Oozie Is Not Allowed to Impersonate Oozie" Error

When trying to run Oozie, you may get the puzzling error:

```
oozie is not allowed to impersonate oozie
```

If you receive this message, make sure the following is defined in the core-site.xml file:

```
<property>
  <name>hadoop.proxyuser.oozie.hosts</name>
    <value>*</value>
</property>

<property>
  <name>hadoop.proxyuser.oozie.groups</name>
    <value>*</value>
</property>
```

If you are using Ambari, make this change (or add the lines) in the Services/HDFS/Config window and restart Hadoop. Otherwise, make the change by hand and restart all the Hadoop daemons.

This setting is required because Oozie needs to impersonate other users to run jobs. The group property can be set to a specific user group or to a wild card. This setting allows the account that runs the Oozie server to run as part of the user's group.

To avoid having to provide the -oozie option with the Oozie URL every time you run the oozie command, set the OOZIE_URL environment variable as follows (using your Oozie server host name in place of "limulus"):

```
$ export OOZIE_URL="http://limulus:11000/oozie"
```

You can now run all subsequent Oozie commands without specifying the -oozie URL option. For instance, using the job ID, you can learn about a particular job's progress by issuing the following command:

```
$ oozie job -info 0000001-150424174853048-oozie-oozi-W
```

The resulting output (line length compressed) is shown in the following listing. Because this job is just a simple test, it may be complete by the time you issue the -info command. If it is not complete, its progress will be indicated in the listing.

```
Job ID : 0000001-150424174853048-oozie-oozi-W
------------------------------------------------------------------------------
Workflow Name : map-reduce-wf
App Path      : hdfs://limulus:8020/user/hdfs/examples/apps/map-reduce
Status        : SUCCEEDED
Run           : 0
User          : hdfs
```

```
Group         : -
Created       : 2015-04-29 20:52 GMT
Started       : 2015-04-29 20:52 GMT
Last Modified : 2015-04-29 20:53 GMT
Ended         : 2015-04-29 20:53 GMT
CoordAction ID: -

Actions
------------------------------------------------------------------------------
ID                                  Status   Ext ID      Ext Status  Err Code
------------------------------------------------------------------------------
0000001-150424174853048-oozie
 -oozi-W@:start:                    OK       -           OK          -
------------------------------------------------------------------------------
0000001-150424174853048-oozie
 -oozi-W@mr-node                    OK   job_1429912013449_0006 SUCCEEDED -
------------------------------------------------------------------------------
0000001-150424174853048-oozie
 -oozi-W@end                        OK       -           OK          -
------------------------------------------------------------------------------
```

The various steps shown in the output can be related directly to the workflow.xml mentioned previously. Note that the MapReduce job number is provided. This job will also be listed in the ResourceManager web user interface. The application output is located in HDFS under the oozie-examples/output-data/map-reduce directory.

Step 3: Run the Oozie Demo Application

A more sophisticated example can be found in the demo directory (oozie-examples /apps/demo). This workflow includes MapReduce, Pig, and file system tasks as well as fork, join, decision, action, start, stop, kill, and end nodes.

Move to the demo directory and edit the job.properties file as described previously. Entering the following command runs the workflow (assuming the OOZIE_URL environment variable has been set):

```
$ oozie job -run -config job.properties
```

You can track the job using either the Oozie command-line interface or the Oozie web console. To start the web console from within Ambari, click on the Oozie service, and then click on the Quick Links pull-down menu and select Oozie Web UI. Alternatively, you can start the Oozie web UI by connecting to the Oozie server directly. For example, the following command will bring up the Oozie UI (use your Oozie server host name in place of "limulus"):

```
$ firefox  http://limulus:11000/oozie/
```

Figure 7.8 shows the main Oozie console window. Note that a link to Oozie documentation is available directly from this window.

Workflow jobs are listed in tabular form, with the most recent job appearing first. If you click on a workflow, the Job Info window in Figure 7.9 will be displayed.

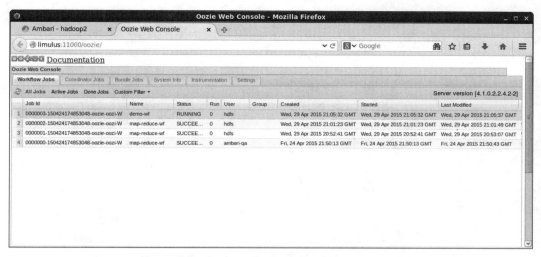

Figure 7.8   Oozie main console window

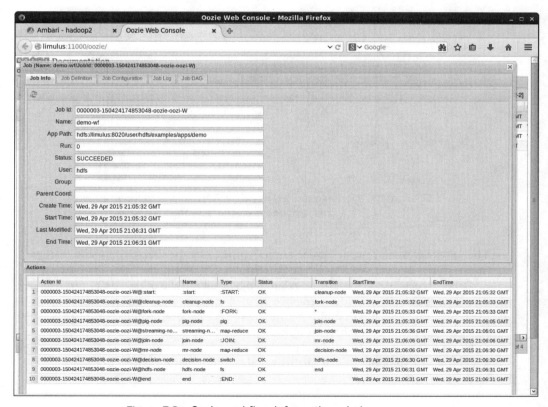

Figure 7.9   Oozie workflow information window

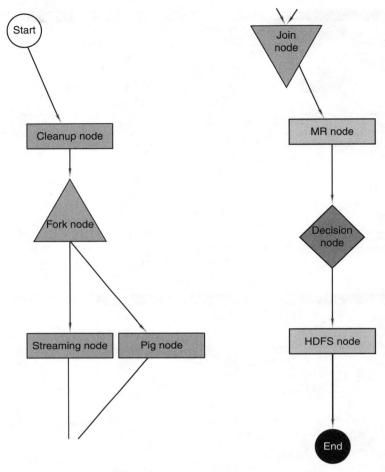

Figure 7.10   Oozie-generated workflow DAG for the demo example,
as it appears on the screen

The job progression results, similar to those printed by the Oozie command line, are
shown in the Actions window at the bottom.

Other aspects of the job can be examined by clicking the other tabs in the window.
The last tab actually provides a graphical representation of the workflow DAG. If the
job is not complete, it will highlight the steps that have been completed thus far. The
DAG for the demo example is shown in Figure 7.10. The actual image was split to
fit better on the page. As with the previous example, comparing this information to
workflow.xml file can provide further insights into how Oozie operates.

A Short Summary of Oozie Job Commands

The following summary lists some of the more commonly encountered Oozie commands. See the latest documentation at http://oozie.apache.org for more information. (Note that the examples here assume OOZIE_URL is defined.)

- Run a workflow job (returns _OOZIE_JOB_ID_):
  ```
  $ oozie job -run -config JOB_PROPERITES
  ```
- Submit a workflow job (returns _OOZIE_JOB_ID_ but does not start):
  ```
  $ oozie job -submit -config JOB_PROPERTIES
  ```
- Start a submitted job:
  ```
  $ oozie job -start _OOZIE_JOB_ID_
  ```
- Check a job's status:
  ```
  $ oozie job -info _OOZIE_JOB_ID_
  ```
- Suspend a workflow:
  ```
  $ oozie job -suspend _OOZIE_JOB_ID_
  ```
- Resume a workflow:
  ```
  $ oozie job -resume _OOZIE_JOB_ID_
  ```
- Rerun a workflow:
  ```
  $ oozie job -rerun _OOZIE_JOB_ID_ -config JOB_PROPERTIES
  ```
- Kill a job:
  ```
  $ oozie job -kill _OOZIE_JOB_ID_
  ```
- View server logs:
  ```
  $ oozie job  -logs _OOZIE_JOB_ID_
  ```

Full logs are available at /var/log/oozie on the Oozie server.

Using Apache HBase

Apache HBase is an open source, distributed, versioned, nonrelational database modeled after Google's Bigtable (http://research.google.com/archive/bigtable.html). Like Bigtable, HBase leverages the distributed data storage provided by the underlying distributed file systems spread across commodity servers. Apache HBase provides Bigtable-like capabilities on top of Hadoop and HDFS. Some of the more important features include the following capabilities:

- Linear and modular scalability
- Strictly consistent reads and writes
- Automatic and configurable sharding of tables
- Automatic failover support between RegionServers
- Convenient base classes for backing Hadoop MapReduce jobs with Apache HBase tables
- Easy-to-use Java API for client access

HBase Data Model Overview

A table in HBase is similar to other databases, having rows and columns. Columns in HBase are grouped into column families, all with the same prefix. For example, consider a table of daily stock prices. There may be a column family called "price" that has four members—price:open, price:close, price:low, and price:high. A column does not need to be a family. For instance, the stock table may have a column named "volume" indicating how many shares were traded. All column family members are stored together in the physical file system.

Specific HBase cell values are identified by a row key, column (column family and column), and version (timestamp). It is possible to have many versions of data within an HBase cell. A version is specified as a timestamp and is created each time data are written to a cell. Almost anything can serve as a row key, from strings to binary representations of longs to serialized data structures. Rows are lexicographically sorted with the lowest order appearing first in a table. The empty byte array denotes both the start and the end of a table's namespace. All table accesses are via the table row key, which is considered its primary key. More information on HBase can be found on the HBase website: http://hbase.apache.org.

HBase Example Walk-Through

For this example, the following software environment is assumed. Other environments should work in a similar fashion.

- OS: Linux
- Platform: CentOS 6.6
- Hortonworks HDP 2.2 with Hadoop version: 2.6
- HBase version: 0.98.4

If you are using the pseudo-distributed installation from Chapter 2 or want to install HBase by hand, see the installation instructions on the HBase website: http://hbase.apache.org. HBase is also installed as part of the Hortonworks HDP Sandbox.

The following example illustrates a small subset of HBase commands. Consult the HBase website for more background. HBase provides a shell for interactive use. To enter the shell, type the following as a user:

```
$ hbase shell
hbase(main):001:0>
```

To exit the shell, type exit.

Various commands can be conveniently entered from the shell prompt. For instance, the status command provides the system status:

```
hbase(main):001:0> status
4 servers, 0 dead, 1.0000 average load
```

Additional arguments can be added to the status command, including 'simple', 'summary', or 'detailed'. The single quotes are needed for proper operation.

For example, the following command will provide simple status information for the four HBase servers (actual server statistics have been removed for clarity):

```
hbase(main):002:0> status 'simple'
4 live servers
    n1:60020 1429912048329
       ...
    n2:60020 1429912040653
       ...
    limulus:60020 1429912041396
       ...
    n0:60020 1429912042885
       ...
0 dead servers
Aggregate load: 0, regions: 4
```

Other basic commands, such as version or whoami, can be entered directly at the hbase(main) prompt. In the example that follows, we will use a small set of daily stock price data for Apple computer. The data have the following form:

Date	Open	High	Low	Close	Volume
6-May-15	126.56	126.75	123.36	125.01	71820387

The data can be downloaded from Google using the following command. Note that other stock prices are available by changing the NASDAQ:AAPL argument to any other valid exchange and stock name (e.g., NYSE: IBM).

```
$ wget -O Apple-stock.csv http://www.google.com/finance/historical
➥?q=NASDAQ:AAPL\&authuser=0\&output=csv
```

The Apple stock price database is in comma-separated format (csv) and will be used to illustrate some basic operations in the HBase shell.

Create the Database

The next step is to create the database in HBase using the following command:

```
hbase(main):006:0> create 'apple', 'price' , 'volume'
0 row(s) in 0.8150 seconds
```

In this case, the table name is apple, and two columns are defined. The date will be used as the row key. The price column is a family of four values (open, close, low, high). The put command is used to add data to the database from within the shell. For instance, the preceding data can be entered by using the following commands:

```
put 'apple','6-May-15','price:open','126.56'
put 'apple','6-May-15','price:high','126.75'
put 'apple','6-May-15','price:low','123.36'
put 'apple','6-May-15','price:close','125.01'
put 'apple','6-May-15','volume','71820387'
```

Note that these commands can be copied and pasted into HBase shell and are available from the book download files (see Appendix A). The shell also keeps a history for the session, and previous commands can be retrieved and edited for resubmission.

Inspect the Database

The entire database can be listed using the scan command. Be careful when using this command with large databases. This example is for one row.

```
scan 'apple'
hbase(main):006:0> scan 'apple'
ROW             COLUMN+CELL
 6-May-15       column=price:close, timestamp=1430955128359, value=125.01
 6-May-15       column=price:high, timestamp=1430955126024, value=126.75
 6-May-15       column=price:low, timestamp=1430955126053, value=123.36
 6-May-15       column=price:open, timestamp=1430955125977, value=126.56
 6-May-15       column=volume:, timestamp=1430955141440, value=71820387
```

Get a Row

You can use the row key to access an individual row. In the stock price database, the date is the row key.

```
hbase(main):008:0> get 'apple', '6-May-15'
COLUMN                          CELL
 price:close                    timestamp=1430955128359, value=125.01
 price:high                     timestamp=1430955126024, value=126.75
 price:low                      timestamp=1430955126053, value=123.36
 price:open                     timestamp=1430955125977, value=126.56
 volume:                        timestamp=1430955141440, value=71820387
5 row(s) in 0.0130 seconds
```

Get Table Cells

A single cell can be accessed using the get command and the COLUMN option:

```
hbase(main):013:0> get 'apple', '5-May-15', {COLUMN => 'price:low'}
COLUMN                          CELL
 price:low                      timestamp=1431020767444, value=125.78
1 row(s) in 0.0080 seconds
```

In a similar fashion, multiple columns can be accessed as follows:

```
hbase(main):012:0> get 'apple', '5-May-15', {COLUMN => ['price:low',
➥'price:high']}
COLUMN                          CELL
 price:high                     timestamp=1431020767444, value=128.45
 price:low                      timestamp=1431020767444, value=125.78
2 row(s) in 0.0070 seconds
```

Delete a Cell

A specific cell can be deleted using the following command:

```
hbase(main):009:0> delete 'apple', '6-May-15' , 'price:low'
```

If the row is inspected using get, the price:low cell is not listed.

```
hbase(main):010:0> get 'apple', '6-May-15'
COLUMN                              CELL
 price:close                        timestamp=1430955128359, value=125.01
 price:high                         timestamp=1430955126024, value=126.75
 price:open                         timestamp=1430955125977, value=126.46
 volume:                            timestamp=1430955141440, value=71820387
4 row(s) in 0.0130 seconds
```

Delete a Row

You can delete an entire row by giving the deleteall command as follows:

```
hbase(main):009:0> deleteall 'apple', '6-May-15'
```

Remove a Table

To remove (drop) a table, you must first disable it. The following two commands remove the apple table from Hbase:

```
hbase(main):009:0> disable 'apple'
hbase(main):010:0> drop 'apple'
```

Scripting Input

Commands to the HBase shell can be placed in bash scripts for automated processing. For instance, the following can be placed in a bash script:

```
echo "put 'apple','6-May-15','price:open','126.56'" | hbase shell
```

The book software page includes a script (input_to_hbase.sh) that imports the Apple-stock.csv file into HBase using this method. It also removes the column titles in the first line. The script will load the entire file into HBase when you issue the following command:

```
$ input_to_hbase.sh Apple-stock.csv
```

While the script can be easily modified to accommodate other types of data, it is not recommended for production use because the upload is very inefficient and slow. Instead, this script is best used to experiment with small data files and different types of data.

Adding Data in Bulk

There are several ways to efficiently load bulk data into HBase. Covering all of these methods is beyond the scope of this chapter. Instead, we will focus on the ImportTsv utility, which loads data in tab-separated values (tsv) format into HBase. It has two distinct usage modes:

- Loading data from a tsv-format file in HDFS into HBase via the put command
- Preparing StoreFiles to be loaded via the completebulkload utility

The following example shows how to use ImportTsv for the first option, loading the tsv-format file using the put command. The second option works in a two-step fashion and can be explored by consulting http://hbase.apache.org/book .html#importtsv.

The first step is to convert the Apple-stock.csv file to tsv format. The following script, which is included in the book software, will remove the first line and do the conversion. In doing so, it creates a file named Apple-stock.tsv.

```
$ convert-to-tsv.sh Apple-stock.csv
```

Next, the new file is copied to HDFS as follows:

```
$ hdfs dfs -put Apple-stock.tsv /tmp
```

Finally, ImportTsv is run using the following command line. Note the column designation in the -Dimporttsv.columns option. In the example, the HBASE_ROW_KEY is set as the first column—that is, the date for the data.

```
$ hbase org.apache.hadoop.hbase.mapreduce.ImportTsv -Dimporttsv.columns=
➥ HBASE_ROW_KEY,price:open,price:high,price:low,price:close,volume
➥ apple /tmp/Apple-stock.tsv
```

The ImportTsv command will use MapReduce to load the data into HBase. To verify that the command works, drop and re-create the apple database, as described previously, before running the import command.

Apache HBase Web Interface

Like many of the Hadoop ecosystem tools, HBase has a web interface. To start the HBase console, shown in Figure 7.11, from within Ambari, click on the HBase service, and then click on the Quick Links pull-down menu and select HBase Master UI. Alternatively, you can connect to the HBase master directly to start the HBase web UI. For example, the following command will bring up the HBase UI (use your HBase master server host name in place of "limulus"):

```
$ firefox http://limulus:60010/master-status
```

The HBase master status (including links to the region servers) is reported by the GUI in addition to statistics for the data tables in the database.

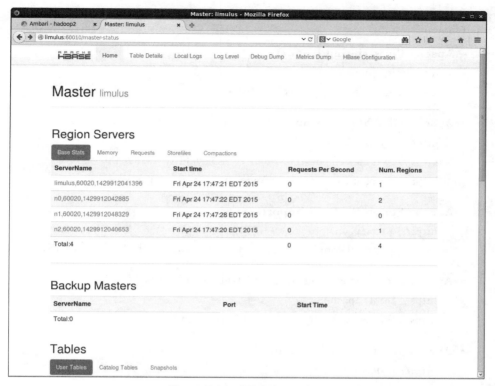

Figure 7.11   HBase web GUI

Summary and Additional Resources

This chapter introduced several essential Hadoop tools and provided at least one complete end-to-end example application of each tool. For each tool, the tool version and Hadoop and operating system distribution were provided, along with references and links to any example data.

The Apache Pig scripting tool enables you to quickly examine data and preprocess raw data for later Hadoop analysis. Apache Hive is an SQL-like interface for Hadoop. The Apache Sqoop application can be used to import and export RDBMS data into HDFS. Apache Flume is used to capture and transport weblog data.

To explore the concept of Hadoop workflows, this chapter also introduced the Oozie workflow management tool. Two examples of Oozie workflows were described, along with the Oozie web GUI.

Finally, the Apache HBase distributed database was introduced. Basic commands were covered, and an example demonstrated the bulk import of external stock market data into HBase.

Additional information and background on each of the tools can be obtained from the following resources.

- **Apache Pig scripting language**
  - http://pig.apache.org/
  - http://pig.apache.org/docs/r0.14.0/start.html

- **Apache Hive SQL–like query language**
  - https://hive.apache.org/
  - https://cwiki.apache.org/confluence/display/Hive/GettingStarted
  - http://grouplens.org/datasets/movielens (data for example)

- **Apache Sqoop RDBMS import/export**
  - http://sqoop.apache.org
  - http://dev.mysql.com/doc/world-setup/en/index.html (data for example)

- **Apache Flume steaming data and transport utility**
  - https://flume.apache.org
  - https://flume.apache.org/FlumeUserGuide.html

- **Apache Oozie workflow manager**
  - http://oozie.apache.org
  - http://oozie.apache.org/docs/4.0.0/index.html

- **Apache HBase distributed database**
  - http://hbase.apache.org/book.html
  - http://hbase.apache.org
  - http://research.google.com/archive/bigtable.html (Google Big Table paper)
  - http://www.google.com/finance/historical?q=NASDAQ:AAPL\&authuser=0\&output=csv (data for example)

8

Hadoop YARN Applications

In This Chapter:

- The YARN Distributed-Shell is introduced as a non-MapReduce application.
- The Hadoop YARN application and operation structure is explained.
- A summary of YARN application frameworks is provided.

The introduction of Hadoop version 2 has drastically increased the number and scope of new applications. By splitting the version 1 monolithic MapReduce engine into two parts, a scheduler and the MapReduce framework, Hadoop has become a general-purpose large-scale data analytics platform. A simple example of a non-MapReduce Hadoop application is the YARN Distributed-Shell described in this chapter. As the number of non-MapReduce application frameworks continues to grow, the user's ability to navigate the data lake increases.

YARN Distributed-Shell

The Hadoop YARN project includes the Distributed-Shell application, which is an example of a Hadoop non-MapReduce application built on top of YARN. Distributed-Shell is a simple mechanism for running shell commands and scripts in containers on multiple nodes in a Hadoop cluster. This application is not meant to be a production administration tool, but rather a demonstration of the non-MapReduce capability that can be implemented on top of YARN. There are multiple mature implementations of a distributed shell that administrators typically use to manage a cluster of machines.

In addition, Distributed-Shell can be used as a starting point for exploring and building Hadoop YARN applications. This chapter offers guidance on how the Distributed-Shell can be used to understand the operation of YARN applications.

Using the YARN Distributed-Shell

For the purpose of the examples presented in the remainder of this chapter, we assume and assign the following installation path, based on Hortonworks HDP 2.2, the Distributed-Shell application:

```
$ export YARN_DS=/usr/hdp/current/hadoop-yarn-client/hadoop-yarn-applications-
distributedshell.jar
```

For the pseudo-distributed install using Apache Hadoop version 2.6.0, the following path will run the Distributed-Shell application (assuming $HADOOP_HOME is defined to reflect the location Hadoop):

```
$ export YARN_DS=$HADOOP_HOME/share/hadoop/yarn/hadoop-yarn-applications-
distributedshell-2.6.0.jar
```

If another distribution is used, search for the file hadoop-yarn-applications-distributedshell*.jar and set $YARN_DS based on its location. Distributed-Shell exposes various options that can be found by running the following command:

```
$ yarn org.apache.hadoop.yarn.applications.distributedshell.Client -jar $YARN_DS
➥ -help
```

The output of this command follows; we will explore some of these options in the examples illustrated in this chapter.

```
usage: Client
 -appname <arg>                             Application Name. Default
                                            value - DistributedShell
 -attempt_failures_validity_interval <arg>  when
                                            attempt_failures_validity_
                                            interval in milliseconds
                                            is set to > 0,the failure
                                            number will not take
                                            failures which happen out
                                            of the validityInterval
                                            into failure count. If
                                            failure count reaches to
                                            maxAppAttempts, the
                                            application will be
                                            failed.
 -container_memory <arg>                    Amount of memory in MB to
                                            be requested to run the
                                            shell command
 -container_vcores <arg>                    Amount of virtual cores to
                                            be requested to run the
                                            shell command
 -create                                    Flag to indicate whether
                                            to create the domain
                                            specified with -domain.
```

-debug	Dump out debug information
-domain <arg>	ID of the timeline domain where the timeline entities will be put
-help	Print usage
-jar <arg>	Jar file containing the application master
-keep_containers_across_application_attempts	Flag to indicate whether to keep containers across application attempts. If the flag is true, running containers will not be killed when application attempt fails and these containers will be retrieved by the new application attempt
-log_properties <arg>	log4j.properties file
-master_memory <arg>	Amount of memory in MB to be requested to run the application master
-master_vcores <arg>	Amount of virtual cores to be requested to run the application master
-modify_acls <arg>	Users and groups that allowed to modify the timeline entities in the given domain
-node_label_expression <arg>	Node label expression to determine the nodes where all the containers of this application will be allocated, "" means containers can be allocated anywhere, if you don't specify the option, default node_label_expression of queue will be used.
-num_containers <arg>	No. of containers on which the shell command needs to be executed
-priority <arg>	Application Priority. Default 0
-queue <arg>	RM Queue in which this application is to be submitted

`-shell_args <arg>`	Command line args for the shell script. Multiple args can be separated by empty space.
`-shell_cmd_priority <arg>`	Priority for the shell command containers
`-shell_command <arg>`	Shell command to be executed by the Application Master. Can only specify either --shell_command or --shell_script
`-shell_env <arg>`	Environment for shell script. Specified as env_key=env_val pairs
`-shell_script <arg>`	Location of the shell script to be executed. Can only specify either --shell_command or --shell_script
`-timeout <arg>`	Application timeout in milliseconds
`-view_acls <arg>`	Users and groups that allowed to view the timeline entities in the given domain

A Simple Example

The simplest use-case for the Distributed-Shell application is to run an arbitrary shell command in a container. We will demonstrate the use of the uptime command as an example. This command is run on the cluster using Distributed-Shell as follows:

```
$ yarn org.apache.hadoop.yarn.applications.distributedshell.Client -jar $YARN_DS
➥ -shell_command uptime
```

By default, Distributed-Shell spawns only one instance of a given shell command. When this command is run, you can see progress messages on the screen but nothing about the actual shell command. If the shell command succeeds, the following should appear at the end of the output:

```
15/05/27 14:48:53 INFO distributedshell.Client: Application completed successfully
```

If the shell command did not work for whatever reason, the following message will be displayed:

```
15/05/27 14:58:42 ERROR distributedshell.Client: Application failed to complete
successfully
```

The next step is to examine the output for the application. Distributed-Shell redirects the output of the individual shell commands run on the cluster nodes into the log files, which are found either on the individual nodes or aggregated onto HDFS, depending on whether log aggregation is enabled.

Assuming log aggregation is enabled, the results for each instance of the command can be found by using the yarn logs command. For the previous uptime example, the following command can be used to inspect the logs:

```
$ yarn logs -applicationId application_1432831236474_0001
```

> **Note**
>
> The applicationId can be found from the program output or by using the yarn application command (see the "Managing YARN Jobs" section in Chapter 10, "Basic Hadoop Administration Procedures").

The abbreviated output follows:

```
Container: container_1432831236474_0001_01_000001 on n0_45454
================================================================
LogType:AppMaster.stderr
Log Upload Time:Thu May 28 12:41:58 -0400 2015
LogLength:3595
Log Contents:
15/05/28 12:41:52 INFO distributedshell.ApplicationMaster: Initializing
ApplicationMaster
[...]
Container: container_1432831236474_0001_01_000002 on n1_45454
================================================================
LogType:stderr
Log Upload Time:Thu May 28 12:41:59 -0400 2015
LogLength:0
Log Contents:

LogType:stdout
Log Upload Time:Thu May 28 12:41:59 -0400 2015
LogLength:71
Log Contents:
 12:41:56 up 33 days, 19:28,  0 users,  load average: 0.08, 0.06, 0.01
```

Notice that there are two containers. The first container (con..._000001) is the ApplicationMaster for the job. The second container (con..._000002) is the actual shell script. The output for the uptime command is located in the second containers stdout after the Log Contents: label.

Using More Containers

Distributed-Shell can run commands to be executed on any number of containers by way of the -num_containers argument. For example, to see on which nodes the Distributed-Shell command was run, the following command can be used:

```
$ yarn org.apache.hadoop.yarn.applications.distributedshell.Client -jar $YARN_DS
➥ -shell_command hostname -num_containers 4
```

If we now examine the results for this job, there will be five containers in the log. The four command containers (2 through 5) will print the name of the node on which the container was run.

Distributed-Shell Examples with Shell Arguments

Arguments can be added to the shell command using the -shell_args option. For example, to do a ls -l in the directory from where the shell command was run, we can use the following commands:

```
$ yarn org.apache.hadoop.yarn.applications.distributedshell.Client -jar $YARN_DS
➥ -shell_command ls -shell_args -l
```

The resulting output from the log file is as follows:

```
total 20
-rw-r--r-- 1 yarn hadoop   74 May 28 10:37 container_tokens
-rwx------ 1 yarn hadoop  643 May 28 10:37 default_container_executor_session.sh
-rwx------ 1 yarn hadoop  697 May 28 10:37 default_container_executor.sh
-rwx------ 1 yarn hadoop 1700 May 28 10:37 launch_container.sh
drwx--x--- 2 yarn hadoop 4096 May 28 10:37 tmp
```

As can be seen, the resulting files are new and not located anywhere in HDFS or the local file system. When we explore further by giving a pwd command for Distributed-Shell, the following directory is listed and created on the node that ran the shell command:

```
/hdfs2/hadoop/yarn/local/usercache/hdfs/appcache/application_1432831236474_0003/
container_1432831236474_0003_01_000002/
```

Searching for this directory will prove to be problematic because these transient files are used by YARN to run the Distributed-Shell application and are removed once the application finishes. You can preserve these files for a specific interval by adding the following lines to the yarn-site.xml configuration file and restarting YARN:

```
<property>
    <name>yarn.nodemanager.delete.debug-delay-sec</name>
    <value>100000</value>
</property>
```

Choose a delay, in seconds, to preserve these files, and remember that all applications will create these files. If you are using Ambari, look on the YARN Configs tab under the Advanced yarn-site options, make the change and restart YARN. (See Chapter 9, "Managing Hadoop with Apache Ambari," for more information on Ambari administration.) These files will be retained on the individual nodes only for the duration of the specified delay.

When debugging or investigating YARN applications, these files—in particular, launch_container.sh—offer important information about YARN processes. Distributed-Shell can be used to see what this file contains. Using DistributedShell, the contents of the launch_container.sh file can be printed with the following command:

```
$ yarn org.apache.hadoop.yarn.applications.distributedshell.Client -jar $YARN_DS
➥ -shell_command cat -shell_args launch_container.sh
```

This command prints the launch_container.sh file that is created and run by YARN. The contents of this file are shown in Listing 8.1. The file basically exports some important YARN variables and then, at the end, "execs" the command (cat launch_container.sh) directly and sends any output to logs.

Listing 8.1 **Distributed-Shell launch_container.sh File**

```
#!/bin/bash

export NM_HTTP_PORT="8042"
export LOCAL_DIRS="/opt/hadoop/yarn/local/usercache/hdfs/appcache/
application_1432816241597_0004,/hdfs1/hadoop/yarn/local/usercache/hdfs/appcache/
application_1432816241597_0004,/hdfs2/hadoop/yarn/local/usercache/hdfs/appcache/
application_1432816241597_0004"
export JAVA_HOME="/usr/lib/jvm/java-1.7.0-openjdk.x86_64"
export NM_AUX_SERVICE_mapreduce_shuffle="AAA0+gAAAAAAAAAAAAAAAAAAAAAAAAAAAAAAAA
AAA=
"
export HADOOP_YARN_HOME="/usr/hdp/current/hadoop-yarn-client"
export HADOOP_TOKEN_FILE_LOCATION="/hdfs2/hadoop/yarn/local/usercache/hdfs/
appcache/application_1432816241597_0004/container_1432816241597_0004_01_000002/
container_tokens"
export NM_HOST="limulus"
export JVM_PID="$$"
export USER="hdfs"
export PWD="/hdfs2/hadoop/yarn/local/usercache/hdfs/appcache/
application_1432816241597_0004/container_1432816241597_0004_01_000002"
export CONTAINER_ID="container_1432816241597_0004_01_000002"
export NM_PORT="45454"
export HOME="/home/"
export LOGNAME="hdfs"
export HADOOP_CONF_DIR="/etc/hadoop/conf"
export MALLOC_ARENA_MAX="4"
export LOG_DIRS="/opt/hadoop/yarn/log/application_1432816241597_0004/
container_1432816241597_0004_01_000002,/hdfs1/hadoop/yarn/log/
application_1432816241597_0004/container_1432816241597_0004_01_000002,/hdfs2/
hadoop/yarn/log/application_1432816241597_0004/
container_1432816241597_0004_01_000002"
exec /bin/bash -c "cat launch_container.sh
1>/hdfs2/hadoop/yarn/log/application_1432816241597_0004/
container_1432816241597_0004_01_000002/stdout 2>/hdfs2/hadoop/yarn/log/
application_1432816241597_0004/container_1432816241597_0004_01_000002/stderr "
hadoop_shell_errorcode=$?
```

```
if [ $hadoop_shell_errorcode -ne 0 ]
then
  exit $hadoop_shell_errorcode
fi
```

There are more options for the Distributed-Shell that you can test. The real value of the Distributed-Shell application is its ability to demonstrate how applications are launched within the Hadoop YARN infrastructure. It is also a good starting point when you are creating YARN applications.

Structure of YARN Applications

A full explanation of writing YARN programs is beyond the scope of this book. The structure and operation of a YARN application are covered briefly in this section. For further information on writing YARN applications, consult *Apache Hadoop YARN: Moving beyond MapReduce and Batch Processing with Apache Hadoop 2* (see the references listed at the end of this chapter).

As mentioned in Chapter 1, "Background and Concepts," the central YARN ResourceManager runs as a scheduling daemon on a dedicated machine and acts as the central authority for allocating resources to the various competing applications in the cluster. The ResourceManager has a central and global view of all cluster resources and, therefore, can ensure fairness, capacity, and locality are shared across all users. Depending on the application demand, scheduling priorities, and resource availability, the ResourceManager dynamically allocates resource containers to applications to run on particular nodes. A container is a logical bundle of resources (e.g., memory, cores) bound to a particular cluster node. To enforce and track such assignments, the ResourceManager interacts with a special system daemon running on each node called the NodeManager. Communications between the ResourceManager and NodeManagers are heartbeat based for scalability. NodeManagers are responsible for local monitoring of resource availability, fault reporting, and container life-cycle management (e.g., starting and killing jobs). The ResourceManager depends on the NodeManagers for its "global view" of the cluster.

User applications are submitted to the ResourceManager via a public protocol and go through an admission control phase during which security credentials are validated and various operational and administrative checks are performed. Those applications that are accepted pass to the scheduler and are allowed to run. Once the scheduler has enough resources to satisfy the request, the application is moved from an accepted state to a running state. Aside from internal bookkeeping, this process involves allocating a container for the single ApplicationMaster and spawning it on a node in the cluster. Often called container 0, the ApplicationMaster does not have any additional resources at this point, but rather must request additional resources from the ResourceManager.

The ApplicationMaster is the "master" user job that manages all application life-cycle aspects, including dynamically increasing and decreasing resource consumption (i.e., containers), managing the flow of execution (e.g., in case of MapReduce jobs, running reducers against the output of maps), handling faults and computation skew, and performing other local optimizations. The ApplicationMaster is designed to run arbitrary user code that can be written in any programming language, as all communication with the ResourceManager and NodeManager is encoded using extensible network protocols (i.e., Google Protocol Buffers, http://code.google.com/p/protobuf/).

YARN makes few assumptions about the ApplicationMaster, although in practice it expects most jobs will use a higher-level programming framework. By delegating all these functions to ApplicationMasters, YARN's architecture gains a great deal of scalability, programming model flexibility, and improved user agility. For example, upgrading and testing a new MapReduce framework can be done independently of other running MapReduce frameworks.

Typically, an ApplicationMaster will need to harness the processing power of multiple servers to complete a job. To achieve this, the ApplicationMaster issues resource requests to the ResourceManager. The form of these requests includes specification of locality preferences (e.g., to accommodate HDFS use) and properties of the containers. The ResourceManager will attempt to satisfy the resource requests coming from each application according to availability and scheduling policies. When a resource is scheduled on behalf of an ApplicationMaster, the ResourceManager generates a lease for the resource, which is acquired by a subsequent ApplicationMaster heartbeat. The ApplicationMaster then works with the NodeManagers to start the resource. A token-based security mechanism guarantees its authenticity when the ApplicationMaster presents the container lease to the NodeManager. In a typical situation, running containers will communicate with the ApplicationMaster through an application-specific protocol to report status and health information and to receive framework-specific commands. In this way, YARN provides a basic infrastructure for monitoring and life-cycle management of containers, while each framework manages application-specific semantics independently. This design stands in sharp contrast to the original Hadoop version 1 design, in which scheduling was designed and integrated around managing only MapReduce tasks.

Figure 8.1 illustrates the relationship between the application and YARN components. The YARN components appear as the large outer boxes (ResourceManager and NodeManagers), and the two applications appear as smaller boxes (containers), one dark and one light. Each application uses a different ApplicationMaster; the darker client is running a Message Passing Interface (MPI) application and the lighter client is running a traditional MapReduce application.

YARN Application Frameworks

One of the most exciting aspects of Hadoop version 2 is the capability to run all types of applications on a Hadoop cluster. In Hadoop version 1, the only processing model available to users is MapReduce. In Hadoop version 2, MapReduce is separated from

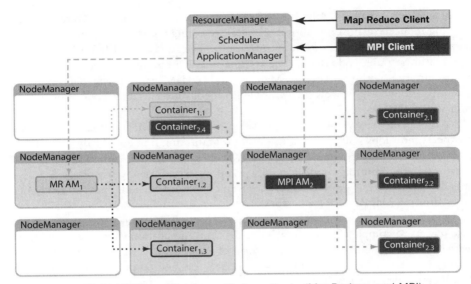

Figure 8.1   YARN architecture with two clients (MapReduce and MPI).
The darker client (MPI AM_2) is running an MPI application, and the lighter
client (MR AM_1) is running a MapReduce application. (From Arun C.
Murthy, et al., *Apache Hadoop™ YARN*, copyright © 2014, p. 45. Reprinted
and electronically reproduced by permission of Pearson Education, Inc.,
New York, NY.)

the resource management layer of Hadoop and placed into its own application framework. Indeed, the growing number of YARN applications offers a high level and mul-
tifaceted interface to the Hadoop data lake discussed in Chapter 1.

YARN presents a resource management platform, which provides services such
as scheduling, fault monitoring, data locality, and more to MapReduce and other
frameworks. Figure 8.2 illustrates some of the various frameworks that will run under
YARN. Note that the Hadoop version 1 applications (e.g., Pig and Hive) run under
the MapReduce framework.

This section presents a brief survey of emerging open source YARN application
frameworks that are being developed to run under YARN. As of this writing, many
YARN frameworks are under active development and the framework landscape is
expected to change rapidly. Commercial vendors are also taking advantage of the
YARN platform. Consult the webpage for each individual framework for full details
of its current stage of development and deployment.

Distributed-Shell

As described earlier in this chapter, Distributed-Shell is an example application
included with the Hadoop core components that demonstrates how to write applications on top of YARN. It provides a simple method for running shell commands and
scripts in containers in parallel on a Hadoop YARN cluster.

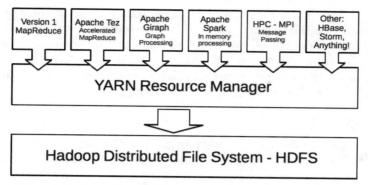

Figure 8.2   Example of the Hadoop version 2 ecosystem. Hadoop version 1 supports batch MapReduce applications only.

Hadoop MapReduce

MapReduce was the first YARN framework and drove many of YARN's requirements. It is integrated tightly with the rest of the Hadoop ecosystem projects, such as Apache Pig, Apache Hive, and Apache Oozie.

Apache Tez

One great example of a new YARN framework is Apache Tez. Many Hadoop jobs involve the execution of a complex directed acyclic graph (DAG) of tasks using separate MapReduce stages. Apache Tez generalizes this process and enables these tasks to be spread across stages so that they can be run as a single, all-encompassing job.

Tez can be used as a MapReduce replacement for projects such as Apache Hive and Apache Pig. No changes are needed to the Hive or Pig applications. For more information, see https://tez.apache.org.

Apache Giraph

Apache Giraph is an iterative graph processing system built for high scalability. Facebook, Twitter, and LinkedIn use it to create social graphs of users. Giraph was originally written to run on standard Hadoop V1 using the MapReduce framework, but that approach proved inefficient and totally unnatural for various reasons. The native Giraph implementation under YARN provides the user with an iterative processing model that is not directly available with MapReduce. Support for YARN has been present in Giraph since its own version 1.0 release. In addition, using the flexibility of YARN, the Giraph developers plan on implementing their own web interface to monitor job progress. For more information, see http://giraph.apache.org.

Hoya: HBase on YARN

The Hoya project creates dynamic and elastic Apache HBase clusters on top of YARN. A client application creates the persistent configuration files, sets up the

HBase cluster XML files, and then asks YARN to create an ApplicationMaster. YARN copies all files listed in the client's application-launch request from HDFS into the local file system of the chosen server, and then executes the command to start the Hoya ApplicationMaster. Hoya also asks YARN for the number of containers matching the number of HBase region servers it needs. For more information, see http://hortonworks.com/blog/introducing-hoya-hbase-on-yarn.

Dryad on YARN

Similar to Apache Tez, Microsoft's Dryad provides a DAG as the abstraction of execution flow. This framework is ported to run natively on YARN and is fully compatible with its non-YARN version. The code is written completely in native C++ and C# for worker nodes and uses a thin layer of Java within the application. For more information, see http://research.microsoft.com/en-us/projects/dryad.

Apache Spark

Spark was initially developed for applications in which keeping data in memory improves performance, such as iterative algorithms, which are common in machine learning, and interactive data mining. Spark differs from classic MapReduce in two important ways. First, Spark holds intermediate results in memory, rather than writing them to disk. Second, Spark supports more than just MapReduce functions; that is, it greatly expands the set of possible analyses that can be executed over HDFS data stores. It also provides APIs in Scala, Java, and Python.

Since 2013, Spark has been running on production YARN clusters at Yahoo!. The advantage of porting and running Spark on top of YARN is the common resource management and a single underlying file system. For more information, see https://spark.apache.org.

Apache Storm

Traditional MapReduce jobs are expected to eventually finish, but Apache Storm continuously processes messages until it is stopped. This framework is designed to process unbounded streams of data in real time. It can be used in any programming language. The basic Storm use-cases include real-time analytics, online machine learning, continuous computation, distributed RPC (remote procedure calls), ETL (extract, transform, and load), and more. Storm provides fast performance, is scalable, is fault tolerant, and provides processing guarantees. It works directly under YARN and takes advantage of the common data and resource management substrate. For more information, see http://storm.apache.org.

Apache REEF: Retainable Evaluator Execution Framework

YARN's flexibility sometimes requires significant effort on the part of application implementers. The steps involved in writing a custom application on YARN include building your own ApplicationMaster, performing client and container management, and handling aspects of fault tolerance, execution flow, coordination, and other concerns. The REEF project by Microsoft recognizes this challenge and factors out several components that are common to many applications, such as storage management, data caching, fault detection, and checkpoints. Framework designers can build their applications on top of REEF more easily than they can build those same applications directly on YARN, and can reuse these common services/libraries. REEF's design makes it suitable for both MapReduce and DAG-like executions as well as iterative and interactive computations. For more information, see http://www.reef-project.org/welcome.

Hamster: Hadoop and MPI on the Same Cluster

The Message Passing Interface (MPI) is widely used in high-performance computing (HPC). MPI is primarily a set of optimized message-passing library calls for C, C++, and Fortran that operate over popular server interconnects such as Ethernet and InfiniBand. Because users have full control over their YARN containers, there is no reason why MPI applications cannot run within a Hadoop cluster. The Hamster effort is a work-in-progress that provides a good discussion of the issues involved in mapping MPI to a YARN cluster (see https://issues.apache.org/jira/browse/MAPRE-DUCE-2911). Currently, an alpha version of MPICH2 is available for YARN that can be used to run MPI applications. For more information, see https://github.com/clarkyzl/mpich2-yarn.

Apache Flink: Scalable Batch and Stream Data Processing

Apache Flink is a platform for efficient, distributed, general-purpose data processing. It features powerful programming abstractions in Java and Scala, a high-performance run time, and automatic program optimization. It also offers native support for iterations, incremental iterations, and programs consisting of large DAGs of operations.

Flink is primarily a stream-processing framework that can look like a batch-processing environment. The immediate benefit from this approach is the ability to use the same algorithms for both streaming and batch modes (exactly as is done in Apache Spark). However, Flink can provide low-latency similar to that found in Apache Storm, but which is not available in Apache Spark.

In addition, Flink has its own memory management system, separate from Java's garbage collector. By managing memory explicitly, Flink almost eliminates the memory spikes often seen on Spark clusters. For more information, see https://flink.apache.org.

Apache Slider: Dynamic Application Management

Apache Slider (incubating) is a YARN application to deploy existing distributed applications on YARN, monitor them, and make them larger or smaller as desired in real time.

Applications can be stopped and then started; the distribution of the deployed application across the YARN cluster is persistent and allows for best-effort placement close to the previous locations. Applications that remember the previous placement of data (such as HBase) can exhibit fast startup times by capitalizing on this feature.

YARN monitors the health of "YARN containers" that are hosting parts of the deployed applications. If a container fails, the Slider manager is notified. Slider then requests a new replacement container from the YARN ResourceManager. Some of Slider's other features include user creation of on-demand applications, the ability to stop and restart applications as needed (preemption), and the ability to expand or reduce the number of application containers as needed. The Slider tool is a Java command-line application. For more information, see http://slider.incubator.apache.org.

Summary and Additional Resources

The Hadoop YARN Distributed-Shell is a simple demonstration of a non-MapReduce program. It can be used to learn about how YARN operates and launches jobs across the cluster. The structure and operation of YARN programs are designed to provide a highly scalable and flexible method to create Hadoop applications. Other resources listed here describe application development with this framework.

YARN application frameworks offer many new capabilities for the Hadoop data lake. Many new algorithms and programming models are available, including an optimized MapReduce engine using Apache Tez. Each framework description in this chapter provides a webpage reference from which to find more information.

- **Apache Hadoop YARN Development**
  - Book: Murthy, A., et al. 2014. *Apache Hadoop YARN: Moving beyond MapReduce and Batch Processing with Apache Hadoop 2*, Boston, MA: Addison-Wesley. http://www.informit.com/store/apache-hadoop-yarn-moving-beyond-mapreduce-and-batch-9780321934505
  - http://hadoop.apache.org/docs/r2.7.0/hadoop-yarn/hadoop-yarn-site/WritingYarnApplications.html
  - MemcacheD on Yarn; http://hortonworks.com/blog/how-to-deploy-memcached-on-yarn/
  - Hortonworks YARN resources; http://hortonworks.com/get-started/yarn
- **Apache Hadoop YARN Frameworks**
  - See the webpage reference at the end of each individual description.

9

Managing Hadoop
with Apache Ambari

In This Chapter:

- A tour of the Apache Ambari graphical management tool is provided.
- The procedure for restarting a stopped Hadoop service is explained.
- The procedure for changing Hadoop properties and tracking configurations is presented.

Managing a Hadoop installation by hand can be tedious and time consuming. In addition to keeping configuration files synchronized across a cluster, starting, stopping, and restarting Hadoop services and dependent services in the right order is not a simple task. The Apache Ambari graphical management tool is designed to help you easily manage these and other Hadoop administrative issues. This chapter provides some basic navigation and usage scenarios for Apache Ambari.

Apache Ambari is an open source graphical installation and management tool for Apache Hadoop version 2. Ambari was used in Chapter 2, "Installation Recipes," to install Hadoop and related packages across a four-node cluster. In particular, the following packages were installed: HDFS, YARN, MapReduce2, Tez, Nagios, Ganglia, Hive, HBase, Pig, Sqoop, Oozie, Zookeeper, and Flume. These packages have been described in other chapters and provide basic Hadoop functionality. As noted in Chapter 2, other packages are available for installation (refer to Figure 2.18). Finally, to use Ambari as a management tool, the entire installation process must be done using Ambari. It is not possible to use Ambari for Hadoop clusters that have been installed by other means.

Along with being an installation tool, Ambari can be used as a centralized point of administration for a Hadoop cluster. Using Ambari, the user can configure cluster services, monitor the status of cluster hosts (nodes) or services, visualize hotspots by service metric, start or stop services, and add new hosts to the cluster. All of these features infuse a high level of agility into the processes of managing and monitoring a distributed computing environment. Ambari also attempts to provide real-time reporting of important metrics.

Apache Ambari continues to undergo rapid change. The description in this chapter is based on version 1.7. The major aspects of Ambari, which will not change, are explained in the following sections. Further detailed information can found at https:// ambari.apache.org.

Quick Tour of Apache Ambari

After completing the initial installation and logging into Ambari (as explained in Chapter 2), a dashboard similar to that shown in Figure 9.1 is presented. The same four-node cluster as created in Chapter 2 will be used to explore Ambari in this chapter. If you need to reopen the Ambari dashboard interface, simply enter the following command (which assumes you are using the Firefox browser, although other browsers may also be used):

```
$ firefox localhost:8080
```

The default login and password are admin and admin, respectively. Before continuing any further, you should change the default password. To change the password, select Manage Ambari from the Admin pull-down menu in the upper-right corner. In the management window, click Users under User + Group Management, and then click the admin user name. Select Change Password and enter a new password. When you are finished, click the Go To Dashboard link on the left side of the window to return to the dashboard view.

To leave the Ambari interface, select the Admin pull-down menu at the left side of the main menu bar and click Sign out.

The dashboard view provides a number of high-level metrics for many of the installed services. A glance at the dashboard should allow you to get a sense of how the cluster is performing.

The top navigation menu bar, shown in Figure 9.1, provides access to the Dashboard, Services, Hosts, Admin, and Views features (the 3 × 3 cube is the Views menu). The status (up/down) of various Hadoop services is displayed on the left using green/orange dots. Note that two of the services managed by Ambari are Nagios and Ganglia; the standard cluster management services installed by Ambari, they are used to provide cluster monitoring (Nagios) and metrics (Ganglia).

Dashboard View

The Dashboard view provides small status widgets for many of the services running on the cluster. The actual services are listed on the left-side vertical menu. These services correspond to what was installed in Chapter 2. You can move, edit, remove, or add these widgets as follows:

- **Moving:** Click and hold a widget while it is moved about the grid.
- **Edit:** Place the mouse on the widget and click the gray edit symbol in the upper-right corner of the widget. You can change several different aspects (including thresholds) of the widget.

- **Remove:** Place the mouse on the widget and click the X in the upper-left corner.

- **Add:** Click the small triangle next to the Metrics tab and select Add. The available widgets will be displayed. Select the widgets you want to add and click Apply.

Some widgets provide additional information when you move the mouse over them. For instance, the DataNodes widget displays the number of live, dead, and decommissioning hosts. Clicking directly on a graph widget provides an enlarged view. For instance, Figure 9.2 provides a detailed view of the CPU Usage widget from Figure 9.1.

The Dashboard view also includes a heatmap view of the cluster. Cluster heatmaps physically map selected metrics across the cluster. When you click the Heatmaps tab, a heatmap for the cluster will be displayed. To select the metric used for the heatmap, choose the desired option from the Select Metric pull-down menu. Note that the scale and color ranges are different for each metric. The heatmap for percentage host memory used is displayed in Figure 9.3.

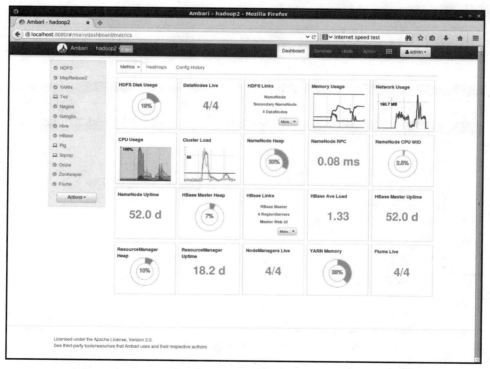

Figure 9.1   Apache Ambari dashboard view of a Hadoop cluster

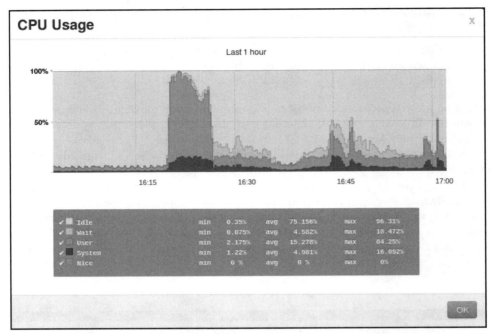

Figure 9.2   Enlarged view of Ambari CPU Usage widget

Figure 9.3   Ambari heatmap for Host memory usage

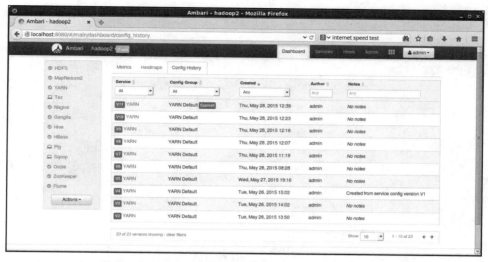

Figure 9.4   Ambari master configuration changes list

Configuration history is the final tab in the dashboard window. This view provides a list of configuration changes made to the cluster. As shown in Figure 9.4, Ambari enables configurations to be sorted by Service, Configuration Group, Data, and Author. To find the specific configuration settings, click the service name. More information on configuration settings is provided later in the chapter.

Services View

The Services menu provides a detailed look at each service running on the cluster. It also provides a graphical method for configuring each service (i.e., instead of hand-editing the /etc/hadoop/conf XML files). The summary tab provides a current Summary view of important service metrics and an Alerts and Health Checks sub-window.

Similar to the Dashboard view, the currently installed services are listed on the left-side menu. To select a service, click the service name in the menu. When applicable, each service will have its own Summary, Alerts and Health Monitoring, and Service Metrics windows. For example, Figure 9.5 shows the Service view for HDFS. Important information such as the status of NameNode, SecondaryNameNode, DataNodes, uptime, and available disk space is displayed in the Summary window. The Alerts and Health Checks window provides the latest status of the service and its component systems. Finally, several important real-time service metrics are displayed as widgets at the bottom of the screen. As on the dashboard, these widgets can be expanded to display a more detailed view.

Clicking the Configs tab will open an options form, shown in Figure 9.6, for the service. The options (properties) are the same ones that are set in the Hadoop XML files. When using Ambari, the user has complete control over the XML files and should manage them only through the Ambari interface—that is, the user should *not* edit the files by hand.

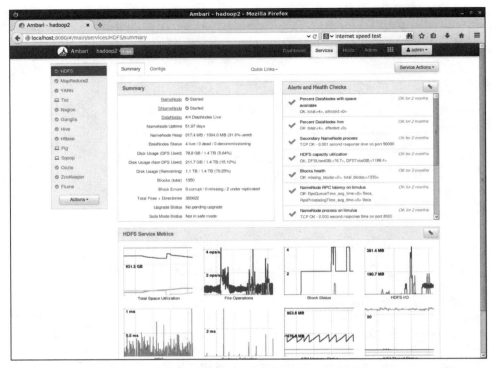

Figure 9.5   HDFS service summary window

The current settings available for each service are shown in the form. The administrator can set each of these properties by changing the values in the form. Placing the mouse in the input box of the property displays a short description of each property. Where possible, properties are grouped by functionality. The form also has provisions for adding properties that are not listed. An example of changing service properties and restarting the service components is provided in the "Managing Hadoop Services" section.

If a service provides its own graphical interface (e.g., HDFS, YARN, Oozie), then that interface can be opened in a separate browser tab by using the Quick Links pull-down menu located in top middle of the window.

Finally, the Service Action pull-down menu in the upper-left corner provides a method for starting and stopping each service and/or its component daemons across the cluster. Some services may have a set of unique actions (such as rebalancing HDFS) that apply to only certain situations. Finally, every service has a Service Check option to make sure the service is working property. The service check is initially run as part of the installation process and can be valuable when diagnosing problems. (See Appendix B, "Getting Started Flowchart and Troubleshooting Guide.")

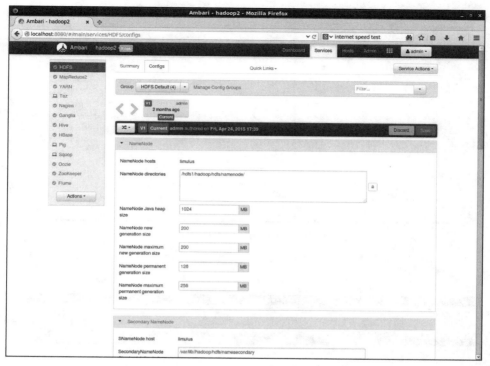

Figure 9.6   Ambari service options for HDFS

Hosts View

Selecting the Hosts menu item provides the information shown in Figure 9.7. The host name, IP address, number of cores, memory, disk usage, current load average, and Hadoop components are listed in this window in tabular form.

To display the Hadoop components installed on each host, click the links in the rightmost columns. You can also add new hosts by using the Actions pull-down menu. The new host must be running the Ambari agent (or the root SSH key must be entered) and have the base software described in Chapter 2 installed. The remaining options in the Actions pull-down menu provide control over the various service components running on the hosts.

Further details for a particular host can be found by clicking the host name in the left column. As shown in Figure 9.8, the individual host view provides three subwindows: Components, Host Metrics, and Summary information. The Components window lists the services that are currently running on the host. Each service can be stopped, restarted, decommissioned, or placed in maintenance mode. The Metrics window displays widgets that provide important metrics (e.g., CPU, memory, disk, and network usage). Clicking the widget displays a larger version of the graphic. The Summary window provides basic information about the host, including the last time a heartbeat was received.

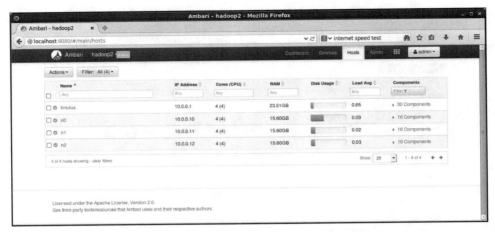

Figure 9.7   Ambari main Hosts screen

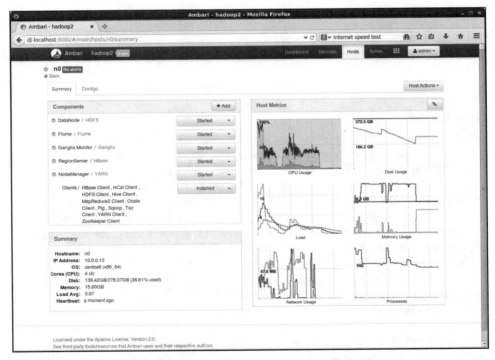

Figure 9.8   Ambari cluster host detail view

Admin View

The Administration (Admin) view provides three options. The first, as shown in Figure 9.9, displays a list of installed software. This Repositories listing generally reflects the version of Hortonworks Data Platform (HDP) used during the installation process. The Service Accounts option lists the service accounts added when the system was installed. These accounts are used to run various services and tests for Ambari. The third option, Security, sets the security on the cluster. A fully secured Hadoop cluster is important in many instances and should be explored if a secure environment is needed. This aspect of Ambari is beyond the scope of this book.

Views View

Ambari Views is a framework offering a systematic way to plug in user interface capabilities that provide for custom visualization, management, and monitoring features in Ambari. Views allows you to extend and customize Ambari to meet your specific needs. You can find more information about Ambari Views from the following source: https://cwiki.apache.org/confluence/display/AMBARI/Views.

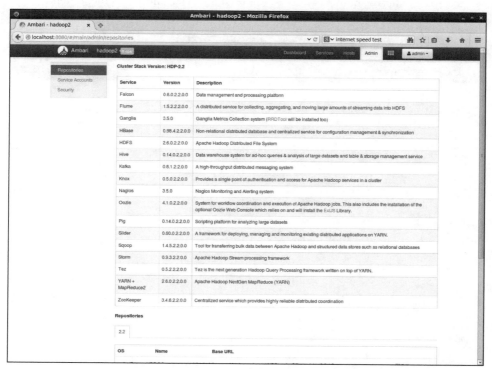

Figure 9.9   Ambari installed packages with versions, numbers, and descriptions

Admin Pull-Down Menu

The Administrative (Admin) pull-down menu provides the following options:

- **About**—Provides the current version of Ambari.
- **Manage Ambari**—Open the management screen where Users, Groups, Permissions, and Ambari Views can be created and configured.
- **Settings**—Provides the option to turn off the progress window. (See Figure 9.15.)
- **Sign Out**—Exits the interface.

Managing Hadoop Services

During the course of normal Hadoop cluster operation, services may fail for any number of reasons. Ambari monitors all of the Hadoop services and reports any service interruption to the dashboard. In addition, when the system was installed, an administrative email for the Nagios monitoring system was required. All service interruption notifications are sent to this email address.

Figure 9.10 shows the Ambari dashboard reporting a down DataNode. The service error indicator numbers next to the HDFS service and Hosts menu item

Figure 9.10   Ambari main dashboard indicating a DataNode issue

indicate this condition. The DataNode widget also has turned red and indicates that 3/4 DataNodes are operating.

Clicking the HDFS service link in the left vertical menu will bring up the service summary screen shown in Figure 9.11. The Alerts and Health Checks window confirms that a DataNode is down.

The specific host (or hosts) with an issue can be found by examining the Hosts window. As shown in Figure 9.12, the status of host n1 has changed from a green dot with a check mark inside to a yellow dot with a dash inside. An orange dot with a question mark inside indicates the host is not responding and is probably down. Other service interruption indicators may also be set as a result of the unresponsive node.

Clicking on the n1 host link opens the view in Figure 9.13. Inspecting the Components sub-window reveals that the DataNode daemon has stopped on the host. At this point, checking the DataNode logs on host n1 will help identify the actual cause of the failure. Assuming the failure is resolved, the DataNode daemon can be started using the Start option in the pull-down menu next to the service name.

When the DataNode daemon is restarted, a confirmation similar to Figure 9.14 is required from the user.

Figure 9.11   Ambari HDFS service summary window indicating a down DataNode

Figure 9.12   Ambari Hosts screen indicating an issue with host n1

Figure 9.13   Ambari window for host n1 indicating the DataNode/HDFS
service has stopped

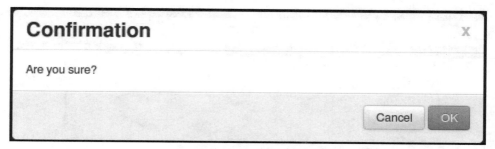

Confirmation   X

Are you sure?

                                                      Cancel   OK

Figure 9.14   Ambari restart confirmation

1 Background Operations Running   X

Operations	Start Time	Duration	Show: All (10)
⚙ Start DataNode ⊛	Today 14:29	6.08 secs	9% ▶
✔ Stop DataNode	Today 14:28	7.75 secs	100% ▶
✔ Start DataNode	Today 14:28	14.64 secs	100% ▶
✔ Stop DataNode	Today 14:13	11.72 secs	100% ▶
✔ Restart all components with Stale Configs for OOZIE	Mon Jun 15 2015 16:27	8.32 secs	100% ▶
✔ Restart components with Stale Configs on limulus	Mon Jun 01 2015 20:52	32.36 secs	100% ▶
✔ Restart all components with Stale	Thu May 28 2015 12:39	50.50 secs	100% ▶

☐ Do not show this dialog again when starting a background operation   OK

Figure 9.15   Ambari progress window for DataNode restart

When a service daemon is started or stopped, a progress window similar to
Figure 9.15 is opened. The progress bar indicates the status of each action. Note that
previous actions are part of this window. If something goes wrong during the action,
the progress bar will turn red. If the system generates a warning about the action, the
process bar will turn orange.

When these background operations are running, the small ops (operations) bubble
on the top menu bar will indicate how many operations are running. (If different service daemons are started or stopped, each process will be run to completion before the
next one starts.)

Once the DataNode has been restarted successfully, the dashboard will reflect
the new status (e.g., 4/4 DataNodes are Live). As shown in Figure 9.16, all four

Figure 9.16   Ambari dashboard indicating all DataNodes are running (The
service error indicators will slowly drop off the screen.)

DataNodes are now working and the service error indicators are beginning to slowly
disappear. The service error indicators may lag behind the real-time widget updates
for several minutes.

Changing Hadoop Properties

One of the challenges of managing a Hadoop cluster is managing changes to cluster-
wide configuration properties. In addition to modifying a large number of properties,
making changes to a property often requires restarting daemons (and dependent daemons) across the entire cluster. This process is tedious and time consuming. Fortunately, Ambari provides an easy way to manage this process.

As described previously, each service provides a Configs tab that opens a form dis-
playing all the possible service properties. Any service property can be changed (or
added) using this interface. As an example, the configuration properties for the YARN
scheduler are shown in Figure 9.17.

The number of options offered depends on the service; the full range of YARN
properties can be viewed by scrolling down the form. Both Chapter 4, "Running
Example Programs and Benchmarks," and Chapter 6, "MapReduce Programming,"

discussed the YARN property `yarn.log-aggregation-enable`. To easily view the application logs, this property must be set to true. This property is normally on by default. As an example for our purposes here, we will use the Ambari interface to disable this feature. As shown in Figure 9.18, when a property is changed, the green Save button becomes activated.

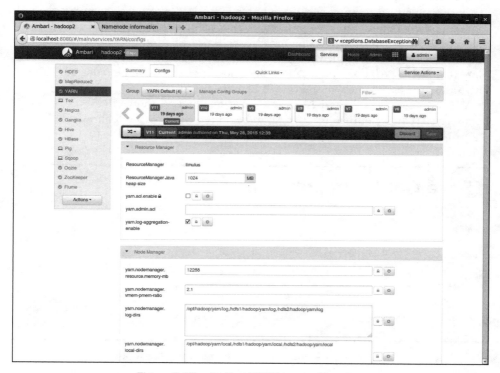

Figure 9.17   Ambari YARN properties view

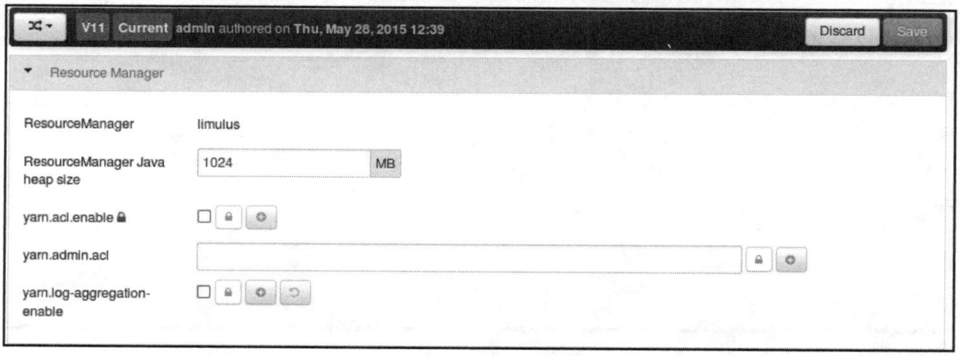

Figure 9.18   YARN properties with log aggregation turned off

Changes do not become permanent until the user clicks the Save button. A save/notes window will then be displayed. It is highly recommended that historical notes concerning the change be added to this window.

Once the user adds any notes and clicks the Save button, another window, shown in Figure 9.20, is presented. This window confirms that the properties have been saved.

Once the new property is changed, an orange Restart button will appear at the top left of the window. The new property will not take effect until the required services are restarted. As shown in Figure 9.21, the Restart button provides two options: Restart All and Restart NodeManagers. To be safe, the Restart All should be used. Note that Restart All does not mean all the Hadoop services will be restarted; rather, only those that use the new property will be restarted.

After the user clicks Restart All, a confirmation window, shown in Figure 9.22 will be displayed. Click Confirm Restart All to begin the cluster-wide restart.

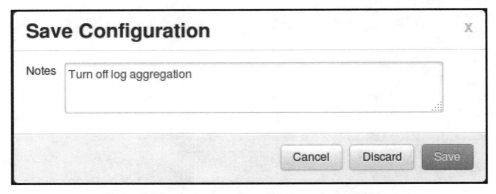

Figure 9.19   Ambari configuration save/notes window

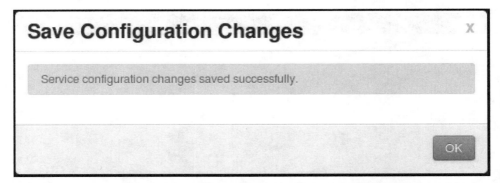

Figure 9.20   Ambari configuration change notification

Figure 9.21   Ambari Restart function appears after changes
in service properties

Figure 9.22   Ambari confirmation box for service restart

Similar to the DataNode restart example, a progress window will be displayed. Again, the progress bar is for the entire YARN restart. Details from the logs can be found by clicking the arrow to the right of the bar (see Figure 9.23).

Once the restart is complete, run a simple example (see Chapter 4) and attempt to view the logs using the YARN ResourceManager Applications UI. (You can access the UI from the Quick Links pull-down menu in the middle of the YARN series window.) A message similar to that in Figure 9.24 will be displayed (compare this message to the log data in Figure 6.1).

Ambari tracks all changes made to system properties. As can be seen in Figure 9.17 and in more detail in Figure 9.25, each time a configuration is changed, a new version is created. Reverting back to a previous version results in a new version. You can reduce the potential for version confusion by providing meaningful comments for each change (e.g., Figure 9.19 and Figure 9.27). In the preceding example, we created version 12 (V12). The current version is indicated by a green Current label in the horizontal version boxes or in the dark horizontal bar. Scrolling though the version boxes

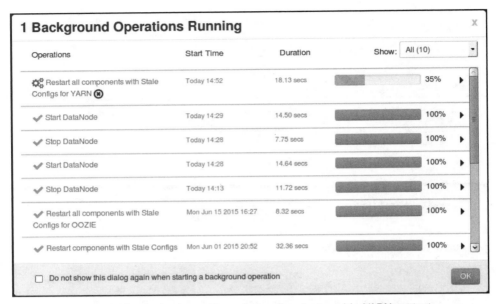

Figure 9.23   Ambari progress window for cluster-wide YARN restart

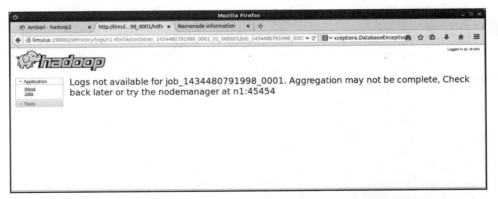

Figure 9.24   YARN ResourceManager interface with log aggregation
turned off (compare to Figure 6.1)

or pulling down the menu on the left-hand side of the dark horizontal bar will display the previous configuration versions.

To revert to a previous version, simply select the version from the version boxes or the pull-down menu. In Figure 9.26, the user has selected the previous version by clicking the Make Current button in the information box. This configuration will return to the previous state where log aggregation is enabled.

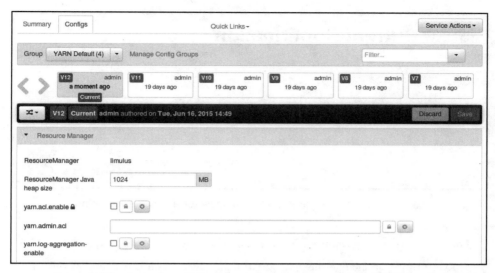

Figure 9.25   Ambari configuration change management for YARN service
(Version V12 is current)

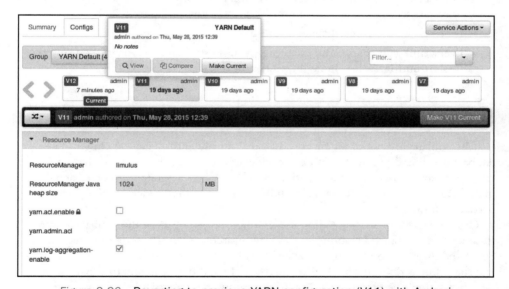

Figure 9.26   Reverting to previous YARN configuration (V11) with Ambari

As shown in Figure 9.27, a confirmation/notes window will open before the new configuration is saved. Again, it is suggested that you provide notes about the change in the Notes text box. When the save step is complete, the Make Current button will restore the previous configuration. The orange Restart button will appear and indicate that a service restart is needed before the changes take effect.

Figure 9.27   Ambari confirmation window for a new configuration

There are several important points to remember about the Ambari versioning tool:

- Every time you change the configuration, a new version is created. Reverting to a previous version creates a new version.
- You can view or compare a version to other versions without having to change or restart services. (See the buttons in the V11 box in Figure 9.26.)
- Each service has its own version record.
- Every time you change the properties, you must restart the service by using the Restart button. When in doubt, restart all services.

Summary and Additional Resources

Apache Ambari provides a single control panel for the entire Hadoop cluster. The Ambari dashboard provides a quick overview of the cluster. Each service has its own summary/status and configuration window. A host's window provides detailed metrics for each host, along with the ability to manage the services running on a particular host.

Other services, including adding users and groups, are part of the Ambari administration features. Each Hadoop service is monitored and all issues are reported via email and displayed on the interface for easy identification. All services can be stopped and started directly from the Ambari interface. In addition, changes to service properties are accomplished by using a simplified form with contextual help. Ambari also provides a versioning system that allows previous cluster configurations to be easily restored.

Apache Ambari is an open source tool that is gaining new features with each release. Currently, it is an efficient and useful tool for all Hadoop 2 clusters. To learn more about Ambari, consult the project website: https://ambari.apache.org.

10

Basic Hadoop Administration Procedures

In This Chapter:

- Several basic Hadoop YARN administration topics are presented, including decommissioning YARN nodes, managing YARN applications, and important YARN properties.
- Basic HDFS administration procedures are described, including using the NameNode UI, adding users, performing file system checks, balancing DataNodes, taking HDFS snapshots, and using the HDFS NFSv3 gateway.
- The Capacity scheduler is discussed.
- Hadoop version 2 MapReduce compatibility and node capacity are discussed.

In Chapter 9, "Managing Hadoop with Apache Ambari," the Apache Ambari web management tool was described in detail. Much of the day-to-day management of a Hadoop cluster can be accomplished using the Ambari interface. Indeed, whenever possible, Ambari should be used to manage the cluster because it keeps track of the cluster state.

Hadoop has two main areas of administration: the YARN resource manager and the HDFS file system. Other application frameworks (e.g., the MapReduce framework) and tools have their own management files. As mentioned in Chapter 2, "Installation Recipes," Hadoop configuration is accomplished through the use of XML configuration files. The basic files and their function are as follows:

- `core-default.xml`: System-wide properties
- `hdfs-default.xml`: Hadoop Distributed File System properties
- `mapred-default.xml`: Properties for the YARN MapReduce framework
- `yarn-default.xml`: YARN properties

You can find a complete list of properties for all these files at http://hadoop.apache
.org/docs/current/ (look at the lower-left side of the page under "Configuration").
A full discussion of all options is beyond the scope of this book. The Apache Hadoop
documentation does provide helpful comments and defaults for each property.

If you are using Ambari, you should manage the configuration files though
the interface, rather than editing them by hand. If some other management tool is
employed, it should be used as described. Installation of Hadoop by hand (as in a
pseudo-distributed mode in Chapter 2) requires that you edit the configuration files
by hand and then copy them to all nodes in the cluster if applicable.

The following sections cover some useful administration tasks that may fall outside
of Ambari, require special configuration, or require more explanation. By no means
does this discussion cover all possible topics related to Hadoop administration; rather,
it is designed to help jump-start your administration of Hadoop version 2.

Basic Hadoop YARN Administration

YARN has several built-in administrative features and commands. To find out
more about them, examine the YARN commands documentation at https://
hadoop.apache.org/docs/current/hadoop-yarn/hadoop-yarn-site/YarnCommands
.html#Administration_Commands. The main administration command is yarn
rmadmin (resource manager administration). Enter yarn rmadmin -help to learn more
about the various options.

Decommissioning YARN Nodes

If a NodeManager host/node needs to be removed from the cluster, it should be
decommissioned first. Assuming the node is responding, you can easily decommission
it from the Ambari web UI. Simply go to the Hosts view, click on the host, and select
Decommission from the pull-down menu next to the NodeManager component. Note
that the host may also be acting as a HDFS DataNode. Use the Ambari Hosts view to
decommission the HDFS host in a similar fashion.

YARN WebProxy

The Web Application Proxy is a separate proxy server in YARN that addresses security issues with the cluster web interface on ApplicationMasters. By default, the proxy
runs as part of the Resource Manager itself, but it can be configured to run in a
stand-alone mode by adding the configuration property yarn.web-proxy.address
to yarn-site.xml. (Using Ambari, go to the YARN Configs view, scroll to the
bottom, and select Custom yarn-site.xml/Add property.) In stand-alone mode,
yarn.web-proxy.principal and yarn.web-proxy.keytab control the Kerberos principal name and the corresponding keytab, respectively, for use in secure mode. These
elements can be added to the yarn-site.xml if required.

Using the JobHistoryServer

The removal of the JobTracker and migration of MapReduce from a system to an application-level framework necessitated creation of a place to store MapReduce job history. The JobHistoryServer provides all YARN MapReduce applications with a central location in which to aggregate completed jobs for historical reference and debugging. The settings for the JobHistoryServer can be found in the `mapred-site.xml` file.

Managing YARN Jobs

YARN jobs can be managed using the `yarn application` command. The following options, including `-kill`, `-list`, and `-status`, are available to the administrator with this command. MapReduce jobs can also be controlled with the `mapred job` command.

```
usage: application
 -appTypes <Comma-separated list of application types>  Works with
                               --list to filter applications based on
                               their type.
 -help                         Displays help for all commands.
 -kill <Application ID>        Kills the application.
 -list                         Lists applications from the RM. Supports optional
                               use of -appTypes to filter applications based
                               on application type.
 -status <Application ID>      Prints the status of the application.
```

Neither the YARN ResourceManager UI nor the Ambari UI can be used to kill YARN applications. If a job needs to be killed, give the `yarn application` command to find the `Application ID` and then use the `-kill` argument.

Setting Container Memory

YARN manages application resource containers over the entire cluster. Controlling the amount of container memory takes place through three important values in the `yarn-site.xml` file:

- `yarn.nodemanager.resource.memory-mb` is the amount of memory the NodeManager can use for containers.
- `scheduler.minimum-allocation-mb` is the smallest container allowed by the ResourceManager. A requested container smaller than this value will result in an allocated container of this size (default 1024MB).
- `yarn.scheduler.maximum-allocation-mb` is the largest container allowed by the ResourceManager (default 8192MB).

Setting Container Cores

You can set the number of cores for containers using the following properties in the `yarn-stie.xml`:

- `yarn.scheduler.minimum-allocation-vcores`: The minimum allocation for every container request at the ResourceManager, in terms of virtual CPU cores. Requests smaller than this allocation will not take effect, and the specified value will be allocated the minimum number of cores. The default is 1 core.

- `yarn.scheduler.maximum-allocation-vcores`: The maximum allocation for every container request at the ResourceManager, in terms of virtual CPU cores. Requests larger than this allocation will not take effect, and the number of cores will be capped at this value. The default is 32.

- `yarn.nodemanager.resource.cpu-vcores`: The number of CPU cores that can be allocated for containers. The default is 8.

Setting MapReduce Properties

As noted throughout this book, MapReduce now runs as a YARN application. Consequently, it may be necessary to adjust some of the `mapred-site.xml` properties as they relate to the map and reduce containers. The following properties are used to set some Java arguments and memory size for both the map and reduce containers:

- `mapred.child.java.opts` provides a larger or smaller heap size for child JVMs of maps (e.g., `--Xmx2048m`).

- `mapreduce.map.memory.mb` provides a larger or smaller resource limit for maps (default = 1536MB).

- `mapreduce.reduce.memory.mb` provides a larger heap size for child JVMs of maps (default = 3072MB).

- `mapreduce.reduce.java.opts` provides a larger or smaller heap size for child reducers.

Basic HDFS Administration

The following section covers some basic administration aspects of HDFS. Advanced topics such as HDFS Federation of high availability are beyond the scope of this chapter. More information on these and other HDFS topics can be found at https://hadoop.apache.org/docs/current/hadoop-project-dist/hadoop-hdfs/HdfsUserGuide.html. (Note the HDFS topic menu available on the left-hand side of this webpage.)

The NameNode User Interface

Monitoring HDFS can be done in several ways. One of the more convenient ways to get a quick view of HDFS status is through the NameNode user interface. This web-based tool provides essential information about HDFS and offers the capability to browse the HDFS namespace and logs.

The web-based UI can be started from within Ambari or from a web browser connected to the NameNode. In Ambari, simply select the HDFS service window and click on the Quick Links pull-down menu in the top middle of the page. Select NameNode UI. A new browser tab will open with the UI shown in Figure 10.1. You can also start the UI directly by entering the following command (the command given here assumes the Firefox browser is used, but other browsers should work as well):

```
$ firefox  http://localhost:50070
```

There are five tabs on the UI: Overview, Datanodes, Snapshot, Startup Progress, and Utilities. The Overview page provides much of the essential information that the command-line tools also offer, but in a much easier-to-read format. The Datanodes tab displays node information like that shown in Figure 10.2.

The Snapshot window (shown later in this chapter in Figure 10.5) lists the "snapshottable" directories and the snapshots. Further information on snapshots can be found in the "HDFS Snapshots" section.

Figure 10.3 provides a NameNode startup progress view. As noted in Chapter 3, "Hadoop Distributed File System Basics," when the NameNode starts, it reads the previous file system image file (fsimage); applies any new edits to the file system image, thereby creating a new file system image; and drops into safe mode until

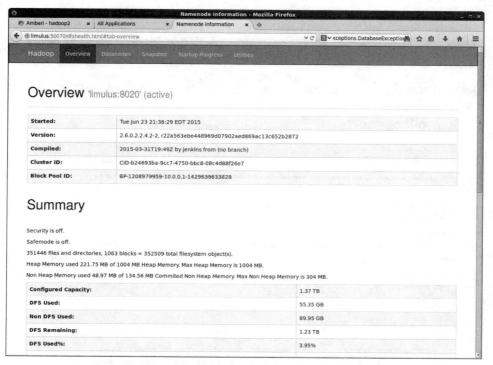

Figure 10.1   Overview page for NameNode user interface

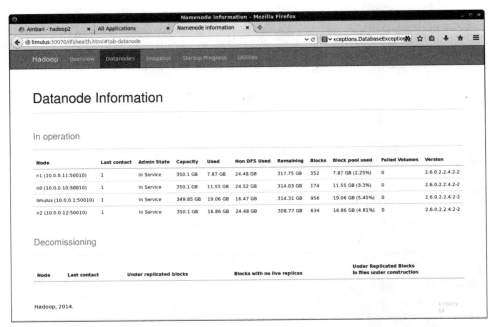

Figure 10.2   NameNode web interface showing status of DataNodes

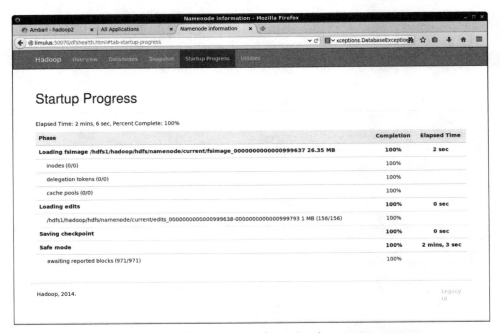

Figure 10.3   NameNode web interface showing startup progress

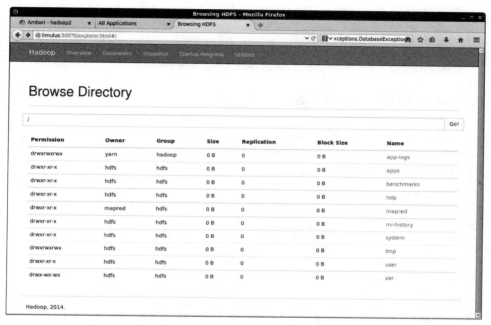

Figure 10.4   NameNode web interface directory browser

enough DataNodes come online. This progress is shown in real time in the UI as the NameNode starts. Completed phases are displayed in bold text. The currently running phase is displayed in italics. Phases that have not yet begun are displayed in gray text. In Figure 10.3, all the phases have been completed, and as indicated in the overview window in Figure 10.1, the system is out of safe mode.

The Utilities menu offers two options. The first, as shown in Figure 10.4, is a file system browser. From this window, you can easily explore the HDFS namespace. The second option, which is not shown, links to the various NameNode logs.

Adding Users to HDFS

For a full explanation of HDFS permissions, see the following document: http://hadoop.apache.org/docs/current/hadoop-project-dist/hadoop-hdfs/HdfsPermissions-Guide.html. Keep in mind that errors that crop up while Hadoop applications are running are often due to file permissions.

To quickly create user accounts manually on a Linux-based system, perform the following steps:

1. Add the user to the group for your operating system on the HDFS client system. In most cases, the groupname should be that of the HDFS superuser, which is often hadoop or hdfs.

   ```
   useradd -G <groupname> <username>
   ```

2. Create the username directory in HDFS.

   ```
   hdfs dfs -mkdir /user/<username>
   ```

3. Give that account ownership over its directory in HDFS.

   ```
   hdfs dfs -chown <username>:<groupname> /user/<username>
   ```

Perform an FSCK on HDFS

To check the health of HDFS, you can issue the hdfs fsck <path> (file system check) command. The entire HDFS namespace can be checked, or a subdirectory can be entered as an argument to the command. The following example checks the entire HDFS namespace.

```
$ hdfs fsck /

Connecting to namenode via http://limulus:50070
FSCK started by hdfs (auth:SIMPLE) from /10.0.0.1 for path / at Fri May 29
14:48:01 EDT 2015
...................................................................
...................................................................
Status: HEALTHY
 Total size:    100433565781 B (Total open files size: 498 B)
 Total dirs:    201331
 Total files:   1003
 Total symlinks:            0 (Files currently being written: 6)
 Total blocks (validated):    1735 (avg. block size 57886781 B) (Total open file
                              blocks (not validated): 6)
 Minimally replicated blocks:       1735 (100.0 %)
 Over-replicated blocks:    0 (0.0 %)
 Under-replicated blocks:   0 (0.0 %)
 Mis-replicated blocks:             0 (0.0 %)
 Default replication factor: 2
 Average block replication:  1.7850144
 Corrupt blocks:            0
 Missing replicas:          0 (0.0 %)
 Number of data-nodes:              4
 Number of racks:           1
FSCK ended at Fri May 29 14:48:03 EDT 2015 in 1853 milliseconds


The filesystem under path '/' is HEALTHY
```

Other options provide more detail, include snapshots and open files, and management of corrupted files.

- -move moves corrupted files to /lost+found.
- -delete deletes corrupted files.
- -files prints out files being checked.

- `-openforwrite` prints out files opened for writes during check.
- `-includeSnapshots` includes snapshot data. The path indicates the existence of a snapshottable directory or the presence of snapshottable directories under it.
- `-list-corruptfileblocks` prints out a list of missing blocks and the files to which they belong.
- `-blocks` prints out a block report.
- `-locations` prints out locations for every block.
- `-racks` prints out network topology for data-node locations.

Balancing HDFS

Based on usage patterns and DataNode availability, the number of data blocks across the DataNodes may become unbalanced. To avoid over-utilized DataNodes, the HDFS balancer tool rebalances data blocks across the available DataNodes. Data blocks are moved from over-utilized to under-utilized nodes to within a certain percent threshold. Rebalancing can be done when new DataNodes are added or when a DataNode is removed from service. This step does not create more space in HDFS, but rather improves efficiency.

The HDFS superuser must run the balancer. The simplest way to run the balancer is to enter the following command:

```
$ hdfs balancer
```

By default, the balancer will continue to rebalance the nodes until the number of data blocks on all DataNodes are within 10% of each other. The balancer can be stopped, without harming HDFS, at any time by entering a Ctrl-C. Lower or higher thresholds can be set using the -threshold argument. For example, giving the following command sets a 5% threshold:

```
$ hdfs balancer -threshold 5
```

The lower the threshold, the longer the balancer will run. To ensure the balancer does not swamp the cluster networks, you can set a bandwidth limit before running the balancer, as follows:

```
$ dfsadmin -setBalancerBandwidth newbandwidth
```

The newbandwidth option is the maximum amount of network bandwidth, in bytes per second, that each DataNode can use during the balancing operation.

Balancing data blocks can also break HBase locality. When HBase regions are moved, some data locality is lost, and the RegionServers will then request the data over the network from remote DataNode(s). This condition will persist until a major HBase compaction event takes place (which may either occur at regular intervals or be initiated by the administrator).

See http://hadoop.apache.org/docs/current/hadoop-project-dist/hadoop-hdfs/
HDFSCommands.html for more information on balancer options.

HDFS Safe Mode

As mentioned in Chapter 3, "Hadoop Distributed File System Basics," when the
NameNode starts, it loads the file system state from the `fsimage` and then applies the
edits log file. It then waits for DataNodes to report their blocks. During this time, the
NameNode stays in a read-only Safe Mode. The NameNode leaves Safe Mode automatically after the DataNodes have reported that most file system blocks are available.

The administrator can place HDFS in Safe Mode by giving the following
command:

```
$ hdfs dfsadmin -safemode enter
```

Entering the following command turns off Safe Mode:

```
$ hdfs dfsadmin -safemode leave
```

HDFS may drop into Safe Mode if a major issue arises within the file system (e.g.,
a full DataNode). The file system will not leave Safe Mode until the situation is
resolved. To check whether HDFS is in Safe Mode, enter the following command:

```
$ hdfs dfsadmin -safemode get
```

Decommissioning HDFS Nodes

If you need to remove a DataNode host/node from the cluster, you should decommission it first. Assuming the node is responding, it can be easily decommissioned
from the Ambari web UI. Simply go to the Hosts view, click on the host, and selected
Decommission from the pull-down menu next to the DataNode component. Note
that the host may also be acting as a Yarn NodeManager. Use the Ambari Hosts view
to decommission the YARN host in a similar fashion.

SecondaryNameNode

To avoid long NameNode restarts and other issues, the performance of the SecondaryNameNode should be verified. Recall that the SecondaryNameNode takes the
previous file system image file (`fsimage*`) and adds the NameNode file system edits
to create a new file system image file for the NameNode to use when it restarts.
The `hdfs-site.xml` defines a property called `fs.checkpoint.period` (called HDFS
Maximum Checkpoint Delay in Ambari). This property provides the time in seconds
between the SecondaryNameNode checkpoints.

When a checkpoint occurs, a new `fsimage*` file is created in the directory corresponding to the value of `dfs.namenode.checkpoint.dir` in the `hdfs-site.xml` file. This file
is also placed in the NameNode directory corresponding to the `dfs.namenode.name.dir`
path designated in the `hdfs-site.xml` file. To test the checkpoint process, a short time
period (e.g., 300 seconds) can be used for `fs.checkpoint.period` and HDFS restarted.

After five minutes, two identical fsimage* files should be present in each of the two previously mentioned directories. If these files are not recent or are missing, consult the NameNode and SecondaryNameNode logs.

Once the SecondaryNameNode process is confirmed to be working correctly, reset the fs.checkpoint.period to the previous value and restart HDFS. (Ambari versioning is helpful with this type or procedure.) If the SecondaryNameNode is not running, a checkpoint can be forced by running the following command:

```
$ hdfs secondarynamenode -checkpoint force
```

HDFS Snapshots

HDFS snapshots are read-only, point-in-time copies of HDFS. Snapshots can be taken on a subtree of the file system or the entire file system. Some common use-cases for snapshots are data backup, protection against user errors, and disaster recovery.

Snapshots can be taken on any directory once the directory has been set as **snap-shottable.** A snapshottable directory is able to accommodate 65,536 simultaneous snapshots. There is no limit on the number of snapshottable directories. Administrators may set any directory to be snapshottable, but nested snapshottable directories are not allowed. For example, a directory cannot be set to snapshottable if one of its ancestors/descendants is a snapshottable directory. More details can be found at https://hadoop.apache.org/docs/current/hadoop-project-dist/hadoop-hdfs/HdfsSnapshots.html.

The following example walks through the procedure for creating a snapshot. The first step is to declare a directory as "snapshottable" using the following command:

```
$ hdfs dfsadmin -allowSnapshot /user/hdfs/war-and-peace-input
Allowing snapshot on /user/hdfs/war-and-peace-input succeeded
```

Once the directory has been made snapshottable, the snapshot can be taken with the following command. The command requires the directory path and a name for the snapshot—in this case, wapi-snap-1.

```
$ hdfs dfs -createSnapshot /user/hdfs/war-and-peace-input wapi-snap-1
Created snapshot /user/hdfs/war-and-peace-input/.snapshot/wapi-snap-1
```

The path of the snapshot is /user/hdfs/war-and-peace-input/.snapshot/wapi-snap-1. The /user/hdfs/war-and-peace-input directory has one file, as shown by issuing the following command:

```
$ hdfs dfs -ls /user/hdfs/war-and-peace-input/
Found 1 items
-rw-r--r--   2 hdfs hdfs    3288746 2015-06-24 19:56 /user/hdfs/war-and-peace-input/war-and-peace.txt
```

If the file is deleted, it can be restored from the snapshot:

```
$ hdfs dfs -rm -skipTrash /user/hdfs/war-and-peace-input/war-and-peace.txt
Deleted /user/hdfs/war-and-peace-input/war-and-peace.txt

$ hdfs dfs -ls /user/hdfs/war-and-peace-input/
```

The restoration process is basically a simple copy from the snapshot to the previous directory (or anywhere else). Note the use of the ~/.snapshot/wapi-snap-1 path to restore the file:

```
$ hdfs dfs -cp /user/hdfs/war-and-peace-input/.snapshot/wapi-snap-1/war-and-peace
.txt /user/hdfs/war-and-peace-input
```

Confirmation that the file has been restored can be obtained by issuing the following command:

```
$ hdfs dfs -ls /user/hdfs/war-and-peace-input/
Found 1 items
-rw-r--r--   2 hdfs hdfs     3288746 2015-06-24 21:12 /user/hdfs/war-and-peace-
input/war-and-peace.txt
```

The NameNode UI provides a listing of snapshottable directories and the snapshots that have been taken. Figure 10.5 shows the results of creating the previous snapshot.
To delete a snapshot, give the following command:

```
$ hdfs dfs -deleteSnapshot /user/hdfs/war-and-peace-input wapi-snap-1
```

To make a directory "*un-snapshottable*" (or go back to the default state), use the following command:

```
$ hdfs dfsadmin -disallowSnapshot /user/hdfs/war-and-peace-input
Disallowing snapshot on /user/hdfs/war-and-peace-input succeeded
```

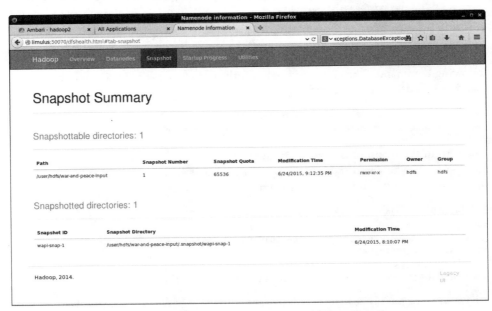

Figure 10.5   Apache NameNode web interface
showing snapshot information

Configuring an NFSv3 Gateway to HDFS

HDFS supports an NFS version 3 (NFSv3) gateway. This feature enables files to be easily moved between HDFS and client systems. The NFS gateway supports NFSv3 and allows HDFS to be mounted as part of the client's local file system. Currently the NFSv3 gateway supports the following capabilities:

- Users can browse the HDFS file system through their local file system using an NFSv3 client-compatible operating system.
- Users can download files from the HDFS file system to their local file system.
- Users can upload files from their local file system directly to the HDFS file system.
- Users can stream data directly to HDFS through the mount point. File append is supported, but random write is *not* supported.

The gateway must be run on the same host as a DataNode, NameNode, or any HDFS client. More information about the NFSv3 gateway can be found at https://hadoop.apache.org/docs/current/hadoop-project-dist/hadoop-hdfs/HdfsNfsGateway.html.

In the following example, a simple four-node cluster is used to demonstrate the steps for enabling the NFSv3 gateway. Other potential options, including those related to security, are not addressed in this example. A DataNode is used as the gateway node in this example, and HDFS is mounted on the main (login) cluster node.

Step 1: Set Configuration Files

Several Hadoop configuration files need to be changed. In this example, the Ambari GUI will be used to alter the HDFS configuration files. See Chapter 9 for information on using Ambari. Do not save the changes or restart HDFS until all the following changes are made. If you are not using Ambari, you must change these files by hand and then restart the appropriate services across the cluster. The following environment is assumed:

- OS: Linux
- Platform: RHEL 6.6
- Hortonworks HDP 2.2 with Hadoop version: 2.6

Several properties need to be added to the /etc/hadoop/config/core-site.xml file. Using Ambari, go to the HDFS service window and select the Configs tab. Toward the bottom of the screen, select the Add Property link in the Custom core-site.xml section. Add the following two properties (the item used for the key field in Ambari is the name field included in this code):

```
<property>
    <name>hadoop.proxyuser.root.groups</name>
    <value>*</value>
</property>
```

```
<property>
  <name>hadoop.proxyuser.root.hosts</name>
  <value>*</value>
</property>
```

The name of the user who will start the Hadoop NFSv3 gateway is placed in the name field. In the previous example, root is used for this purpose. This setting can be any user who starts the gateway. If, for instance, user nfsadmin starts the gateway, then the two names would be hadoop.proxyuser.nfsadmin.groups and hadoop.proxyuser.nfsadmin.hosts. The * value, entered in the preceding lines, opens the gateway to all groups and allows it to run on any host. Access is restricted by entering groups (comma separated) in the group's property. Entering a host name for the host's property can restrict the host running the gateway.

Next, move to the Advanced hdfs-site.xml section and set the following property:

```
<property>
    <name>dfs.namenode.accesstime.precision</name>
    <value>3600000</value>
  </property>
```

This property ensures client mounts with access time updates work properly. (See the mount default atime option.)

Finally, move to the Custom hdfs-site section, click the Add Property link, and add the following property:

```
property>
    <name>dfs.nfs3.dump.dir</name>
    <value>/tmp/.hdfs-nfs</value>
</property>
```

The NFSv3 dump directory is needed because the NFS client often reorders writes. Sequential writes can arrive at the NFS gateway in random order. This directory is used to temporarily save out-of-order writes before writing to HDFS. Make sure the dump directory has enough space. For example, if the application uploads 10 files, each of size 100MB, it is recommended that this directory have 1GB of space to cover a worst-case write reorder for every file.

Once all the changes have been made, click the green Save button and note the changes you made to the Notes box in the Save confirmation dialog. Then restart all of HDFS by clicking the orange Restart button.

Step 2: Start the Gateway

Log into a DataNode and make sure all NFS services are stopped. In this example, DataNode n0 is used as the gateway.

```
# service rpcbind stop
# service nfs stop
```

Next, start the HDFS gateway by using the `hadoop-daemon` script to start `portmap` and nfs3 as follows:

```
# /usr/hdp/2.2.4.2-2/hadoop/sbin/hadoop-daemon.sh start portmap
# /usr/hdp/2.2.4.2-2/hadoop/sbin/hadoop-daemon.sh start nfs3
```

The `portmap` daemon will write its log to

```
/var/log/hadoop/root/hadoop-root-portmap-n0.log
```

The nfs3 daemon will write its log to

```
/var/log/hadoop/root/hadoop-root-nfs3-n0.log
```

To confirm the gateway is working, issue the following command. The output should look like the following:

```
# rpcinfo -p n0
   program vers proto   port  service
    100005   2   tcp    4242  mountd
    100000   2   udp     111  portmapper
    100000   2   tcp     111  portmapper
    100005   1   tcp    4242  mountd
    100003   3   tcp    2049  nfs
    100005   1   udp    4242  mountd
    100005   3   udp    4242  mountd
    100005   3   tcp    4242  mountd
    100005   2   udp    4242  mountd
```

Finally, make sure the mount is available by issuing the following command:

```
# showmount -e n0
Export list for n0:
/ *
```

If the `rpcinfo` or `showmount` command does not work correctly, check the previously mentioned log files for problems.

Step 3: Mount HDFS

The final step is to mount HDFS on a client node. In this example, the main login node is used. To mount the HDFS files, exit from the gateway node (in this case node n0) and create the following directory:

```
# mkdir /mnt/hdfs
```

The mount command is as follows. Note that the name of the gateway node will be different on other clusters, and an IP address can be used instead of the node name.

```
# mount -t nfs -o vers=3,proto=tcp,nolock n0:/  /mnt/hdfs/
```

Once the file system is mounted, the files will be visible to the client users. The following command will list the mounted file system:

```
# ls /mnt/hdfs
app-logs  apps  benchmarks  hdp  mapred  mr-history  system  tmp  user  var
```

The gateway in the current Hadoop release uses AUTH_UNIX-style authentication and requires that the login user name on the client match the user name that NFS passes to HDFS. For example, if the NFS client is user admin, the NFS gateway will access HDFS as user admin and existing HDFS permissions will prevail.

The system administrator must ensure that the user on the NFS client machine has the same user name and user ID as that on the NFS gateway machine. This is usually not a problem if you use the same user management system, such as LDAP/NIS, to create and deploy users to cluster nodes.

Capacity Scheduler Background

The Capacity scheduler is the default scheduler for YARN that enables multiple groups to securely share a large Hadoop cluster. Developed by the original Hadoop team at Yahoo!, the Capacity scheduler has successfully run many of the largest Hadoop clusters.

To use the Capacity scheduler, one or more queues are configured with a predetermined fraction of the total slot (or processor) capacity. This assignment guarantees a minimum amount of resources for each queue. Administrators can configure soft limits and optional hard limits on the capacity allocated to each queue. Each queue has strict ACLs (Access Control Lists) that control which users can submit applications to individual queues. Also, safeguards are in place to ensure that users cannot view or modify applications from other users.

The Capacity scheduler permits sharing a cluster while giving each user or group certain minimum capacity guarantees. These minimum amounts are not given away in the absence of demand (i.e., a group is always guaranteed a minimum number of resources is available). Excess slots are given to the most starved queues, based on the number of running tasks divided by the queue capacity. Thus, the fullest queues as defined by their initial minimum capacity guarantee get the most needed resources. Idle capacity can be assigned and provides elasticity for the users in a cost-effective manner.

Administrators can change queue definitions and properties, such as capacity and ACLs, at run time without disrupting users. They can also add more queues at run time, but cannot delete queues at run time. In addition, administrators can stop queues at run time to ensure that while existing applications run to completion, no new applications can be submitted.

The Capacity scheduler currently supports memory-intensive applications, where an application can optionally specify higher memory resource requirements than the default. Using information from the NodeManagers, the Capacity scheduler can then place containers on the best-suited nodes.

The Capacity scheduler works best when the workloads are well known, which helps in assigning the minimum capacity. For this scheduler to work most effectively, each queue should be assigned a minimal capacity that is less than the maximal expected workload. Within each queue, multiple jobs are scheduled using hierarchical (first in, first out) FIFO queues similar to the approach used with the stand-alone FIFO scheduler. If there are no queues configured, all jobs are placed in the default queue.

The ResourceManager UI provides a graphical representation of the scheduler queues and their utilization. Figure 10.6 shows two jobs running on a four-node cluster. To select the scheduler view, click the Scheduler option at the bottom of the left-side vertical menu.

Information on configuring the Capacity scheduler can be found at https://hadoop. apache.org/docs/current/hadoop-yarn/hadoop-yarn-site/CapacityScheduler.html and from *Apache Hadoop YARN: Moving beyond MapReduce and Batch Processing with Apache Hadoop 2.* (See the list of resources at the end of this chapter.)

In addition to the Capacity scheduler, Hadoop YARN offers a Fair scheduler. More information can be found on the Hadoop website.

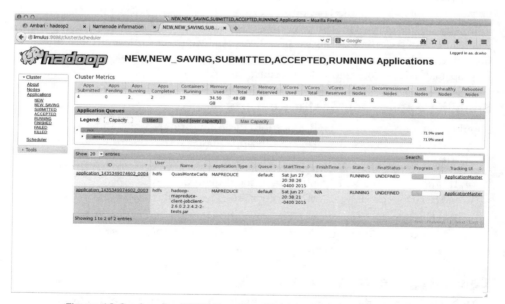

Figure 10.6   Apache YARN ResourceManager web interface showing
Capacity scheduler information

Hadoop Version 2 MapReduce Compatibility

Hadoop version 1 is essentially a monolithic MapReduce engine. Moving this technology to YARN as a separate application framework was a complex task because MapReduce requires many important processing features, including data locality, fault tolerance, and application priorities. See Chapter 8, "Hadoop YARN Applications," for more background on the structure of YARN applications.

To provide data locality, the MapReduce ApplicationMaster is required to locate blocks for processing and then request containers on these blocks. To implement fault tolerance, the capability to handle failed map or reduce tasks and request them again on other nodes was needed. Fault tolerance moved hand-in-hand with the complex intra-application priorities.

The logic to handle complex intra-application priorities for map and reduce tasks had to be built into the ApplicationMaster. There was no need to start idle reducers before mappers finished processing enough data. Reducers were now under control of the ApplicationMaster and were not fixed, as they had been in Hadoop version 1. This design actually made Hadoop version 2 much more efficient and increased cluster throughput.

The following sections provide basic background on how the MapReduce framework operates under YARN. The new Hadoop version 2 MapReduce (often referred to as MRv2) was designed to provide as much backward compatibility with Hadoop version 1 MapReduce (MRv1) as possible. As with the other topics in this chapter, the following discussion provides an overview of some of the important considerations when administering the Hadoop version 2 MapReduce framework. For more information, consult https://hadoop.apache.org/docs/current/hadoop-mapreduce-client/hadoop-mapreduce-client-core/MapReduceTutorial.html.

Enabling ApplicationMaster Restarts

Should an error occur in a MapReduce job, the ApplicationMaster can be automatically restarted by YARN. To enable ApplicationMaster restarts, set the following properties:

- Inside `yarn-site.xml`, you can tune the property `yarn.resourcemanager.am.max-retries`. The default is 2.
- Inside `mapred-site.xml`, you can more directly tune how many times a MapReduce ApplicationMaster should restart with the property `mapreduce.am.max-attempts`. The default is 2.

Calculating the Capacity of a Node

YARN has removed the hard-partitioned mapper and reducer slots of Hadoop version 1. To determine the MapReduce capacity of a cluster node, new capacity calculations are required. Estimates as to the number of mapper and reducer tasks that can efficiently run on a node help determine the amount of computing resources made available to Hadoop users. There are eight important parameters for calculating a node's

MapReduce capacity; they are found in the `mapred-site.xml` and `yarn-site.xml` files.

- `mapred-site.xml`
  - `mapreduce.map.memory.mb`
    `mapreduce.reduce.memory.mb`

    The hard limit enforced by Hadoop on the mapper or reducer task.
  - `mapreduce.map.java.opts`
    `mapreduce.reduce.java.opts`

    The heap size of the `jvm -Xmx` for the mapper or reducer task. Remember to leave room for the JVM Perm Gen and Native Libs used. This value should always be smaller than `mapreduce.[map|reduce].memory.mb`.
- `yarn-site.xml`
  - `yarn.scheduler.minimum-allocation-mb`

    The smallest container YARN will allow.
  - `yarn.scheduler.maximum-allocation-mb`

    The largest container YARN will allow.
  - `yarn.nodemanager.resource.memory-mb`

    The amount of physical memory (RAM) on the compute node for containers. It is important that this value is not equal to the total RAM on the node, as other Hadoop services also require RAM.
  - `yarn.nodemanager.vmem-pmem-ratio`

    The amount of virtual memory each container is allowed. It is calculated with the following formula:

    `containerMemoryRequest*vmem-pmem-ratio`.

As an example, consider a configuration with the settings in Table 10.1. Using these settings, we have given each map and reduce task a generous 512MB of overhead for

Table 10.1   **Example YARN MapReduce Settings**

Property	Value
`mapreduce.map.memory.mb`	1536
`mapreduce.reduce.memory.mb`	2560
`mapreduce.map.java.opts`	-Xmx1024m
`mapreduce.reduce.java.opts`	-Xmx2048m
`yarn.scheduler.minimum-allocation-mb`	512
`yarn.scheduler.maximum-allocation-mb`	4096
`yarn.nodemanager.resource.memory-mb`	36864
`yarn.nodemanager.vmem-pmem-ratio`	2.1

the container, as seen with the difference between the mapreduce.[map|reduce]
.memory.mb and the mapreduce.[map|reduce].java.opts.

Next, we have configured YARN to allow a container no smaller than 512MB and
no larger than 4GB. Assuming the compute nodes have 36GB of RAM available for
containers, and with a virtual memory ratio of 2.1 (the default value), each map can
have as much as 3225.6MB of RAM and a reducer can have 5376MB of virtual RAM.
Thus our compute node configured for 36GB of container space can support up to
24 maps or 14 reducers, or any combination of mappers and reducers allowed by the
available resources on the node.

Running Hadoop Version 1 Applications

To ease the transition from Hadoop version 1 to version 2 with YARN, a major goal
of YARN and the MapReduce framework implementation on top of YARN is to
ensure that existing MapReduce applications that were programmed and compiled
against previous MapReduce APIs (MRv1 applications) can continue to run with little
work on top of YARN (MRv2 applications).

Binary Compatibility of org.apache.hadoop.mapred APIs

For the vast majority of users who use the org.apache.hadoop.mapred APIs, MapReduce
on YARN ensures full binary compatibility. These existing applications can run on YARN
directly without recompilation. You can use jar files of your existing application that code
against MapReduce APIs and use bin/hadoop to submit them directly to YARN.

Source Compatibility of org.apache.hadoop.mapreduce APIs

Unfortunately, it has proved difficult to ensure full binary compatibility of applications that were originally compiled against MRv1 org.apache.hadoop.mapreduce
APIs. These APIs have gone through lots of changes. For example, many of the classes
stopped being abstract classes and changed to interfaces. The YARN community
eventually reached a compromise on this issue, supporting source compatibility only
for org.apache.hadoop.mapreduce APIs. Existing applications using MapReduce
APIs are source compatible and can run on YARN either with no changes, with simple recompilation against MRv2 jar files that are shipped with Hadoop version 2, or
with minor updates.

Compatibility of Command-Line Scripts

Most of the command-line scripts from Hadoop 1.x should work without any tweaking.
The only exception is mradmin, whose functionality was removed from MRv2 because
the JobTracker and TaskTracker no longer exist. The mradmin functionality has been
replaced with rmadmin. The suggested method to invoke rmadmin is through the command line, even though you can directly invoke the APIs. In YARN, when mradmin
commands are executed, warning messages will appear, reminding users to use YARN
commands (i.e., rmadmin commands). Conversely, if the user's applications program-
matically invoke mradmin, those applications will break when running on top of YARN.
There is no support for either binary or source compatibility under YARN.

Running Apache Pig Scripts on YARN

Pig is one of the two major data process applications in the Hadoop ecosystem, with the other being Hive (see Chapter 7, "Essential Hadoop Tools"). Thanks to the significant efforts made by the Pig community, Pig scripts of existing users do not need any modifications. Pig on YARN in Hadoop 0.23 has been supported since version 0.10.0, and Pig working with Hadoop 2.x has been supported since version 0.10.1.

Existing Pig scripts that work with Pig 0.10.1 and beyond will work just fine on top of YARN. In contrast, versions earlier than Pig 0.10.x may not run directly on YARN due to some of the incompatible MapReduce APIs and configuration.

Running Apache Hive Queries on YARN

Hive queries of existing users do not need any changes to work on top of YARN, starting with Hive 0.10.0, thanks to the work done by Hive community. Support for Hive to work on YARN in the Hadoop 0.23 and 2.x releases has been in place since version 0.10.0. Queries that work in Hive 0.10.0 and beyond will work without changes on top of YARN. However, as with Pig, earlier versions of Hive may not run directly on YARN, as those Hive releases do not support Hadoop 0.23 and 2.x.

Running Apache Oozie Workflows on YARN

Like the Pig and Hive communities, the Apache Oozie community worked to ensure existing Oozie workflows would run in a completely backward-compatible manner on Hadoop version 2. Support for Hadoop 0.23 and 2.x is available starting with Oozie release 3.2.0. Existing Oozie workflows can start taking advantage of YARN in versions 0.23 and 2.x with Oozie 3.2.0 and above.

Summary and Additional Resources

Administering an Apache Hadoop cluster may involve many different services and issues. The two core Hadoop services are the YARN ResourceManager and the HDFS. The Apache Ambari management GUI, presented in Chapter 9, is a good tool for making changes to these services. Several basic YARN administration topics were presented in this chapter, including using the `rmadmin` tool, taking advantage of the YARN Web Proxy, decommissioning YARN nodes, managing YARN applications, and setting important YARN properties.

Important topics and procedures related to basic HDFS administration were described as well. These include exploring the NameNode UI and learning how to add HDFS users, run file system checks, balance DataNodes, create HDFS snapshots, and start an HDFS NFSv3 gateway. In addition, this chapter provided background information on HDFS Safe Mode and the SecondaryNameNode.

The Capacity scheduler offers key functionality within Hadoop version 2, as discussed in this chapter. An example of the Scheduler view on the YARN Resource-Manager UI was provided in this chapter as well. Finally, Hadoop version 2 MapReduce compatibility and node capacity are issues that many programmers need to address.

Additional information can be found from the following sources:

- **Apache Hadoop YARN Administration**
  - http://hadoop.apache.org/docs/current/ (Scroll down to the lower left-hand corner under "Configuration.")
  - https://hadoop.apache.org/docs/current/hadoop-yarn/hadoop-yarn-site/YarnCommands.html#Administration_Commands (YARN Administration Commands)
  - Book: Murthy, A., et al. 2014. *Apache Hadoop YARN: Moving beyond MapReduce and Batch Processing with Apache Hadoop 2*. Boston, MA: Addison-Wesley. http://www.informit.com/store/apache-hadoop-yarn-moving-beyond-mapreduce-and-batch-9780321934505

- **HDFS Administration:**
  - https://hadoop.apache.org/docs/current/hadoop-project-dist/hadoop-hdfs/HdfsUserGuide.html (Notice the HDFS topic menu on the left-hand side of the page.)
  - http://hadoop.apache.org/docs/current/hadoop-project-dist/hadoop-hdfs/HdfsPermissionsGuide.html (HDFS permissions)
  - http://hadoop.apache.org/docs/current/hadoop-project-dist/hadoop-hdfs/HDFSCommands.html (HDFS commands)
  - https://hadoop.apache.org/docs/current/hadoop-project-dist/hadoop-hdfs/HdfsSnapshots.htm (HDFS snapshots)
  - https://hadoop.apache.org/docs/current/hadoop-project-dist/hadoop-hdfs/HdfsNfsGateway.html (HDFS NFSv3 gateway)

- **Capacity Scheduler Administration**
  - https://hadoop.apache.org/docs/current/hadoop-yarn/hadoop-yarn-site/CapacityScheduler.html (Capacity scheduler configuration)
  - Book: Murthy, A., et al. 2014. *Apache Hadoop YARN: Moving beyond MapReduce and Batch Processing with Apache Hadoop 2*. Boston, MA: Addison-Wesley. http://www.informit.com/store/apache-hadoop-yarn-moving-beyond-mapreduce-and-batch-9780321934505 (See "Apache Hadoop YARN Administration/")

- **MapReduce Version 2 (MRv2) Administration**
  - https://hadoop.apache.org/docs/current/hadoop-mapreduce-client/hadoop-mapreduce-client-core/MapReduceTutorial.html (MapReduce with YARN)
  - Book: Murthy, A., et al. 2014. *Apache Hadoop YARN: Moving beyond MapReduce and Batch Processing with Apache Hadoop 2*. Boston, MA: Addison-Wesley. http://www.informit.com/store/apache-hadoop-yarn-moving-beyond-mapreduce-and-batch-9780321934505

A

Book Webpage and Code Download

A webpage with code downloads, a question and answer forum, resource links, and updated information is available from the following link. All of the code and examples used in this book can be downloaded from this page.

http://www.clustermonkey.net/Hadoop2-Quick-Start-Guide

Getting Started Flowchart and Troubleshooting Guide

The flowchart helps you get to the book content that you need, while the trouble-shooting section walks you through basic rules and tips.

Getting Started Flowchart

For those who are new to Hadoop, the flowchart depicted in Figures B.1, B.2, and B.3 provides some guidance on how to use the book and where to find specific topics.

General Hadoop Troubleshooting Guide

It is impossible to predict and handle all the potential errors and problems you may have with a Hadoop installation. There are some basic approaches and places to look for issues, however. In addition, the type of errors and their resolution may depend upon on your specific hardware and software environment.

The following general rules and tips may help you if something goes wrong. Keep in mind that, as with the rest of this book, the following information is designed to get you started. The complete resolution of an issue may take some effort and provide an opportunity to learn something about the Hadoop ecosystem.

Rule 1: Don't Panic

Errors happen. In a complex system of tools and applications like Hadoop, things can go wrong (and most likely will go wrong). The underlying cause can be anything from a simple file system issue to an actual bug in some Hadoop component.

Looking for a Needle in a Haystack

Hadoop services are very verbose and will usually provide enough information from the console and/or the logs to enable you to find the problem (or at least point you in the right direction). The amount of information may be daunting to new users.

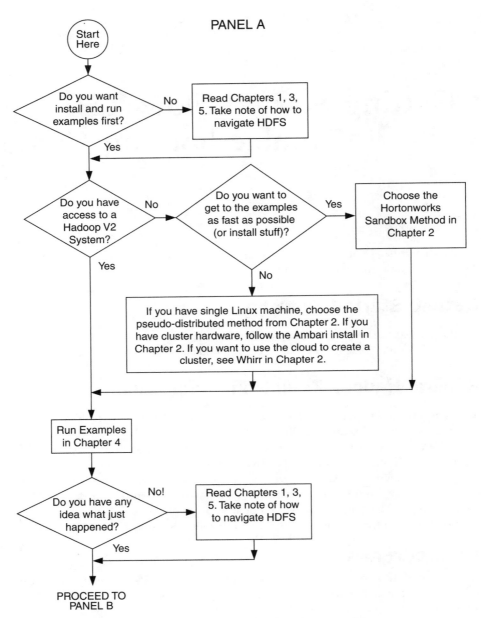

Figure B.1   Book navigation flowchart panel A

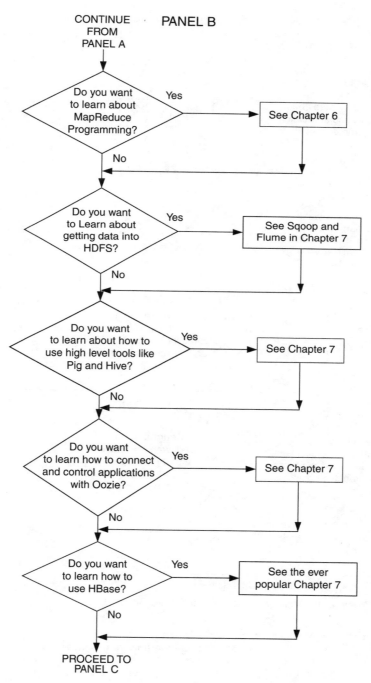

Figure B.2   Book navigation flowchart panel B

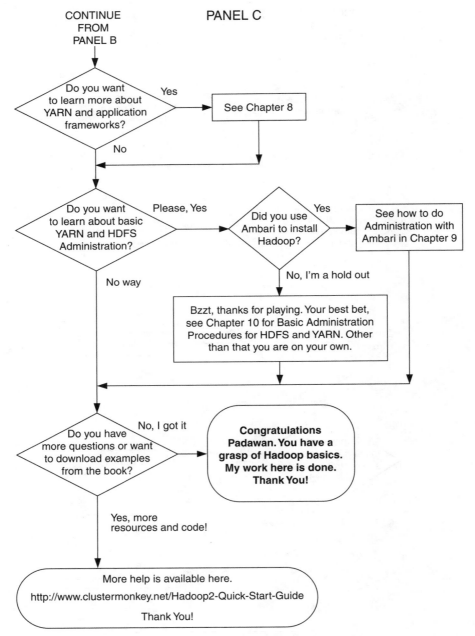

Figure B.3   Book navigation flowchart panel C

Thus, some patience is required when first getting started with Hadoop systems. And remember—it is almost impossible to learn about Hadoop without getting a "haystack" of error messages in which you need to find a "needle" of help.

Acquainting yourself with the options and capabilities of the various components that seem to be causing the problem (or are not working as expected) is also helpful. The Apache Hadoop documentation pages (http://hadoop.apache.org/docs/current/, see the left-hand menu) have a large amount of *current* information on the core components (HDFS, YARN, and MapReduce).

Understanding Java Errors and Messages

If you are new to Java applications, a Java error often looks worse than the actual problem. For instance, consider the error message (highlighted in bold) that is buried in these program trace messages. This error results from running the wordcount.jar program in Chapter 6 with an existing output directory.

```
$ hadoop jar wordcount.jar  WordCount war-and-peace war-and-peace-output
15/07/18 15:56:25 INFO impl.TimelineClientImpl: Timeline service address:
http://limulus:8188/ws/v1/timeline/
15/07/18 15:56:25 INFO client.RMProxy: Connecting to ResourceManager at
limulus/10.0.0.1:8050
Exception in thread "main"
org.apache.hadoop.mapred.FileAlreadyExistsException: Output directory
hdfs://limulus:8020/user/hdfs/war-and-peace-output already exists
    at org.apache.hadoop.mapreduce.lib.output.FileOutputFormat.checkOutputSpecs(File
OutputFormat.java:146)
    at org.apache.hadoop.mapreduce.JobSubmitter.checkSpecs(JobSubmitter.java:562)
    at org.apache.hadoop.mapreduce.JobSubmitter.submitJobInternal(JobSubmitter.
java:432)
    at org.apache.hadoop.mapreduce.Job$10.run(Job.java:1296)
    at org.apache.hadoop.mapreduce.Job$10.run(Job.java:1293)
    at java.security.AccessController.doPrivileged(Native Method)
    at javax.security.auth.Subject.doAs(Subject.java:415)
    at org.apache.hadoop.security.UserGroupInformation.doAs(UserGroupInformation.
java:1628)
    at org.apache.hadoop.mapreduce.Job.submit(Job.java:1293)
    at org.apache.hadoop.mapreduce.Job.waitForCompletion(Job.java:1314)
    at WordCount.main(WordCount.java:59)
    at sun.reflect.NativeMethodAccessorImpl.invoke0(Native Method)
    at sun.reflect.NativeMethodAccessorImpl.invoke(NativeMethodAccessorImpl.java:57)
    at sun.reflect.DelegatingMethodAccessorImpl.invoke(DelegatingMethodAccessorImpl.
java:43)
    at java.lang.reflect.Method.invoke(Method.java:606)
    at org.apache.hadoop.util.RunJar.run(RunJar.java:221)
    at org.apache.hadoop.util.RunJar.main(RunJar.java:136)
```

There is plenty of information printed to aid you in debugging, but the important message can be found near the beginning:

```
Output directory hdfs://limulus:8020/user/hdfs/war-and-peace-output
already exists
```

To resolve this problem, remove the war-and-peace-output directory and run the application again.

Rule 2: Install and Use Ambari

From an administrative standpoint, tools like Apache Ambari are a great help. These types of tools manage the complex state of a Hadoop cluster. The alternative is to use shell scripts and tools like pdsh (see Chapter2, "Installation Recipes"). In addition to automatically managing and monitoring services, Ambari will make sure the right package versions and dependencies are installed. If you are creating a Hadoop cluster with four or more servers, seriously consider Apache Ambari.

Rule 3: Check the Logs

System logs are there for a reason. Although the logs seem complex and full of extraneous messages, the answer to your issue is probably buried in the logs somewhere. If you find something in the logs and do not understand the issue, the next best strategy is to search the Internet for a similar problem. This approach often helps resolve the issue or, at minimum, gets you closer to the source of problem.

Check the System Logs First: Maybe the Problem Is Not Hadoop

When an issue or error occurs, a quick check of the system logs is a good idea. There could be a file permission error or some local non-Hadoop service that is causing problems.

Check the Hadoop Service and Application Logs

If the system logs look fine, check the Hadoop service and application logs. The service logs—that is, those logs that report from the running services—should be examined to ensure the service is working. The nature of the error should help point you in the direction of the Hadoop service log. That is, if you have an HDFS issue, then look in the NameNode and DataNode logs, not the ResourceManager or NodeManager logs. Do not assume that just because a service shows up in the Java jps command that it is working correctly. When in doubt, check the service log. Many services are robust enough to keep running while some error condition exists. (In such a case, the service is assuming the condition may get resolved.) Also, some services will start and run for a short period of time and then stop.

The steps for examining the application logs are covered in Chapter 6, "MapReduce Programming."

Keep in mind that the logs are not necessarily in the standard log location (e.g., /var/log). The log file location is set in the service's XML configuration file.

For example, if Oozie is not working, and the Oozie log file has been set to write to /opt/oozie/logs, then searching for the log in /var/log will lead to a dead end.

By default, Hadoop system log files are cumulative. That is, if you are having trouble starting a service, the log will contain all the output from previous attempts. Make sure you are looking at the *end* of the log. Logs are managed by the log4j package (http://logging.apache.org/log4j).

Rule 4: Simplify the Situation

A time-tested debugging technique is to simplify the issue and see if it can be reproduced in a less complicated environment. Hadoop MapReduce applications can be easily run as a single pseudo-distributed or sandbox node or, for example, Pig and Hive can run natively on the local machine. The amount of data can also be reduced. In general, MapReduce applications should scale up (or down) without any changes to the user's program.

In terms of services, if all the servers running the DataNodes and NodeManagers have been configured in the same fashion, then if one works (or does not work), they should all work (or not). Debug these types of issues with a small number (one or two) of the cluster nodes first and then scale up to the full complement of systems when the solution has been tested.

Rule 5: Ask the Internet

As mentioned previously, searching the Internet for similar error messages can be very effective. Remember to strip any system-specific data (e.g., system names, file paths) from the error message to make it more general.

Apache Hadoop is an open source project and is part of the Apache Foundation (http://www.apache.org/). Community involvement is encouraged and information about the Apache Hadoop project can be found at the project website: http://hadoop.apache.org.

In addition, active discussions can be found in Apache's JIRA issue tracker system. Issues, ideas, and many important discussions take place on this site. You can see all the Hadoop JIRAs by consulting the following site:

https://issues.apache.org/jira/secure/BrowseProjects.jspa#10292

Please do not post basic errors and issues to the JIRA site unless you are sure you have found a real bug or problem. Other helpful sites such as StackOverflow (http://stackoverflow.com) have tags for many Hadoop questions and issues (hadoop, hdfs, hive, mapreduce, apache-pig, hbase, and others). Finally, vendor sites, including those operated by Hortonworks, Cloudera, and MapR, have support forms that deal with many commonly asked questions.

Other Helpful Tips

The following tips may also be helpful for troubleshooting.

Controlling MapReduce Information Streams

The first time users run a Hadoop job, they are usually struck by the amount of data that is produced. When you are first exploring Hadoop or developing applications, these data can be invaluable. Sometimes, however, this information is not needed and becomes cumbersome. For instance, consider the output from the simple word count program (see Chapter 6, "MapReduce Programming").

```
$ hadoop jar wordcount.jar  WordCount war-and-peace-input war-and-peace-output
15/07/18 16:21:44 INFO impl.TimelineClientImpl: Timeline service address: http://
limulus:8188/ws/v1/timeline/
15/07/18 16:21:44 INFO client.RMProxy: Connecting to ResourceManager at
limulus/10.0.0.1:8050
15/07/18 16:21:44 WARN mapreduce.JobSubmitter: Hadoop command-line option parsing
not performed. Implement the Tool interface and execute your application with
ToolRunner to remedy this.
15/07/18 16:21:45 INFO input.FileInputFormat: Total input paths to process : 1
15/07/18 16:21:45 INFO mapreduce.JobSubmitter: number of splits:1
15/07/18 16:21:45 INFO mapreduce.JobSubmitter: Submitting tokens for job:
job_1435349074602_0012
15/07/18 16:21:45 INFO impl.YarnClientImpl: Submitted application
application_1435349074602_0012
15/07/18 16:21:45 INFO mapreduce.Job: The url to track the job: http://
limulus:8088/proxy/application_1435349074602_0012/
15/07/18 16:21:45 INFO mapreduce.Job: Running job: job_1435349074602_0012
15/07/18 16:21:50 INFO mapreduce.Job: Job job_1435349074602_0012 running in uber
mode : false
15/07/18 16:21:50 INFO mapreduce.Job:  map 0% reduce 0%
15/07/18 16:21:56 INFO mapreduce.Job:  map 100% reduce 0%
15/07/18 16:22:01 INFO mapreduce.Job:  map 100% reduce 100%
15/07/18 16:22:01 INFO mapreduce.Job: Job job_1435349074602_0012 completed
successfully
15/07/18 16:22:01 INFO mapreduce.Job: Counters: 49
    File System Counters
        FILE: Number of bytes read=630143
        FILE: Number of bytes written=1489265
        FILE: Number of read operations=0
        FILE: Number of large read operations=0
        FILE: Number of write operations=0
        HDFS: Number of bytes read=3288878
        HDFS: Number of bytes written=467839
        HDFS: Number of read operations=6
        HDFS: Number of large read operations=0
        HDFS: Number of write operations=2
    Job Counters
        Launched map tasks=1
        Launched reduce tasks=1
        Data-local map tasks=1
```

```
        Total time spent by all maps in occupied slots (ms)=3875
        Total time spent by all reduces in occupied slots (ms)=2816
        Total time spent by all map tasks (ms)=3875
        Total time spent by all reduce tasks (ms)=2816
        Total vcore-seconds taken by all map tasks=3875
        Total vcore-seconds taken by all reduce tasks=2816
        Total megabyte-seconds taken by all map tasks=5952000
        Total megabyte-seconds taken by all reduce tasks=4325376
    Map-Reduce Framework
        Map input records=65336
        Map output records=565456
        Map output bytes=5469729
        Map output materialized bytes=630143
        nput split bytes=132
        Combine input records=565456
        Combine output records=41965
        Reduce input groups=41965
        Reduce shuffle bytes=630143
        Reduce input records=41965
        Reduce output records=41965
        Spilled Records=83930
        Shuffled Maps =1
        Failed Shuffles=0
        Merged Map outputs=1
        GC time elapsed (ms)=58
        CPU time spent (ms)=4190
        Physical memory (bytes) snapshot=1053450240
        Virtual memory (bytes) snapshot=3839856640
        vTotal committed heap usage (bytes)=1337458688
    Shuffle Errors
        BAD_ID=0
        CONNECTION=0
        IO_ERROR=0
        WRONG_LENGTH=0
        WRONG_MAP=0
        WRONG_REDUCE=0
    File Input Format Counters
        Bytes Read=3288746
    File Output Format Counters
        Bytes Written=467839
```

One way to quickly reduce the amount of information produced by this program is to set the `$HADOOP_ROOT_LOGGER` environment variable. The following lines will turn off the INFO messages for the job:

```
$ export HADOOP_ROOT_LOGGER="console"
$ hadoop jar wordcount.jar  WordCount war-and-peace-input war-and-peace-output
```

Although no messages are printed, the output of the job can be confirmed by examining the output directory.

```
hdfs dfs -ls war-and-peace-output
Found 2 items
-rw-r--r--   2 hdfs hdfs          0 2015-07-18 16:30 war-and-peace-output/_SUCCESS
-rw-r--r--   2 hdfs hdfs     467839 2015-07-18 16:30 war-and-peace-output/
part-r-00000
```

The default can be restored by unsetting the $HADOOP_ROOT_LOGGER variable. The message level can be permanently set in the log4j.properties file in the Hadoop configuration directory. See the following line:

```
hadoop.root.logger=INFO,console
```

The allowable levels are OFF, FATAL, ERROR, WARN, INFO, DEBUG, TRACE and ALL.

Starting and Stopping Hadoop Daemons

If you are not using something like Ambari to manage the Hadoop daemons, the following tips may be helpful.

If you are using the Hadoop scripts to start and stop services, you may receive the following notice when trying to stop a service:

```
# /opt/hadoop-2.6.0/sbin/yarn-daemon.sh stop resourcemanager

no resourcemanager to stop
```

When you check the system, however, you will see that the ResourceManager is still running. The reason for this confusion is that the user who started the Hadoop service must stop that service. Unlike system processes, the root user cannot kill whatever Hadoop process is running. Of course, the root user can kill the Java process running the service, but this is not a clean method.

There is also a preferred order for starting and stopping Hadoop services. Although it is possible to start the services in any order, a more ordered method helps minimize startup issues. The core services should be started as follows.

For HDFS, start in this order (shut down in the opposite order):

1. NameNode
2. All DataNodes
3. SecondaryNameNode

For YARN, start in this order (shut down in the opposite order)

1. ResourceManager
2. All NodeManagers
3. MapReduceHistoryServer

The HDFS and YARN services can be started independently. Apache Ambari manages the startup/shutdown order automatically.

NameNode Reformatting

Like any other file system, the format operation in HDFS deletes all data. If you choose to reformat a previously installed and running HDFS system, be aware that the DataNodes and/or SecondaryNameNode will not start with the newly formatted NameNode. If you examine the DataNode logs, you will see something similar to the following:

```
2015-07-20 12:00:56,446 FATAL org.apache.hadoop.hdfs.server.datanode.DataNode:
Initialization failed for Block pool <registering> (Datanode Uuid unassigned)
service to localhost/127.0.0.1:9000. Exiting.
java.io.IOException: ncompatible clusterIDs in /var/data/hadoop/hdfs/dn: namenode
clusterID = CID-b611ee00-cbce-491f-8efd-c46a6dd6587a; datanode
clusterID = CID-9693dc8e-3c5c-4c34-b8b6-1039460183a7
```

The new format of NameNode has given it a new clusterID (CID-b611ee00-cbce-491f-8efd-c46a6dd6587a). The DataNodes are using the old clusterID (CID-9693dc8e-3c5c-4c34-b8b6-1039460183a7). The solution is to remove all the data created by the DataNodes and SecondaryNameNode and then restart the daemons. For instance, the following commands will clean out the old *local* DataNode directory. (These steps assume the SecondaryNameNode and all DataNodes are stopped.)

```
$ rm -r /var/data/hadoop/hdfs/dn/current/
$ /opt/hadoop-2.6.0/sbin/hadoop-daemon.sh start datanode
```

The path to the DataNode used here is set in the hdfs-site.xml file. This step must be performed for each of the individual data nodes. In a similar fashion, the SecondaryNameNode must be reset using the following commands:

```
$ rm -r /var/data/hadoop/hdfs/snn/current
$ /opt/hadoop-2.6.0/sbin/hadoop-daemon.sh start namenode
```

The DataNodes and SecondaryNameNode should start and a new clean (empty) HDFS image should be available for use. Keeping and reclaiming old data on the DataNodes (i.e., do not delete the current directory) is not possible unless you can recover the NameNode metadata and change clusterIDs to match the new NameNode.

NameNode Failure and Possible Recovery Methods

The following general hints may help with NameNode issues. Proceed with caution—and be advised that when dealing with some NameNode issues, data loss may result.

The NameNode is essential for HDFS operation. For this reason, on production systems, it should be implemented in High Availability mode or at a minimum on a resilient server (i.e., redundant power supplies and disk). A first layer of redundancy can be created by configuring the NameNode to write to multiple storage directories, including, if possible, one remote NFS mount (use NFS soft mounting). The extra directories are mirrors of the main directory. A NameNode with corrupted or lost file systems can be recovered from the mirrored data.

If all else fails, and a previously working Namenode refuses to start and shows error messages similar to the following, **do not reformat the NameNode.** These messages indicate that the previously working NameNode service cannot find a valid NameNode directory.

```
2015-07-20 09:15:19,207 WARN org.apache.hadoop.hdfs.server.namenode.FSNamesystem:
Encountered exception loading fsimage
java.io.IOException: NameNode is not formatted.
```

```
2015-07-20 09:10:49,651 WARN org.apache.hadoop.hdfs.server.namenode.FSNamesystem:
Encountered exception loading fsimage
org.apache.hadoop.hdfs.server.common.InconsistentFSStateException:
Directory /var/data/hadoop/hdfs/nn is in an inconsistent state: storage
directory does not exist or is not accessible.
```

These errors are usually due to a failed, corrupt, or unavailable local machine file system. Check that the directory in the hdfs-site.xml file, set in the following property, is mounted and functioning correctly. As mentioned previously, this property can include multiple directories for redundancy.

```
<property>
    <name>dfs.namenode.name.dir</name>
    <value>file:/var/data/hadoop/hdfs/nn</value>
</property>
```

If the NameNode directory (or directories) is not recoverable, then you can use the mirrored copy to restore the NameNode state. As a last resort, the latest checkpoint, if intact, can be used to restore the NameNode. Note that some data may be lost in this process. The latest checkpoint can be imported to the NameNode if all other copies of the image and the edits files are lost. The following steps will restore the latest NameNode checkpoint:

1. Create an empty directory specified in the dfs.namenode.name.dir configuration variable.

2. Specify the location of the checkpoint directory in the configuration variable dfs.namenode.checkpoint.dir.

3. Start the NameNode with the -importCheckpoint option:

```
$ hadoop-daemon.sh start namenode -importCheckpoint
```

The NameNode will upload the checkpoint from the dfs.namenode.checkpoint.dir directory and then save it to the NameNode directory(s) set in dfs.namenode.name.dir. The NameNode will fail if a legal image is contained in dfs.namenode.name.dir. The

NameNode verifies that the image in `dfs.namenode.checkpoint.dir` is consistent, but does not modify it in any way.

After completing step 3, attempt to start the DataNodes. If they do not start, check the logs—there could be a clusterID issue. If the DataNodes start, HDFS will most likely be in Safe Mode and need a file system check. First, check for Safe Mode:

```
$ hdfs dfsadmin -safemode get
```

If Safe Mode is on, turn it off. If Safe Mode will not turn off, there may be larger issues. Check the NameNode log:

```
$ hdfs dfsadmin -safemode leave
```

Next, check the file system for problems:

```
$ hdfs fsck /
```

If there are corrupted blocks or files, delete them with the following command:

```
$ hdfs fsck / -delete
```

Your HDFS files system should be usable, but there is no guarantee that all the files will be available.

Summary of Apache Hadoop Resources by Topic

The following is a summary of resources listed by chapter topic. An online version of this list (with updates and clickable links) is available on the book webpage (see Appendix A).

General Hadoop Information

- Main Apache Hadoop website: http://hadoop.apache.org
- Apache Hadoop documentation website: http://hadoop.apache.org/docs/current/index.html
- Wikipedia: http://en.wikipedia.org/wiki/Apache_Hadoop
- Book: Murthy, Arun C., et al. (2014). *Apache Hadoop YARN: Moving beyond MapReduce and Batch Processing with Apache Hadoop 2*, Boston, MA: Addison-Wesley. http://www.informit.com/store/apache-hadoop-yarn-moving-beyond-mapreduce-and-batch-9780321934505
- Video training: *Hadoop Fundamentals LiveLessons, 2nd Edition.* http://www.informit.com/store/hadoop-fundamentals-livelessons-video-training-9780134052403

Hadoop Installation Recipes

Additional information and background on the installation methods can be found from the following resources.

- **Apache Hadoop XML configuration files description**
  - https://hadoop.apache.org/docs/stable/ (scroll down to the lower left-hand corner under Configuration)
- **Officially Hadoop sources and supported Java versions**
  - http://www.apache.org/dyn/closer.cgi/hadoop/common/
  - http://wiki.apache.org/hadoop/HadoopJavaVersions

- **Oracle VirtualBox**
  - https://www.virtualbox.org
- **Hortonworks Hadoop Sandbox (virtual machine)**
  - http://hortonworks.com/hdp/downloads
- **Ambari project page**
  - https://ambari.apache.org/
- **Ambari installation guide**
  - http://docs.hortonworks.com/HDPDocuments/Ambari-1.7.0.0/Ambari_Install_v170/Ambari_Install_v170.pdf
- **Ambari troubleshooting guide**
  - http://docs.hortonworks.com/HDPDocuments/Ambari-1.7.0.0/Ambari_Trblshooting_v170/Ambari_Trblshooting_v170.pdf
- **Apache Whirr cloud tools**
  - https://whirr.apache.org

HDFS

- **HDFS background**
  - http://hadoop.apache.org/docs/stable1/hdfs_design.html
  - http://developer.yahoo.com/hadoop/tutorial/module2.html
  - http://hadoop.apache.org/docs/stable/hdfs_user_guide.html
- **HDFS user commands**
  - http://hadoop.apache.org/docs/stable/hadoop-project-dist/hadoop-hdfs/HDFSCommands.html
- **HDFS Java programming**
  - http://wiki.apache.org/hadoop/HadoopDfsReadWriteExample
- **HDFS libhdfs programming in C**
  - http://hadoop.apache.org/docs/stable/hadoop-project-dist/hadoop-hdfs/LibHdfs.html

Examples

- **Pi benchmark**
  - https://hadoop.apache.org/docs/current/api/org/apache/hadoop/examples/pi/package-summary.html
- **Terasort benchmark**
  - https://hadoop.apache.org/docs/current/api/org/apache/hadoop/examples/terasort/package-summary.html

- **Benchmarking and stress testing a Hadoop cluster**
  - http://www.michael-noll.com/blog/2011/04/09/benchmarking-and-stress-testing-an-hadoop-cluster-with-terasort-testdfsio-nnbench-mrbench (uses Hadoop V1, will work with V2)

MapReduce

- https://developer.yahoo.com/hadoop/tutorial/module4.html (based on Hadoop version 1, but still a good MapReduce background)
- http://en.wikipedia.org/wiki/MapReduce
- http://research.google.com/pubs/pub36249.html

MapReduce Programming

- **Apache Hadoop Java MapReduce example**
  - http://hadoop.apache.org/docs/current/hadoop-mapreduce-client/hadoop-mapreduce-client-core/MapReduceTutorial.html#Example:_WordCount_v1.0
- **Apache Hadoop streaming example**
  - http://hadoop.apache.org/docs/r1.2.1/streaming.html
  - http://www.michael-noll.com/tutorials/writing-an-hadoop-mapreduce-program-in-python
- **Apache Hadoop Pipes example**
  - http://wiki.apache.org/hadoop/C++WordCount
  - https://developer.yahoo.com/hadoop/tutorial/module4.html#pipes
- **Apache Hadoop Grep example**
  - http://wiki.apache.org/hadoop/Grep
  - https://developer.yahoo.com/hadoop/tutorial/module4.html#chaining
- **Debugging MapReduce**
  - http://wiki.apache.org/hadoop/HowToDebugMapReducePrograms
  - http://hadoop.apache.org/docs/current/hadoop-mapreduce-client/hadoop-mapreduce-client-core/MapReduceTutorial.html#Debugging

Essential Tools

- **Apache Pig scripting language**
  - http://pig.apache.org/
  - http://pig.apache.org/docs/r0.14.0/start.html

- **Apache Hive SQL–like query language**
  - https://hive.apache.org/
  - https://cwiki.apache.org/confluence/display/Hive/GettingStarted
  - http://grouplens.org/datasets/movielens (data for example)
- **Apache Sqoop RDBMS import/export**
  - http://sqoop.apache.org
  - http://dev.mysql.com/doc/world-setup/en/index.html (data for example)
- **Apache Flume steaming data and transport utility**
  - https://flume.apache.org
  - https://flume.apache.org/FlumeUserGuide.html
- **Apache Oozie workflow manager**
  - http://oozie.apache.org
  - http://oozie.apache.org/docs/4.0.0/index.html
- **Apache HBase distributed database**
  - http://hbase.apache.org/book.html
  - http://hbase.apache.org
  - http://research.google.com/archive/bigtable.html (Google Big Table paper)
  - http://www.google.com/finance/historical?q=NASDAQ:AAPL\&authuser=0\&output=csv (data for example)

YARN Application Frameworks

- **Apache Hadoop YARN development**
  - Book: Murthy, Arun C., et al. (2014). *Apache Hadoop YARN: Moving beyond MapReduce and Batch Processing with Apache Hadoop 2*. Boston, MA: Addison-Wesley. http://www.informit.com/store/apache-hadoop-yarn-moving-beyond-mapreduce-and-batch-9780321934505
  - http://hadoop.apache.org/docs/r2.7.0/hadoop-yarn/hadoop-yarn-site/WritingYarnApplications.html
  - MemcacheD on YARN: http://hortonworks.com/blog/how-to-deploy-memcached-on-yarn/
  - Hortonworks YARN resources: http://hortonworks.com/get-started/yarn
- **Apache Hadoop YARN frameworks**
  - See the webpage references at the end of the individual descriptions

Ambari Administration

- https://ambari.apache.org

Basic Hadoop Administration

- **Apache Hadoop YARN administration**
  - http://hadoop.apache.org/docs/current/ (scroll down to the lower left-hand corner under "Configuration")
  - https://hadoop.apache.org/docs/current/hadoop-yarn/hadoop-yarn-site/YarnCommands.html#Administration_Commands (YARN administration commands)
  - Book: Murthy, Arun C., et al. (2014). *Apache Hadoop YARN: Moving beyond MapReduce and Batch Processing with Apache Hadoop 2*. Boston, MA: Addison-Wesley. http://www.informit.com/store/apache-hadoop-yarn-moving-beyond-mapreduce-and-batch-9780321934505

- **HDFS administration**
  - https://hadoop.apache.org/docs/current/hadoop-project-dist/hadoop-hdfs/HdfsUserGuide.html (note the HDFS topic menu on the left-hand side of the page)
  - http://hadoop.apache.org/docs/current/hadoop-project-dist/hadoop-hdfs/HdfsPermissionsGuide.html (HDFS permissions)
  - http://hadoop.apache.org/docs/current/hadoop-project-dist/hadoop-hdfs/HDFSCommands.html (HDFS commands)
  - https://hadoop.apache.org/docs/current/hadoop-project-dist/hadoop-hdfs/HdfsSnapshots.htm (HDFS snapshots)
  - https://hadoop.apache.org/docs/current/hadoop-project-dist/hadoop-hdfs/HdfsNfsGateway.html (HDFS NFSv3 gateway)

- **Capacity scheduler administration**
  - https://hadoop.apache.org/docs/current/hadoop-yarn/hadoop-yarn-site/CapacityScheduler.html (Capacity scheduler configuration)
  - Book: Murthy, Arun C., et al. (2014). *Apache Hadoop YARN: Moving beyond MapReduce and Batch Processing with Apache Hadoop 2*. Boston, MA: Addison-Wesley. http://www.informit.com/store/apache-hadoop-yarn-moving-beyond-mapreduce-and-batch-9780321934505

- **MapReduce version 2 (MRv2) administration**
  - https://hadoop.apache.org/docs/current/hadoop-mapreduce-client/hadoop-mapreduce-client-core/MapReduceTutorial.html (MapReduce with YARN)
  - Murthy, Arun C., et al. (2014). *Apache Hadoop YARN: Moving beyond MapReduce and Batch Processing with Apache Hadoop 2*. Boston, MA: Addison-Wesley. http://www.informit.com/store/apache-hadoop-yarn-moving-beyond-mapreduce-and-batch-9780321934505

D

Installing the Hue
Hadoop GUI

Hue (Hadoop User Experience) is a browser-based environment that enables you to easily interact with a Hadoop installation. Hue includes several easy-to-use applications that help you work with many of the Hadoop components discussed previously. Hue applications run in a web browser and require no web client software installation. The current version supports an HDFS file browser, ResourceManager interface, Hive, Pig, Oozie, HBase, and more. Hue works in Chrome, Firefox, and Safari. Internet Explorer 9 and 10 are also supported.

The Hue interface is used by the Hortonworks virtual Hadoop sandbox introduced in Chapter 2, "Installation Recipes." The full Hue interface can be explored by using the sandbox installation or by using the following Ambari installation instructions. You can install Hue by hand, but it is easiest to use with the Cloudera, Hortonworks, or MapR distribution.

The following instructions explain how to install Hue on Hortonworks HDP 2.2 with Ambari. More information and tutorials can be found at the Hue website: http://gethue.com/.

Hue Installation

For this example, the following software environment is assumed. This Ambari environment is the same as that used in Chapter 2, "Installation Recipes," and Chapter 9, "Managing Hadoop with Apache Ambari."

- OS: Linux
- Platform: RHEL 6.6
- Hortonworks HDP 2.2.4 with Hadoop version: 2.6
- Hue version: 2.6.1-2

Installing Hue requires several configuration steps. In this appendix, the Hadoop XML configuration files will be changed using Ambari and the hue.ini files will be edited by hand. More detailed instructions are provided in the Hortonworks HDP documentation: http://docs.hortonworks.com/HDPDocuments/HDP2/HDP-2.1.7/ bk_installing_manually_book/content/rpm-chap-hue.html.

Steps Performed with Ambari

We will use Ambari to change various properties needed for Hue. Changing properties is covered in Chapter 9, "Managing Hadoop with Apache Ambari." Briefly, for each property mentioned here, go to the Services Tab in Ambari, select the service, and click on the Config tab. The configuration form should appear in the window. In some cases, the property will need to be added. Do not edit the Hadoop configuration files by hand.

When you are adding properties, an Add Property link is displayed in the custom XML file section for each service. The <name> field used in the new properties is the value used for the Key field in the example dialog window in Figure D.1. Also, do not forget to add notes when requested to do so by Ambari.

Step 1: Modify the HDFS Service and Proxy Users

Open up the Ambari console and move to HDFS under the services tab and select Config. Make sure the `dfs.webhdfs.enabled` property is enabled under the General heading in the configuration form. If it is not, check the enable box. This setting corresponds to the following setting in the `hdfs-site.xml` file located in the `/etc/hadoop/conf` directory:

```
<property>
  <name>dfs.webhdfs.enabled</name>
  <value>true</value>
</property>
```

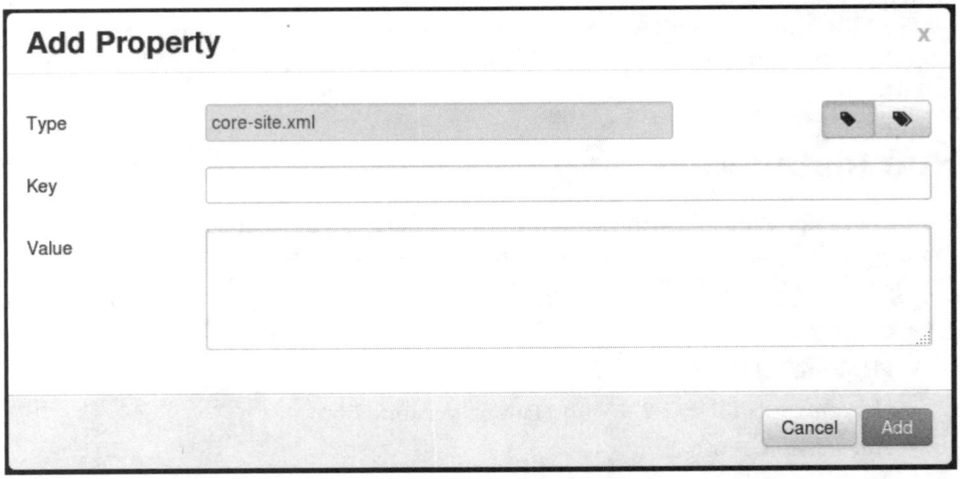

Figure D.1   Ambari Add Property example window

Next, look further down in the HDFS properties form for the Custom core-site heading and click the small triangle to open the drop-down form. Using the Add Property... link at the bottom of the form, add the following properties and values. (Recall that the <name> tag here refers to the Key field in the input form.) These additions correspond to the settings in the `core-site.xml` file located in the `/etc/hadoop/conf` directory. When you are finished, select Save and add your notes, but do not restart the services.

```
<property>
  <name>hadoop.proxyuser.hue.hosts</name>
  <value>*</value>
</property>


<property>
  <name>hadoop.proxyuser.hue.groups</name>
  <value>*</value>
</property>


<property>
  <name>hadoop.proxyuser.hcat.groups</name>
  <value>*</value>
</property>


<property>
  <name>hadoop.proxyuser.hcat.hosts</name>
  <value>*</value>
</property>
```

Step 2: Modify the Hive Webhcat Service

Move to the Hive Services window and look for the Custom webhcat-site heading. Open this form and add the following two properties. These properties are placed (by Ambari) in the `webhcat-site.xml` file located in the `/etc/hive-webhcat/conf` directory. When you are finished, select Save and add your notes, but do not restart the services.

```
<property>
  <name>webhcat.proxyuser.hue.hosts</name>
  <value>*</value>
</property>


<property>
  <name>webhcat.proxyuser.hue.groups</name>
  <value>*</value>
</property>
```

Step 3: Modify the Oozie Workflow Service

Finally, move to the Oozie Service window and open the Custom oozie-site form. Add the following properties to the form. These properties are placed (by Ambari) in the oozie-site.xml file located in the /etc/oozie/conf directory. When you are finished, select Save and add your notes, but do not restart the services.

```
<property>
  <name>oozie.service.ProxyUserService.proxyuser.hue.hosts</name>
  <value>*</value>
</property>


<property>
  <name>oozie.service.ProxyUserService.proxyuser.hue.groups</name>
  <value>*</value>
</property>
```

Step 4: Restart All Services

Once you have made the changes, the services can be restarted. Restart HDFS first, then continue with YARN and the rest of the services that are requesting a restart. All services should restart without issues (assuming they had no previous issues).

Install and Configure Hue

Hue installation is needed on only a single Hue client node. It does not need to be installed across the cluster. The following command will install all the HUE packages:

```
# yum install hue
```

Once Hue is installed, you need to modify the /etc/hue/conf/hue.ini file for your system. This example does not configure the ssl (https) version of Hue.

Under the [desktop] heading, set the secret_key value. (Do not use the one here because it is not a secret.)

```
# Set this to a random string, the longer the better.
# This is used for secure hashing in the session store.
secret_key=rhn7&*mmsdmm.ssss;sns7%n)*icnq
```

Next, set the time zone variable to your time zone. (See https://en.wikipedia.org/wiki/List_of_tz_database_time_zones for values.)

```
time_zone=America/New_York
```

Under the [hadoop] [[[default]]] sections, change the following to reflect the host name on which the services are run. These values should match the corresponding host names and port values in your core-site.xml and hdfs-site.xml files. In the example here, localhost was changed to limulus.

```
# Enter the filesystem uri
fs_defaultfs=hdfs://limulus:8020
# Use WebHdfs/HttpFs as the communication mechanism. To fallback to
# using the Thrift plugin (used in Hue 1.x), this must be uncommented
# and explicitly set to the empty value.
webhdfs_url=http://limulus:50070/webhdfs/v1/
```

Under the [beeswax] section, uncomment the line ## hive_conf_dir=
/etc/hive/conf to look like the following:

```
# Hive configuration directory, where ## hive-site.xml is located
  hive_conf_dir=/etc/hive/conf
```

Starting Hue

Hue is started as a service. Once its configuration is complete, it can be started with
the following command:

```
# service hue start
```

As Hue starts, the console output should look like the following:

```
Detecting versions of components...
HUE_VERSION=2.6.1-2
HDP=2.2.4
Hadoop=2.6.0
Pig=0.14.0
Hive-Hcatalog=0.14.0
Oozie=4.1.0
Ambari-server=1.7-169
HBase=0.98.4
Knox=0.5.0
Storm=0.9.3
Falcon=0.6.0
Starting hue:                                          [  OK  ]
```

Hue User Interface

To get to the Hue users interface, use a browser to open http://localhost:8000. For
example, with Firefox, the command is as follows:

```
$ firefox http://localhost:8000
```

The first time you connect to Hue, the window in Figure D.2 is presented. The
user name and password used for this first login will be the administrator for Hue. In
this example, the user name hue-admin and password admin are used.

Figure D.2   **Hue initial login screen**

Once you log in, the configuration window in Figure D.3 is shown. To make sure everything is working correctly, click on the Check for misconfiguration tab below the green bar.

If the configuration is valid, Hue will display the message shown in Figure D.4. For any invalid configurations, Hue displays a red alert icon on the top green navigation icon bar.

Once you have confirmed a valid installation was completed, you need to add users. If you click on the Users icon, which is surrounded by dark green in Figure D.5, the Hue Users window in Figure D.5 is displayed. From here, you can add users to the Hue interface.

Finally, the Hue navigation icon bar shown in Figure D.6 provides interfaces to the various components. The icons represent the following functions (moving from left to right): About Hue, Hive Beeswax Interface, Pig, HCatalog, File Browser, Job Browser, Job Designer, Oozie Editor Dashboard, User Admin, and Help.

You can learn more about Hue and the included Hadoop components from the Help icon and by consulting the tutorials at http://gethue.com/.

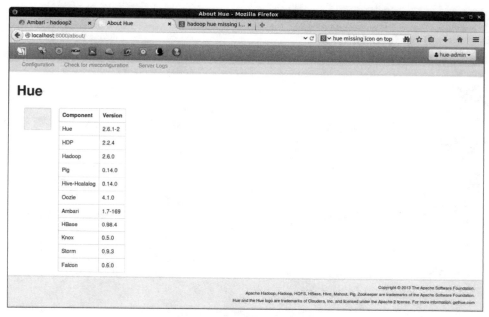

Figure D.3   Hue configuration screen

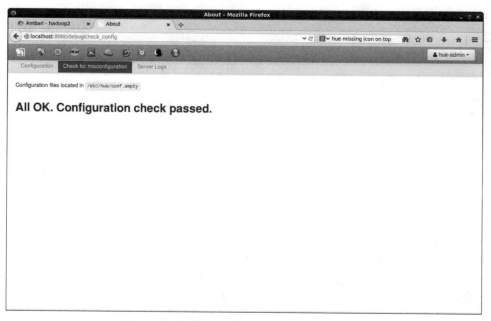

Figure D.4   Hue configuration check screen

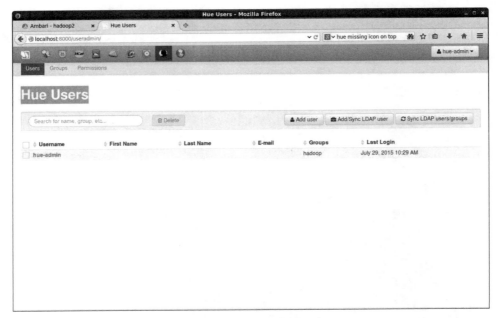

Figure D.5   Hue Users administration screen

Figure D.6   Hue main icon bar

E

Installing Apache Spark

As mentioned in Chapter 8, "Hadoop YARN Applications," Apache Spark is a fast, in-memory data processing engine. Spark differs from the classic MapReduce model in two ways. First, Spark holds intermediate results in memory, rather than writing them to disk. Second, Spark supports more than just MapReduce functions, greatly expanding the set of possible analyses that can be executed over HDFS data stores. It also provides APIs in Scala, Java, and Python. Spark has been fully integrated to run under YARN.

As of this writing, Apache Spark has not been fully integrated into the Hortonworks HDP Hadoop distribution version 2.2.4. The next release will include Spark as a fully integrated Ambari and HDP component.

As demonstrated in this appendix, Spark can be installed and used alongside an HDP installation.

Spark Installation on a Cluster

For this installation example, the following software environment is assumed. The cluster is the same four-node system used in Chapter 2, "Installation Recipes," and Chapter 9, "Managing Hadoop with Apache Ambari."

- OS: Linux
- Platform: RHEL 6.6
- Hortonworks HDP 2.2.4 with Hadoop version: 2.6
- Spark Version: 1.4.1–bin–hadoop2.6

Installing Spark is done outside of Ambari. In this example, Spark is installed in /usr, although any location can be used as long as it is the same on all nodes. The installation is performed as root.

1. Download the binary tar file version of Spark that matches your Hadoop version from http://spark.apache.org/downloads.html. The version used for this install is spark-1.4.1-bin-hadoop2.6.tgz. Save the package in /tmp.

2. Extract the Spark binary package on the master node.

```
# cd /usr
# tar xvzf /tmp/spark-1.4.1-bin-hadoop2.6.tgz
```

3. Extract the package in the same location on every node that you want to run Spark. In this case, the pdsh command introduced in Chapter 2 can be used as follows. Copy the Spark binary tar file to an NSF shared directory (e.g., /home). Then use pdsh to extract the file. Note that pdcp is not installed on nodes and cannot be used for this step. If you do not have pdsh installed, these steps can be completed by hand or with a suitable bash script.

```
# cp /tmp/spark-1.4.1-bin-hadoop2.6.tgz /home/
# pdsh -w n[0-2] "cd /usr; tar xvzf /home/spark-1.4.1-bin-hadoop2.6.tgz "
# /bin/rm /home/spark-1.4.1-bin-hadoop2.6.tgz
```

4. Move to the Spark conf directory (/usr/spark-1.4.1-bin-hadoop2.6/conf), create the slaves file, and enter the slave nodes. The following example is for the four-node cluster used previously with a master (limulus) and three worker nodes (n0, n1, n2). The localhost entry will start a Spark worker on the master node.

```
# A Spark Worker will be started on each of the machines listed below.
localhost
n0
n1
n2
```

Starting Spark across the Cluster

Finally, define $SPARK_HOME and move to the sbin directory on the master node. Once there, use the start-all.sh script to start Spark on the master and worker nodes.

```
#   export SPARK_HOME=/usr/spark-1.4.1-bin-hadoop2.6/
# cd $SPARK_HOME/sbin
# ./start-all.sh
```

The logs will be placed in the $SPARK_HOME/logs directory of each machine. For instance, the following logs (a master log and a worker log) are present on the master. Unlike Hadoop log files, the Spark log files end with an out tag.

```
spark-root-org.apache.spark.deploy.master.Master-1-limulus.out
spark-root-org.apache.spark.deploy.worker.Worker-1-limulus.out
```

The three worker nodes will have one log. For instance on node n0, a single log file will be created with the following name:

```
spark-root-org.apache.spark.deploy.worker.Worker-1-n0.out
```

Check the logs for any issues. In particular, if iptables (or some other firewall) is running, make sure it is not blocking the slave nodes from contacting the master node. If everything worked correctly, messages similar to the following should appear in the master log. The successful registration of all four worker nodes, including the local node, should be listed. The Spark master URL is also provided in the output (spark://limulus:7077).

```
...
INFO Master: Starting Spark master at spark://limulus:7077
INFO Master: Running Spark version 1.4.1
WARN Utils: Service 'MasterUI' could not bind on port 8080. Attempting port 8081.
INFO Utils: Successfully started service 'MasterUI' on port 8081.
INFO MasterWebUI: Started MasterWebUI at http://10.0.0.1:8081
INFO Master: I have been elected leader! New state: ALIVE
INFO Master: Registering worker 10.0.0.1:54856 with 4 cores, 22.5 GB RAM
INFO Master: Registering worker 10.0.0.11:34228 with 4 cores, 14.6 GB RAM
INFO Master: Registering worker 10.0.0.12:49932 with 4 cores, 14.6 GB RAM
INFO Master: Registering worker 10.0.0.10:36124 with 4 cores, 14.6 GB RAM
```

Spark provides a web UI, whose address is given as part of the log. As indicated, the MasterWebUI is http://10.0.0.1:8081. Placing this address in a browser on the master node displays the interface in Figure E.1. Note that Ambari uses the default port 8080. In this case, Spark used 8081.

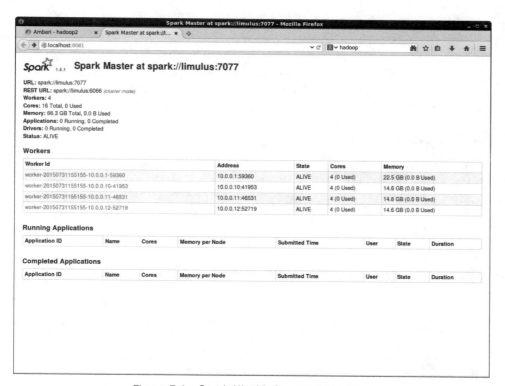

Figure E.1   Spark UI with four worker nodes

Installing and Starting Spark on the Pseudo-distributed Single-Node Installation

In Chapter 2, "Installation Recipes," a single-node (desktop/laptop) Hadoop pseudo-distributed installation was described. Spark can be easily installed in this mode as well.

1. Download the binary tar file version of Spark that matches your Hadoop version from http://spark.apache.org/downloads.html. The version used for this install is spark-1.4.1-bin-hadoop2.6.tgz. Save the package in /tmp.

2. Extract the Spark binary package on the master node.

```
# cd /opt
# tar xvzf /tmp/spark-1.4.1-bin-hadoop2.6.tgz
```

3. Define $SPARK_HOME, move to that directory, and run the start-all.sh script. Spark will start the master node and one worker node on the host.

```
# export SPARK_HOME=/opt/spark-1.4.1-bin-hadoop2.6/
# cd $SPARK_HOME
# ./sbin/start-all.sh
```

4. Inspect the logs to make sure both the master and the worker started properly. Files similar to the following should appear in the $SPARK_HOME/logs directory (the host name is norbert).

```
spark-root-org.apache.spark.deploy.master.Master-1-norbert.out
spark-root-org.apache.spark.deploy.worker.Worker-1-norbert.out
```

5. Open the Spark web GUI as described previously. Note that the MasterWebUI will use port 8080 because Ambari is not running. Check the master log for the exact URL.

Run Spark Examples

To run the Spark examples, log in as a non-root user and try the following. Your $SPARK_HOME path may vary.

```
$ export SPARK_HOME=/usr/spark-1.4.1-bin-hadoop2.6/
$ cd $SPARK_HOME
$ ./bin/run-example SparkPi
$ ./bin/spark-submit $SPARK_HOME/examples/src/main/python/pi.py
```

You can start the Spark shell with the following command:

```
$ $SPARK_HOME/bin/spark-shell
```

Finally, to access Hadoop HDFS data from Spark, use the Hadoop NameNode URL. This URL is typically hdfs://<namenode>:8020/path (for HDP installations) or hdfs://namenode>:9000 (for ASF source installations). The HDFS NameNode URL can be found in the /etc/hadoop/conf/core-site.xml file.

More information on using Spark can be found at http://spark.apache.org.

Index